FAMILY AND ECONOMY IN MODERN SOCIETY

Edited by

Paul Close and Rosemary Collins

Foreword by David Morgan

M

**MACMILLAN
PRESS**

First published 1985
Reprinted 1988

Published by
THE MACMILLAN PRESS LTD
Houndmills, Basingstoke, Hampshire RG21 2XS
and London
Companies and representatives
throughout the world

Typeset by
Styleset Limited
Warminster, Wiltshire

Printed in Hong Kong

British Library Cataloguing in Publication Data
Family and economy in modern society
1. Family—Economic aspects
I. Title   II. Close, Paul
III. Collins, Rosemary
306.8′5   HQ518
ISBN 0-333-37437-1 (hardcover)
ISBN 0-333-37438-X (paperback)

To Alexander, Christopher and Megan

Contents

List of Tables and Figures

Notes on the Contributors

Jon Bernardes lectures in Sociology and Methodology at Wolverhampton Polytechnic. Conducting research on alternative sociological theory of family life. Awarded Ph.D. in Sociology by the University of Hull, 1981.

Lois Bryson is Assistant Director General, Program Development in the Department of Community Welfare Services, Victoria, Australia. Formerly, Associate Professor and Head of School of Sociology, the University of New South Wales. Written extensively on the family, gender divisions, poverty and welfare.

Judith Chaney is Assistant Registrar for Technology, the Council for National Academic Awards, London. Formerly lectured in Sociology at Sunderland Polytechnic. Conducted research for the Equal Opportunities Commission on patterns of women's employment.

Paul Close is a Senior Lecturer in Sociology at Teesside Polytechnic. Conducting research on the content, distribution and significance of domestic labour. Written on the family, domestic labour and gender divisions. Awarded Ph.D. in Sociology by the University of Kent, 1977.

Rosemary Collins teaches Sociology at Teesside Polytechnic. Formerly, research assistant in Sociology. Conducting research on the division of domestic labour for Ph.D. in Sociology. Written on domestic labour and gender divisions.

David Morgan – Department of Sociology, University of Manchester – is the author of, among other works, the highly influential *Social Theory and the Family* (London: Routledge & Kegan Paul, 1975).

Linda Murgatroyd currently works in economic and social statistics. Studied Economics at the University of Cambridge and Sociology at the University of Oxford, where she was a founder member of the Oxford Women's Studies Committee. Conducted research with the Lancaster Regionalism Group.

Jennie Popay lectures in Medical Sociology with the Open University. Formerly a Research Officer with the Study Commission on the Family. Current research on the implications of unemployment for health and social service professionals. Written several publications on unemployment and health.

Jens Qvortrup is Associate Professor at the Institute of East-West Research, University Centre of South Jutland. Formerly, Scientific Coordinator of Comparative Family Research, Vienna Centre. Written on living conditions and social policy in socialist societies. Graduate of the University of Copenhagen.

Graham Thomas is with the Science Policy Research Unit, University of Sussex. Research on household technology and time-budgeting of domestic labour. Written on the changing patterns of time-use and domestic labour.

Clare Ungerson is Lecturer in Social Administration at the University of Kent. Formerly, Senior Research Fellow with the Institute of Race Relations, and a Research Officer with the Centre for Environmental Studies. Written extensively on women and caring, gender divisions, and urban and planning issues.

Christine Zmroczek is with the Science Policy Research Unit, University of Sussex. Research on household technology and time-budgeting of domestic labour. Written on the changing patterns of time-use and domestic labour.

Foreword

DAVID MORGAN

The essays collected in this volume represent an area of study which has seen considerable expansion in recent years – that of the examination of issues lying at the intersection of family, economy, class and gender. While it is with the first two items that the volume is chiefly concerned, all the contributors are aware that questions of class and especially of gender cannot be excluded from their explorations. The sociology of the family, which was once in danger of becoming a parochial and atheoretical back-water, has been given a new importance and excitement precisely because contemporary researchers are interested not simply in the family as an isolated area of study but in placing it within the wider context of economy, class and gender. The essays here further this promising convergence of topics.

The book contains chapters which have been informed by social history, economic analysis, and problems of social administration and social policy as well as by specifically sociological concerns and insights. By focusing on the interrelationship between family and economy in a way which deploys several disciplines and methodologies they reflect a development which has not been confined to studies in Britain, as demonstrated by two chapters in particular. It is salutary to be reminded of the continuing important contribution of debates coming from Scandinavian countries, just as it is to be made aware of the ferment surrounding issues of family and gender currently taking place in Australia.

One of the main influences on recent developments has been the growth of feminism, especially through its impact upon the theory and practice of sociology. This has not been simply a political or an ethical movement, seeking to right various wrongs, distortions and omissions within the discipline. It has also entailed a large-scale reconceptualisation and re-examination of many key issues and concerns. In many cases, this has involved not so much a discovery of new facts as a shift in focus to looking at old facts and problems in a new and critical light. It has often meant statements of 'the obvious' (for instance, that workers are gendered subjects; that gender is a major line of division within marriage and family), but an 'obvious' which has been long obscured by the androcentric bias of much routine sociological and other academic practice.

A second major influence, and one clearly reflected in this volume, has been that of unemployment. The slow realisation that unemployment is not some temporary hiccup but very probably a permanent feature of late capitalist society, has brought about a questioning of some of the established and key assumptions within the sociology of work. The identification of work with paid employment; the portrayal of work as a 'central life interest' and a major element in the acquisition of full adult status; the Protestant work ethic; the sharp opposition between work and leisure – these and other assumptions have been brought under scrutiny by changes in patterns of employment and unemployment over recent years.

Together, the joint impact of feminism and of alterations in employment and the labour market has resulted in a critical review of the family, the economy and the relationship between them. To take the question of 'family', there has been a growing appreciation of the protean and variable nature of the concept along with associated terms such as 'household', 'marriage' and 'home'. This has led to some claims that there is no such thing as 'the British family' or 'the industrial family'; and more generally to increased pressure for greater conceptual clarity, for recognition of crucial differences between 'family', 'household' and 'network', and for enhanced awareness of the temporal dimension within family living.

Similarly, the taken-for-granted assumptions about the gender division of labour within the home have been called into question. The myth of the male breadwinner has been recognised within sociological enquiry for some time, even though it still permeates some studies of family, economy and stratification. What remains a matter of interest is the way in which the myth continues to affect everyday practices along with many areas of public policy. Yet, to call into question some of the more traditional notions of the gender division of labour is not to succumb to the further myth of increasing equality or symmetricality between spouses. Several of the pieces in this volume are representative of recent studies which have demonstrated the remarkable resilience of the conventional model on both the level of practice and the level of ideology. Such resilience, even in the face of greater female participation in the paid labour force, at all social levels and among a wide range of industrial countries, is one of the most impressive social facts of our time. The finding that the growing involvement of women in the paid labour force has not been accompanied by a reciprocal trend in the participation of men in the home holds true whether we are considering socialist, social democratic or capitalist industrial societies. Moreover, as at least one of the essays here argues, the growing participation of men in some aspects of domestic life (especially in parenting) will not necessarily be to the benefit of women, whose domestic role and expertise has already been eroded by state, professional and commercial encroachments and whose involvement in the paid labour force is largely marginal and intermittent.

To explain such an impressive persistence we need to take seriously issues of ideology, issues barely addressed in some more restricted treatments of the family. To talk about this, as these essays remind us in different ways, is to consider something which has very deep roots. It is not simply a matter of political or media indoctrination. To explore the issue at any great depth entails asking questions about how language works and about some very fundamental taboos and sentiments in our culture.

If notions of family and household have come under increasing critical attention, the same is true of 'employment' and 'the economy' together with related terms such as 'work' and 'career'. Mention has already been made of the assumption that the worker is a man. Yet it is not enough to argue for recognition of the growing proportion of women within the paid labour force. We should be prepared to accept gender as a relevant category in the analysis of all workers, men and women.

Of equal importance is the reconceptualisation of 'work' itself, involving a severing of its traditional association with 'paid employment'. There is a growing acceptance, reflected within these pages, of the need to broaden the scope of our understanding of the term 'economic activity'. This will include not simply a further and deeper understanding of the economic significance of housework, domestic labour and caring (together with all the activities often euphemistically labelled 'community care'), but also an assessment of the significance of the part played by children within the home. In addition, the familiar distinction between work and leisure will need to be re-examined.

There are further areas related to economic activity which, while they have not been ignored in sociological enquiry, require fuller incorporation into our analyses. For example, the notion of 'the consumer' will have to be reconstructed and brought into the analysis of the relationship between work and family life. This applies especially with respect to the identities of women and children. Likewise, the various direct and indirect interventions of the state need to be absorbed more fruitfully into these discussions and not relegated to some other area of study.

As we have seen an increasing willingness to look critically at the concepts of 'family' and 'work', the relationship between the two areas has come under increasing scrutiny. Gone are the certainties of the single-stranded link through the male breadwinner, assisted in the opposite direction by the housewife, that were so much a feature of traditional functionalist and Marxist analysis. Gone too is the notion of the unambiguous separation of home and work, so much part of received textbook wisdom. In place of this there is a recognition of both separation and unity, of fundamental experiential and theoretical linkages between home and work, and the complexities which follow are explored in the chapters here.

One way of viewing the contributions to this volume is as 'work in progress'. As worthy and as valuable as they are, they nevertheless illustrate the point that the task of reassessing the relationship between family and economy is a still-to-be-completed process. Looking to the future, I would welcome elaborations of the suggestions made at various locations in this volume that the interweave of family and work needs to be explored over time, along the lines of a 'life course' approach. Finally, if we are to assume that both the feminist critique and the widespread presence of unemployment are to be with us for some years to come, we should begin to move beyond an analysis of present dilemmas towards a systematic and thoughtful discussion of alternative models. Studies such as the ones collected in this volume should help us make a start in this direction.

Acknowledgements

The editors wish to thank Reg Smythe for kindly allowing 'Andy and Flo' to appear on the front cover, Lesley Holmes for the skill and effort she put into typing the manuscript, and Karen Fletcher and Stephen Collins for their patient support and encouragement.

The editors and publishers are grateful to Merlin Press for giving permission for use of copyright material in 'The Production of People and Domestic Labour Revisited' by Linda Murgatroyd.

Introduction

PAUL CLOSE AND ROSEMARY COLLINS

It has become commonplace to acclaim the revitalised interest in the study of family life led by feminists, Marxists and critical psychologists. The fresh directions of discourse, however, return time and time again to a longstanding theme — the relationship between the family and the economy. A hundred years ago, Marx proclaimed that the 'capitalist system . . . creates a new economic foundation for a higher form of the family and of relations between the sexes' (Marx, 1974 [originally 1887], p. 460). Ever since, analysts of the family as diverse as Emile Durkheim, Talcott Parsons, Michael Young and Peter Willmott, Christopher Harris, the Conference of Socialist Economists, and radical feminists such as Shulamith Firestone have consistently assigned major explanatory importance to the links between family relations and economic relations.

This collection of essays feeds into the new awareness by exploring signficant aspects of the family's relationship with the economy *in modern society*. It reflects the breadth and variety of facets to this relationship, while focusing on the crucial mediating feature of the social divisions and inequalities which exist within and between families. Throughout, there is tacit recognition of the substantial contribution families make to the operation of economic mechanisms, not only by way of their members' participation in industrial or 'public' production but also by way of their constituent activities, roles and relationships. The book carries the message that in order to understand both the family and the economy in modern society it is essential to grasp the manner in which each is intimately dependent upon the other.

The chapters variously select for attention substantive, conceptual and theoretical issues. Equally, they encompass several explanatory orientations and objectives. The opening chapter by Paul Close sets the theme for the book by reviewing background debates and problems concerning the interplay between family and economy. Close assesses and relates recent notable attempts to account for the development of the modern family in terms of accompanying changes in economic factors and forces.

1

He shows that even when accounts begin from sharply divided theoretical stances, including those of Marxism and functionalism, they nevertheless proceed to adopt common assumptions and to arrive at shared conclusions about the direction in which the family has moved and why. The different approaches converge, not only in crediting 'the economic' with considerable explanatory importance, but also in locating more precisely the principal source of influence on family life. It is generally argued that, although the family has been left with a part to play in relation to the economy, the particular process of *industrialisation* has denuded families of their status as 'units of economic production'. The family's demise in this sense is then usually presented as being fundamental to the development of the further features which help distinguish a modern dominant family form.

Paul Close does not dispute the presence of a dominant family form in modern society, but on the basis of an examination of recent empirical evidence and historical insights in conjunction with an exposition of prevalent concepts and theory, he argues that its origins lie squarely in the advent and progress of *capitalism*. He concludes that the modern family – its dominant form, variations of type, and contradictions – can only be explained primarily in terms of its 'articulation' with the capitalist mode of production. Close rounds off by raising the possibility that, after all, families in modern society not only retain activities which attach them to the economy, but also remain 'units of production' firmly entrenched within the economy. An acceptance of this possibility would pave the way for developing Marxian theory to counter the attack that it cannot be used to analyse the internal character of family life. It has been argued recently that because Marx's theory was designed specifically for the purpose of dealing with 'industrial production' within the 'public domain' of society, its central notions are inapplicable to the highly personalised relations which constitute the 'private domain' of the family (Stacey, 1981).

However, in the second chapter, Linda Murgatroyd meets the challenge to extend Marx's categories into modern family relations. Murgatroyd accepts the view that Marxism, in common with other theoretical approaches, has concentrated on analysing 'economic production' within the public, or 'market', sector of society. But she establishes a point of departure by arguing that it has therefore neglected to take into account that *production* which takes place within the private sphere of the household and family. For Murgatroyd, families in modern society *are* 'units of production'. Moreover, *domestic* labour results in precisely the same types of product as wage-labour, namely *both* goods or the means of subsistence *and* 'people'. Within the family, the production of goods and the production of people are tied together, and especially through 'people production' the family sustains a relationship with capitalism. The family provides the wage-labour, or labour power, upon which capitalist production depends. In turn, families, their activities and relations of production (those between the sexes), are conditioned by the requirements and relations of production which characterise the public sphere of production. While recognising that private production is embedded in somewhat *distinctive* family relationships, divisions and inequalities, Murgatroyd argues against the assumption that it can be analysed separately from public production. After noting the inherent difficulty of drawing a clear boundary between the two types of production which take place in both spheres, she ventures a conceptual scheme as a basis for their integrated analysis.

The concept of 'domestic labour' occupies a central place in a number of Marxian informed accounts of the family. Essentially, these accounts have been concerned with the links which domestic labour secures between the family and the economy via the reproduction of labour power, intra- and inter-generationally (Seccombe, 1974). In addition, feminists have accorded the concept a similar place in their accounts, singling out the way in which gender divisions of domestic labour reflect and reinforce the inequalities women suffer within both family and economic relations (Hartmann, 1979). In Chapter 3, Rosemary Collins uses her research findings on a sample of families in the north-east of England to demonstrate how traditional conjugal divisions of domestic labour have been maintained with the help of ideological rationalisations. The data show that men provide quite a lot of help with the performance of domestic labour (and perhaps more than they used to); that their help increases when their wives are employed; and that it also increases when they are *un*employed. However, what men tend to provide is, literally, *help*. Women are left with the greater share of *doing* domestic labour, and more significantly of the burden of *being responsible* for its performance and completion. This applies whatever the employment status or the social class of the women involved. Traditional divisions, although hidden to some extent behind men's increased help and modern pretensions in support of 'equality', are confirmed in practice by the effects of conventional beliefs and values about the proper places of women and men in the broad sweep of the social division of labour.

Rosemary Collins argues that women's identification with the family may be understood primarily in terms of their continuing material and emotional dependence on men. For Collins, this dependency is rooted in men's more advantageous position in relation to the external economy, which in turn provides legitimation for men's exercise of power and domination within family relations. Collins's argument is supported in the fourth chapter by Lois Bryson's interpretation of the findings from thirty years of research on conjugal divisions in Australia. Bryson's survey reveals that there have been increases in men's participation in a range of tasks in Australian households. This applies especially to those tasks connected with child caring and rearing. However, men's involvement in 'fathering' has been traditionally high compared with their involvement in other, purely domestic, chores. Bryson shows that because men's increased participation in the latter has been relatively limited, their overall share of the performance of domestic labour has been raised only slightly. In line with Collins's conclusions, Bryson argues that any significant alteration in the conjugal divisions of domestic labour will be conditional upon women's entry into paid employment on equal terms with men, and so on the removal of their subordination within the external economy and wider society in general. She postulates that in the absence of such changes, the overall position of women may well decline in so far as men do make inroads into the domestic arena where women have traditionally enjoyed a degree of 'autonomous control'.

There have been claims that women's opportunities in relation to the external economy have improved, and will continue to improve, by virtue of changes *within* the domestic sphere centred on the development and utilisation of household technology. It has been argued that the way women in the past were tied to the household has been weakened by advances in 'labour saving' devices (Berger and Berger, 1983, ch. 4). In Chapter 5, Graham Thomas and Christine Zmroczek investigate this possibility. They address themselves to the issue of the effects of household technology on the content, distribution and organisation of domestic labour, and the way in which in turn the social organisation of domestic labour influences the development of such technology. On the basis of a comparison of time-budget surveys carried out since the 1960s, they are able to document the changes which have occurred in the time spent on individual domestic activities, and the accompanying changes and continuities in the way the burden of domestic labour is divided between husbands and wives. Thomas and Zmroczek demonstrate that, despite a reduction in the drudgery involved in its performance, domestic labour still places considerable demands on time and energy. Moreover, they confirm the findings of both Collins and Bryson that women continue to assume the major share of the burden. They assess the factors which lie behind the persistence of the traditional organisation of domestic labour, and conclude that the promotion of women's 'liberation' is dependent upon broad social change rather than narrow 'technical fixes'.

A large portion of the continuing burden of domestic labour, and one which still falls mainly on the shoulders of women, is concerned with child caring and rearing. As already noted, through this type of domestic labour the family plays a role in the inter-generational production of labour power (in 'people production') on behalf of the economy in modern society. Moreover, there is general agreement that the family has become 'child-centred'; that the everyday lives of adults (especially mothers) have become primarily geared to satisfying the needs of children, and through them the requirements of modern society. Indeed, it has been argued that 'childhood' is a relatively recent *social* construction (Ariès, 1973). A corresponding development would seem to have been a dramatic increase in the academic interest in children. On the topic of 'the history of childhood' alone, whereas during the whole of the 1930s there were about ten books and articles published, during the period 1971 to 1976 there were over nine hundred publications (Tucker, 1984, p. 150). However, in accordance with the everyday treatment of children – the separation of children from the world of adults behind the closed doors of the home and the high walls of the school – academic writings have tended to leave them 'hidden from history', devoid of having played a notable part *as children* in social and economic developments.

Jens Qvortrup, in the sixth chapter, reveals that, on the contrary, children have contributed and continue to contribute to such developments. He employs historical and recent evidence to dispel the myth that children have simply been a burden on adults; merely beneficiaries of adult domestic labour and wage-labour. Children have consistently played an active, reciprocal, part in a broadened notion of the social division of labour. As well as their direct incorporation into economic production, especially during the early stages of industrial-capitalism, children have occupied a crucial place in the 'economic' division of labour through participating in their own socialisation within the family and other agencies, such as schools. Only by recognising the economic role of children is it possible to comprehend the alterations which have occurred in adult treatment and expectations of them; to explain the consolidation of the child-centred family along with the expansion of the system of formal education. Children's activities and relationships are largely conditioned by their indispensability to the maintenance of economic production in modern society. But their importance in this respect is obscured behind the view of them as purely 'dependents'. Accordingly, they are denied the social rights (enjoyed by adults) commensurate with their actual social contribution. They are instead subjected to control by adults, and in particular by their parents, who take charge of their upbringing. For Qvortrup, the fact that it is primarily parents who take on the burden of child caring and rearing presents a paradox. After all, he argues, it is 'society' by way of the economy which benefits from parent–child relations viewed in the context of the social division of labour. However, again, parents will continue to cope with this burden in so far as the economic importance of childhood remains hidden (helped by the clouding of sentiments which surround parenthood).

Just as women within the conjugal division of labour take on the largest share of caring for children, and without any remuneration in recognition of the resulting benefit to the economy, so they assume the main burden of (unpaid) caring in general. In Chapter 7, Clare Ungerson assesses the significance for women of their role as 'carers' for sick and elderly relatives. Using empirical evidence, she argues that the trend towards an ageing population is likely to result in a problem over caring, not for the state, but for women. This is because women tend to perform automatically the task of caring for elderly relatives as an extension of their traditional roles as wives and mothers, while being increasingly drawn into paid employment in the external economy. In a similar way to Rosemary Collins, Ungerson posits the continuing strength of an ideology which stresses that 'a woman's place is primarily in the home' as a principal factor influencing women to try to weave *paid* labour around the servicing requirements of elderly relatives among family members in general. She supports her case by documenting how ideological pressures on women manifest themselves in the 'mothering' taboos and guilt which surround the task of caring. Ungerson points out that women's propensity to care for the 'nation's elderly' is reinforced by the continued existence of substantial disparities between the sexes in earnings and opportunities through wage-labour. The increasing likelihood, nevertheless, of married women taking on paid employment (albeit on a part-time basis) could mean that in the near future they will be regularly performing a 'triple shift', in so far as they will also be caring for husbands and children as well as their elderly relatives. When women find that this round of tasks becomes exhausting or impossible to maintain, they will be likely to give up paid work in favour of unpaid caring. Ungerson proposes that the immediate solution is for women to press for an extension of the state provision of 'services in kind' to relieve them of the burden of being 'carers'.

The suggestion that women's identity with and responsibility for domestic labour in its various guises conditions their approach to paid employment is developed by Judith Chaney in Chapter 8. Thus Chaney argues that women's orientations towards paid employment are fashioned by the character of their relationships with husbands, their obligations to family members in general, along with the constraints imposed by *local* labour markets. She demonstrates the influence of these factors using evidence on the 'return to work' of women in a working-class district in the north-east of England. She argues that, within the limitations of a local labour market, women's chances and choices of paid employment are dependent upon their 'social networks' as channels of information and assistance. At the same time, however, the co-operative aspect of these networks is founded upon a shared understanding among those involved about the primacy of women's domestic responsibilities. Hence, such networks serve to confirm traditional gender identities and divisions. Chaney further reveals how the onus on women to find jobs which fit in with their families' requirements may result in them undergoing a sequence of withdrawals and re-entries into paid employment. The effect of this is to 'de-skill' women in proportion to the frequency of their 'returns', reinforcing their disadvantages and vulnerability within the external economy and thereby their tendency to assume the major share of domestic responsibilities.

The constraints imposed by the labour market in general, but by some labour markets in particular (such as within the north-east of England). have become considerably greater during the 1970s and 1980s due to the massive increase in structural unemployment. In Chapter 9, Jennie Popay examines unemployment's psychological, social and economic consequences as they penetrate family life. By reviewing available evidence, she is able to point out that both being unemployed and facing the prospect of unemployment can have deleterious consequences, and not only for those directly involved, but also those indirectly affected through family ties. Thus, when men are unemployed the consequences are shared by, in particular, their wives – even to the point where their wives display very similar psychological effects. Turning to the consequences of female unemployment, Popay reveals that they vary with the marital status of the women involved. Single women appear to suffer more psychologically, but they are spared the problems faced by married women arising out of their obligations to husbands and children. The consequences for married women reflect their dual burden of being responsible for domestic labour and (increasingly) of being important contributors to family finances. The precarious divide between women being employed and unemployed has become increasingly critical for whether or not their families are in poverty. In that the more dire consequences of female unemployment depend not so much on women's marital status *per se* as on the presence or absence of dependent relatives, it is far more insidious overall in its impact because of the accompanying increases in divorce and lone-parenthood.

For Popay, the effects of unemployment — that is, of changes in the demand for wage-labour stemming from alterations in the requirements and fortunes of the external economy and of those who organise it — vary according to family type. Because of a trend towards a more pronounced diversity of family types, and in particular towards higher proportions of single-parent and dual-worker families, the adverse impact of unemployment is that much greater. The topic of family diversity and its significance for 'the family' in relation to modern economic structures and processes is examined in the final chapter by Jon Bernardes. For Bernardes, it is germane to the theme of the book to consider the issue of both everyday and social scientific notions of 'what the family is' in modern society. He argues that sociologists have been prone to accept a single 'ideal type' model of 'the family', which they then impose on society in the face of evidence of considerable family diversity. The adoption and popularity of this misplaced notion, however, facilitates the easier handling of family life for the purpose of social scientific discourse and theorising. At the same time, it reflects (and in turn helps perpetuate) everyday misconceptions. Bernardes discusses the way in which ideology plays a part in allowing members of modern society to live in 'real', highly diverse, family situations and yet share with sociologists their view of the uniformity of '*the* family'. According to Bernardes, the ideologically informed everyday notion of 'the family' serves the purpose of helping to sustain current social and economic structures. But, he points out, given the aim of social scientific enquiry into the relationship between family life and the economy, it is necessary for sociologists to look beyond *mis*-informed notions of 'the family' in seeking conceptualisations which are sensitive to the *reality* of the diversity and complexity involved.

It is hoped that the purview of the following collection of essays will provide a firm grounding in the 'reality' of the family and its crucial interdependence with the economy in modern society.

1 Family Form and Economic Production

PAUL CLOSE

This chapter examines arguments about the main features of the relationship between the family and the economy in modern society with a view to establishing a general framework within which the issues of the remaining chapters may be located and understood. It considers the possibility that, by virtue of the family's relationship with economic structures and processes, there is a dominant family form in advanced industrial capitalist societies (exemplified by modern Britain). It investigates competing theoretical approaches to the analysis of the modern family, and in particular those which attribute primary explanatory importance to either the process of industrialisation or the progress of capitalism. It assesses the recurring claim that underlying the emergence and development of the modern family has been the demise of families as 'units of economic production'.

It is useful to begin by clarifying the meaning of certain central terms. To speak of 'the family' in modern society, or any society, does not in itself infer a particular 'family form'. The term 'the family' is employed in the same way as the terms 'the economy' and 'the polity', to specify an area of social life whatever form or forms it manifests. It refers to that area of social life covering and circumscribed by kinship (blood or consanguineal relationships) and marriage (conjugal and other affinal relationships) (Fox, 1967, ch. 1). The application of the term in this sense does not presume that in practice there will necessarily be an area of social life which is exclusive to the family. It is conceptually possible for family relationships and, for example, economic relationships to be empirically indistinguishable. As we shall see, the view that in feudal society family relationships were also economic relationships lies behind the idea that in this kind of society families were 'units of economic production'. The term 'a family' then refers to any social group based on consanguineal and/or affinal relationships.[1]

Any instance of a family will be at the same time an instance of one or more 'family types', depending on its composition, content or character.[2] Thus a family may belong to the 'nuclear family' type, if it is composed of a man and a woman and their dependent offspring; to the 'one-parent family' type; to the 'child-centred family' type, and so on. In addition, a range of families and of family types may belong to the same 'family form' in so far as they display a similar overall shape or outward appearance in relation to the rest of society. For example, a set of nuclear families *and* one-parent families may be similarly 'closed' in relation to external kin and community; they may exhibit similar degrees of 'relative autonomy' in relation to other families (Morgan, 1979); their relationships with the economy may be similarly dependent upon the supply of wage-labour, and so on. Moreover, it may be argued that there is in any particular society a family form which is *dominant.* This may be done on various grounds, including the discovery that most families belong to this family form; that all families are converging towards it; that there is a cultural or ideological emphasis on it; that the dominant economic structures and processes are best 'articulated' with it (Harris, 1983), and so on.[3] Thus, it has been widely argued (albeit, as we shall see, in the face of some notable opposition) that modern societies tend to be characterised by a distinctive, dominant family form whereby the 'conjugal family of procreation' is prominent. This is accompanied by further widespread agreement that the source of the dominant 'conjugal family form' lies largely within the economy, even though there is dissension over precisely where within the economy.

The term 'the economy' may be conveniently defined as that area of social life covering and circumscribed by the production, distribution and exchange of goods and services (Sandford, 1982). There is a well-established tradition within the social sciences of formulating *general* theories of society which locate the principal determining or conditioning factors within the economy. However, within this tradition there are 'competing interpretations' of the development of modern society, and 'one major line of division around which different views tend to cluster' (Giddens, 1982, p. 29). Anthony Giddens distinguishes 'the theory of industrial society' from 'the theory of capitalist society'. According to the first, the

> most significant set of changes to be found in the contemporary world is to do with the transition from 'traditional' societies, based on agriculture, on the one hand, to 'industrial societies' based on mechanised production and exchange of goods, on the other. (ibid, p. 33)

It follows from this assumption that there will be 'an essential unity to the industrial order wherever it emerges'. Clark Kerr, for instance, has proposed a 'logic of industrialism' which 'inexorably leads industrial societies to become increasingly alike in their basic institutions, however they may have been originally' (ibid, p. 35; Kerr *et al*, 1973). Whereas the theory of industrial society gives explanatory primacy to the process of industrialisation, the theory of capitalist society has been guided by Marx to give this primacy to the progress of capitalism. Giddens summarises:

> Marx regarded capitalism as both a form of economic enterprise and, since he believed other institutions to be closely involved with this mode of economic organisation, a type of society. Fundamental to Marx's view is the presumption that the origins of capitalism, as a type of economic enterprise, were established well before the industrial revolution, and in fact provided the stimulus for the onset of industrialisation. Capitalist economic enterprise, according to Marx, involves two essential structuring elements. One, of course, is capital. 'Capital' is simply any asset that can be invested so as to secure further assets: it thus includes . . . the means that make production possible [and therefore] after the phase of industrialisation, factories and machines. (Giddens, 1982, p. 43)

The transition to capitalism involves the transformation of the means of production into 'capital', for the purpose of profit and capital accumulation, and it therefore depends on a class of people who own the means of production as capital. But this class in turn depends on 'the second element involved in the constitution of capitalistic enterprise. The accumulation of capital presupposes the formation of "wage-labour", this referring to workers who, in Marx's phrase, have been "expropriated from their means of production"' (ibid, p. 44). Capitalism depends on a class of non-owners of capital which needs to sell its labour power to the capitalist class for wages. In this way, the non-owning class is brought into 'relations of production' with the capitalist class within which it labours and is, thereby, 'exploited' for the purpose of profit and capital accumulation.

For Marx, a particular type of *relations of production* predicated by people's relationships to the means of production is the distinguishing feature of any particular *mode of production*. That is, a 'mode of production', as Chris Harris has put it, 'refers to a set of relations of production specified in terms of different relations to the means of production, and this specification in turn involves relations of possession and the legal categories which give these relations form' (Harris, 1983, pp. 110–11). The set of relations of production predicated by the existence of a class of people who legally own the means of production as 'capital' and the concomitant 'existence of a class of people who can only produce by selling their labour power' (ibid, p. 184) distinguishes the *capitalist* mode of production (CMP) from, for instance, the *feudal* mode of production.[4] Historically, the .CMP developed within feudal society (that is when the feudal mode of production was still *dominant*), but it eventually became dominant, transforming society into 'capitalist society'. This occurrence was the precursor to the eighteenth-century (in England) Industrial Revolution. The latter is specified with reference to major advances in 'machino-facture' and to an associated shift to the factory system of production; but as such, for Marx, it represents a transformation of the means of production *within* rather than *of* the established dominant mode of economic production.

According to the 'theory of capitalist society', the CMP not only remains the dominant mode of production in modern 'advanced industrial' societies such as Britain and the United States, it also continues to be the principal factor conditioning the rest of society (Miliband, 1969; for an alternative view, see Dahrendorf, 1959). It follows that modern capitalist societies will be characterised by institutions which, first of all, will have originated prior to the advent of 'industrial society', and second, will be significantly different from those found in any contemporary societies with distinct dominant modes of production. Thus, whereas in advanced industrial *capitalist* societies 'class relationships directly link the economic organisation of capitalism to the institutions comprising the rest of society' (Giddens, 1982, p. 45), in any advanced industrial *socialist* society there would be no (following Marx) such intervening exploitative relationships (Bottomore and Rubel, 1963, part five).

The competing interpretations of modern society pervade the various accounts of the development of the family. At the same time, however, the prevailing theoretical divide is bridged by certain shared assumptions about the impact of economic change on the family. It is commonly assumed that there has been a fundamental alteration in the family's relationship with the economy, so that whereas families once constituted 'units of economic production' they no longer do so. It is assumed that in this way the family has been removed from its integral place within economic structures and processes, and thereby from its central position within society as a whole. The family's demise in this respect is then thought to have been largely behind the development of the dominant conjugal family form. Moreover, even among those who ostensibly adopt the theory of capitalist society approach to the family, there is nevertheless a tendency to assume that the destruction of families as units of economic production occurs with *and because of* the process of industrialisation.

The theory of industrial society is favoured by those who have provided functionalist accounts of the family. That is, 'Most functionalists have attempted to characterise the modern societal form by reference to the *means* of production utilised. Hence, they refer to modern Western societies as *industrial* societies' (Harris, 1983, p. x). The most influential functionalist account has been that of Talcott Parsons, for whom the Industrial Revolution marks a 'great divide' (ibid, p. 95) between dominant family forms (Parsons, 1964a; Parsons, 1971a; Parsons, 1971b; Parsons, 1959; Parsons, 1952; Parsons and Bales, 1956). He argues, essentially, that the family changed to suit the other characteristics of industrial society, and more precisely that a new dominant family form emerged in response to the *needs* of industrialisation. Parsons asserts that the 'relative absence of any structural bias in favour of solidarity with ascendant and descendant families in any one line of descent has enormously increased the structural isolation of the individual conjugal family. This isolation . . . is the most distinctive feature of the American kinship system' (Parsons, 1964a, pp. 184–5). The American case is indicative of a general trend in industrial societies, in which the 'most stringent kinship obligations' are to be found within 'the conjugal family of procreation isolating this in a relative sense from wider kinship units' (Parsons, 1952, p. 186). Parsons claims, in other words, that in industrial societies marriage brings with it culturally imposed obligations on a husband and wife to each other and to their dependent children, and that such obligations take precedence over any they may have to their respective conjugal families of origin and external kin in general. In this sense, the conjugal family of procreation is *relatively structurally isolated*. It follows that this family form will be the *dominant* family form. As Parsons puts it, 'Ours then is a "conjugal" system in that it is made up exclusively of interlocking conjugal families' (Parsons, 1964a, p. 180); one manifestation of this system being that the 'isolated conjugal family' constitutes the 'normal household unit' (ibid, p. 183).

It may be objected that Parsons's portrayal of the modern family appears inaccurate in the light of evidence from the United States and Britain which demonstrates the continuing salience of 'extended kin relationships',[5] involving such things as considerable contact, the exchange of services and provision of aid, and close emotional ties (Harris, pt 1, s. II; Morgan, 1975, ch. 2). Parsons himself has responded to this discovery by arguing that it is not inconsistent with his claims. According to Parsons, all that it signifies is that 'extended kin constitute a resource which may be selectively taken advantage of within considerable limits'. The members of nuclear families are able to exercise *choices* in relation to extended kin within limits imposed by cultural rules favouring the conjugal family form. In as much as choices are involved, the so-called 'extended families' of industrial societies 'do not form firmly structured units of the social system' (Parsons, 1971a).

Parsons's conclusions have received support from a number of writers (B. Adams, 1971; Harris, 1983). Thus, Chris Harris has agreed that what he labels 'the nuclear family system' does characterise modern, advanced industrial, societies. Moreover, he argues that Parsons's view 'that the nuclear family system is the most *functional* form of family system in an industrial society . . . remains unchallenged' (Harris, 1983, p. 84, my emphasis). Harris clarifies his support for Parsons as follows:

> The *nuclear* family is a social group composed of spouses and *immature* children. Such groups are regularly formed in industrialised societies, and the vast majority of children in these societies are raised in nuclear-family households . . . There can be little doubt that while [extended families] are formed in industrial societies, their incidence is infinitely less frequent than that of nuclear family formation or of the existence of active, extended kinship *networks*. (ibid, pp. 92–3)

Here Harris makes a distinction between 'bounded' extended family *groups*, which subsume nuclear families, and 'unbounded' extended kinship *networks* (ibid, pp. 47–9). Modern societies tend to be characterised by the latter rather than the former because, while there is no feature of the nuclear family system which prevents the formation of families larger than the nuclear family, 'in such a system the formation of extended family groups must remain a matter of private enterprise on the part of the individuals concerned. Such groups are formed as a result of negotiated agreements between autonomous persons' (ibid, p. 93). In other words, Harris argues in line with Parsons that in modern societies there is a cultural emphasis on the conjugal family of procreation; the 'families formed in [such] societies . . . may be termed "conjugal"' (ibid, p. 93); the *dominant* family form is the *conjugal* family form.

Although it may be accepted that extended families are infrequent, it may still be objected that there is evidence which nevertheless contradicts the conclusion that the conjugal family form is *dominant*. It has been argued that in modern Britain there is *no* dominant family form;

that there is evidence instead of a growing *diversity* of family forms. According to Peter Laslett, for instance, ' "The British Family" is not the phrase to use, but a phrase consciously to abandon. For there is now no single British family, but a rich variety of forms . . . a plurality' (Laslett, 1982, p. xii). Laslett claims, more specifically, that 'the stereotype of group consisting of a father, mother and at least two residing children, young children, is entirely misleading in contemporary Britain. A majority of our households now consists of solitaries, people living with persons not their relatives, couples (married and unmarried) without accompanying offspring, or single-parent households' (ibid, p. xii). In other words, as far as Laslett is concerned there is evidence against the view that the conjugal family is dominant and in favour of the alternative view that there is a growing diversity of family forms to be found in modern *household composition*.[6]

Robert and Rhona Rapoport concur with Laslett on the basis of their interpretation of the details on household composition (R. and R. Rapoport, 1982).[7] They assert that 'the conventional family was an adaptive solution to the social and economic circumstance of early industrial society [but] it is no longer [the] dominant form' (ibid, p. 476). Their 'argument is that . . . families in Britain today are in transition from coping in a society in which there was a single overriding norm of what family life should be like to a society in which a plurality of norms is recognised as legitimate and, indeed, desirable' (ibid, p. 477). They have detected in modern Britain, as 'an expression of diverse needs and wishes', an 'emergent diversity of family patterns' (ibid, p. 477).[8] In support of their argument the Rapoports rely very much on the 'diversity recognised in official statistics' on 'household types' during the late 1970s (ibid, p. 479). These statistics, while showing that the 'two or more families' household type accounts for a meagre 1 per cent of all households, demonstrate that 'married couple with children' households account for about 40 per cent. They therefore confirm that 'nuclear family households' do make up only a minority of households. However, apart from the fact that they constitute a *substantial* minority, a problem emerges over whether this figure can be legitimately interpreted as evidence against the view that there is a dominant conjugal family form in modern Britain. That is, the 'married couple, no children' household type is the next most frequent with 27 per cent of the total. If, instead of applying a 'static' interpretation, this figure is perceived in terms of the 'dynamic' process of the 'family life-cycle', it must be taken to include a large proportion of couples who intend to have, will have, or have had children. Thus, Chris Harris has noted how 'central childbearing is to marriage both normatively and practically, and [how] recent studies suggest it continues to be central [even though] child-bearing and rearing will occupy a smaller part of the life course of a contemporary marriage than ever before in history' (Harris, 1983, p. 217). It is likely, given prevailing patterns of fertility, that at any point in time 'married couple, no children' households *will* make up a smaller proportion of all households than in the past, but that just as many will be heading towards or will have recently emerged from the 'nuclear family type' (Rimmer, 1981; *Social Trends*, 1983).

The statistics also show that the 'one-parent family' type household contributes about 8 per cent to the total. However, apart from this figure being relatively small and similar to that for the early 1960s (*Social Trends*, 1981), it is reasonable to assume that a large proportion of these households will be 'in transit' towards the 'nuclear family' type. This follows from the probability that over 60 per cent of them will have been created through divorce or separation, and the further probability that most divorcees will end up remarrying (Harris, 1983, pp. 211–13). It is certainly unlikely that very many one-parent households will be created out of choice or preference, especially when they are the result of the death of a spouse or of extra-marital conception. There is no evidence of any significant increase in the proportions of unmarried women or men choosing to be single parents (ibid, ch. 11).

Finally, the Rapoports' statistics show that the 'one-person' type household involves 21 per cent of the total. However, this includes a figure of 15 per cent which is accounted for by people 'over retirement age'. Again, viewed in terms of the family life-cycle, a large section of this category will represent households in the post-nuclear phase. It is likely that few of them will be the outcome of choice or preference, but that even so they will be on the increase. This will be due to the gains made in longevity, combined with the continuing imbalance in this respect in favour of women. The 'one-person' type household also includes a figure of 6 per cent of all households in which the person is 'under retirement age'. However, given the still considerable popularity of marriage (Dunnell, 1979; Cherlin, 1980), it would seem appropriate to interpret the size of and increase in this figure in accordance with the claim that:

> It seems likely . . . that an increasing (if still small) number of young people are living independently of their families of origin prior to establishing their own nuclear families . . . If this assumption is correct, it constitutes a further move in the direction of a nuclear family system in the sense of the predominant form of domestic group containing parents and *dependent* children only. (Harris, 1983, p. 219)

In other words, in concert with the cultural rules underlying the dominant conjugal family form in modern society, children on reaching 'independence' are increasingly leaving home as part of their preparation for setting up fresh 'relatively structurally isolated conjugal families of procreation'.

The statistics on household composition in modern Britain demonstrate that there is a, perhaps increasing, plurality of household types, and that at any point in time the 'nuclear family' type is not *statistically* normal. However, this cannot be interpreted as evidence against the conclusion that the 'nuclear family household' is *culturally* normal nor, especially, against the view that the *conjugal family form* is culturally prescribed and in this sense 'dominant'. Here, a crucial analytical distinction is being made and a basic methodological principle is being inferred. A household type is not necessarily conterminous with a 'family type' or 'family form', or information about the former does not by itself allow us to draw conclusions about the latter. As Lutz Berkner has put it: 'Valid statements about family structure require an analysis based on the function of kinship ties, the developmental [or family life-cycle] process, the rules of behaviour, not on the composition of narrowly defined residential groups' (Berkner, 1975, p. 738; see also Berkner, 1973). The additional, qualitative information mentioned by the Rapoports in support of their argument is very limited and highly ambiguous (R. and R. Rapoport, 1982, pp. 479–96); it does not mitigate the plausible view in the light of the foregoing discussion that the information on household composition in modern Britain favours, if anything, the conclusion that the 'nuclear family household' and the conjugal family form *are* dominant.

Support for Parsons's depiction of the modern dominant family form should not be confused with support for his explanation of it. According to Parsons, the emergence and predominance of the conjugal family form is explicable in terms of industrialisation's dependency on an economic system within which the incumbents of positions are treated and recruited on the basis of the values of 'universalism' and 'achievement'. In industrial society, therefore, the dominant culture stresses values which contrast with those which underlie family relationships. However, the family adapts to the needs of industrialisation, so that the dominant family form becomes the one which is most suited to the effective operation of the dominant cultural values within the economic system. In this way, Parsons explains not only the relative structural isolation of the nuclear family but also (what he sees as) the characteristic conjugal segregation of roles. Parsons's view of the *functionality* of these two features of modern family life is neatly summarised by Chris Harris:

Major conflict is . . . avoided by *two* types of segregation. The nuclear family is cut off from *wider* kin in the sense that the most stringent ties are confined within it, and because its members do not perform economic roles opposite one another it is also segregated from the *economic system*, except for the husband. In this way intrusion of family values into the sphere of work is avoided and work values do not disrupt the solidarity of the family. (Harris, 1983, p. 58)

For Parsons, the efficiency of the economic system together with the continuing viability of the family is assisted by a conjugal division whereby the husband assumes responsibility for the externally oriented 'instrumental' task of being the (at least principal) holder of an occupation within the economic sphere. The wife, on the other hand, is mainly responsible for the internally oriented 'expressive' tasks of the socialisation of children and the 'stabilisation of the adult personalities' (Parsons and Bales, 1956, p. 17).[9] The wife is therefore responsible for those tasks which, in Parsons's view, explain the persistence of the family in *some* form in modern society. Through her tasks the family continues to perform functions within industrial society and, in particular, for the economic system, in that her responsibilities are those of preparing children for *their* adult roles and of providing stabilising support for her husband to help him cope with the strains arising from his occupation.

But, for Parsons, the family in industrial society performs only *indirect* functions in relation to the economy; it no longer performs any *direct* function. Prior to industrialisation, it is families which co-ordinate economic activity, and more specifically constitute 'units of economic production'. With, and because of, the process of industrialisation the family loses its function of economic production to specialist agencies, such as factories. This occurs as part of a more general 'evolutionary' process involving an increase in task specialisation and social differentiation (Parsons, 1964b).

The removal of the function of economic production has important consequences for family solidarity. It results in the weakening of ties which bind nuclear families into more inclusive family groups. It therefore facilitates the emergence of the conjugal family form in accordance with the requirements of the process of industrialisation. Because the nuclear family, or more precisely the husband, is no longer 'bound to a particular residential location by the occupational, property, or status interests of other [family] members', it is capable of meeting the achievement needs of the now separate economic system (Parsons, 1959, p. 263); hence the relatively high rates of geographical and social mobility in industrial society which further weaken (but do not necessarily destroy) extended kinship relationships.

Parsons's account of the modern family has been the subject of a considerable amount of scrutiny and criticism, usefully assessed elsewhere (Morgan, 1975, part one; Harris, 1983, part one, section II).[10] Of particular relevance to the theme of the present discussion is Chris Harris's point about the 'inadequacy of the concept of industrialisation' as *the* vehicle for explaining the modern family (Harris, 1983, p. 69). Harris argues that 'an attempt to formulate a type of society on the basis of a specification of the means of production alone is unlikely to succeed' (ibid, p. 85; see also Harris, 1977). He questions whether 'industrial society' constitutes a 'coherent theoretical type', claiming that:

> it is difficult to see how it is possible at a theoretical level to derive a description of a societal form from a description of the means of production. 'Industrial' is, therefore, a descriptor which denotes an empirical class of societies. It has no theoretical weight. However, a theoretical basis for the analysis of societal forms is exactly what is required if we are to explain, rather than merely describe, the emergence of the modern family. (Harris, 1983, p. x)

For Harris, the required theoretical basis may be achieved through the adoption of Marxian categories, the central one being, for the purpose of explaining the emergence of the modern family, that of 'mode of production'. This category, as we have already noted, subsumes the further one of 'means of production'. Harris argues that the 'transformation of family life would appear always the resultant of the transformation of economic life' (Harris, 1983, p. 184), and accordingly assumes the theoretical principle that 'family forms must be understood in terms of the part they play in a system of production, either directly or indirectly' (ibid, p. 117), and more specifically in the *dominant* mode of production. He proposes that it is theoretically justifiable 'to characterise social formations in terms of their dominant or predominant mode of production and associated family form' (ibid, p. 117), even though this dominant family form will show some variation, in particular by social class, and the family (its various forms and types) will not be simply *determined* by the dominant mode of production. In line with the *historical*-materialist approach within the Marxist tradition, family forms cannot be explained merely in terms of a mode of production. Their 'explanation always requires reference to conditions which are historically determined and incidental to the mode of production itself' (ibid, p. xi). Thus, in the particular case of capitalist social formations:

What is required is that we show the way in which the development of the capitalist mode of production affected pre-existent family forms, and investigate the outcome of such transformations in terms of their tendency to maintain or undermine the stability of the formation concerned. (ibid, p. 181)

The CMP has not, as such, 'determined' the family, its forms and development; it has merely been the major factor 'conditioning' the family through its interaction with the pre-capitalist family. Moreover, in a consistent fashion, the family will have continued to be involved in what Marxists refer to as a *dialectical* process with the CMP (Zeitlin, 1967, ch. 1).

For Harris, it is axiomatic that the modern dominant family form has its origins in the genesis of capitalism and so in an historical period prior to the Industrial Revolution. He claims that the adoption of Marxian categories requires 'that we see the emergence of modern societal and family forms as occurring not . . . during the process of industrialisation, but . . . with the beginning of the rise of the capitalist mode of production and the bourgeoisie' (Harris, 1983, p. x). He then adds, in accordance with the notion of 'dialectic', that the development of capitalism and its associated family form were pre-*conditions* of the process of industrialisation conceptualised as a transformation *within* the CMP:

> The *first stage* of the industrialisation process requires a concentration *of capital*, and the development of an ideology to justify those who control it . . . Capital concentration destroys the economic base of authority structure of the family while the new ideologies, which justify the concentration of capital and its control, remove its legitimation. It must therefore be inconsistent with the traditional kinship systems of descent-group societies . . . Historically the ideological and economic changes preceded the adoption of industrial means of production and seem to have been a precondition of autonomous industrial growth. It is not surprising, therefore, to discover that the 'conjugal' family also antedated industrialisation. (Harris, 1983, p. 69)

Despite Harris's theoretical and historical tenets, however, it is commonplace for summary statements about the development of the modern family to be made along the following lines: 'The industrial revolution brought about a change in the economic structure of society, the factory replacing the family as the unit of production, and with it certain changes in the social structure, the disintegration of the extended family interdependence and the assumption by the state of many functions previously confined to the family' (Clarke and Ogus, 1978, p. 1). In addition, it is by no means unusual to discover *since Parsons* purportedly original accounts of family development relying on arguments which attribute, if not the sole 'cause', at least considerable explanatory importance to the process of industrialisation. This applies to the accounts not only by other functionalists such as William Goode (Goode, 1963),[11] but also by 'empiricists' such as Michael Young and Peter Willmott (Young and Willmott, 1975), by 'interactionists' such as Brigitte and Peter Berger (Berger and Berger, 1983), and by 'Marxists' such as (in practice) Chris Harris himself.[12]

Young and Willmott suggest that the family form in modern Britain has three main features which distinguish it from earlier forms. In the first place, as claimed by Parsons, 'the nuclear family has become relatively more isolated' (Young and Willmott, 1975, p. 30). Second, 'the couple, and their children, are very much centred on the home' (ibid, p. 29), or, following John Goldthorpe, are more 'privatised' (Goldthorpe *et al.*, 1969). Young and Willmott then argue, in apparent violation of Parsons's view of the modern family, that the 'third and most vital characteristic is that inside the family of marriage the roles of the sexes have become less segregated' (Young and Willmott, 1975, p. 30). This shift, moreover, has been accompanied by one towards greater 'equality' between the sexes. On the grounds that conjugal relationships display a continuing degree of 'difference' (in that a 'division of labour is still the rule') along with 'a measure of egalitarianism', Young and Willmott label the modern family form 'the symmetrical family' (ibid, p. 31).[13]

Young and Willmott argue that underlying the modern family's features is its 'unity' which has been 'restored around its function not of production but of consumption' (ibid, p. 28). The idea that the modern family's relationships with the economy operates to a large degree through its (new) 'function' of consumption is accepted by a wide range of writers (Harris, 1983; Berger and Berger, 1983; Brennan, 1973), even though the designation '*unit* of consumption' has received some sharp criticism (Delphy, 1979). Here, however, Young and Willmott are alluding to a further point – that the family has recently (since the beginning of the twentieth century) emerged out of a stage of disunity and 'disruption' brought about by its previous loss of the function of 'economic production'. Thus they claim that in pre-industrial Britain families were usually units of economic production, in that 'For the most part, men, women and children worked together in home and field.' But this 'economic partnership' was destroyed during the eighteenth and nineteenth centuries because the Industrial Revolution 'outmoded old techniques of production' and brought many new 'forms of employment which shared one vital feature, that the employees worked for wages'. This led to a new family form arising, in the first place, within the working class because its members were the ones who were 'caught up in the new economy as individual wage-earners. The collective was undermined' (Young and Willmott, 1975, pp. 28–9).

In their account of the development of the modern family, Young and Willmott give considerable *theoretical weight* to the process, and in particular the arrival, of industrialisation. For them, the Industrial Revolution had the crucial effect of destroying the specific 'unity' of pre-industrial families based on their location within the economy as 'units of production'. It did this by drawing out family members to work with the new 'techniques of production' as *individual* wage-earners. A similar view of the impact of industrialisation appears to be held by Brigitte and Peter Berger (Berger and Berger, 1983, ch. 4), even though they otherwise emphasise that industrialisation is not the *original* source of the modern family. They argue that the emergence of the modern family can be traced back to well before the Industrial Revolution, to the preceding development of capitalism.

The Bergers label the modern family 'the peculiar Western family', on the grounds that it is 'a significant deviation from the "common human pattern"'. They claim that the 'central idea of [this] nuclear family' is that 'the household consists of only a married couple and their children'. But it has other features: it is 'domesticated', 'privatised' and child-centred. In addition it is characterised by a distinctive type of conjugal relationship, in that the relation between the spouses is 'one of intense mutual affection and respect'. Moreover, within 'the household, at least, the woman is seen as equal if not dominant.'[14] The Bergers also apply the label 'bourgeois family' because, they claim, the modern family occurred 'first and foremost in the bourgeoisie'. They then charge the bourgeoisie, its family and culture, with considerable influence on social change since the period of the Industrial Revolution. Thus, from the end of the eighteenth century 'the history of the West is, in a very basic sense, the history of the bourgeois class and its culture'. During the nineteenth century the bourgeois family gradually became the model for all social classes, and by the middle of the twentieth century it had been adopted throughout all Western societies.

The diffusion of the bourgeois family has been the outcome of the '"evangelistic", or missionary' zeal of the bourgeoisie, helped by the 'power of the state', the 'rise in standards of living made possible by industrial technology', and the 'technological transformation of the household' which has led to 'an extraordinary reduction in women's menial tasks'.[15] For the Bergers, the development of the modern family has in turn been more than merely incidental to the process of industrialisation. It has even been the 'pivotal institution' in this process. The Bergers argue, in effect, that the bourgeois family has been of major *functional* importance in relation to the process of industrialisation, which together with urbanisation they identify as 'modernisation'. They propose that this family form has been 'small and mobile enough to allow individuals to participate in modernisation, and at the same time tightly knit enough to make this participation humanly tolerable'. What the Bergers have in mind here is made clear by their suggestions as to the advantages of being a housewife in modern society. Within the domestic sphere, women enjoy ' "liberation" from the discontents of the marketplace'. In other words, housewives are *free* of having to cope with the situation of 'the working father', for whom 'the home becomes the locale of withdrawal from the tensions and worries of the job, a place of refuge and renewal, where the "real life" of the individual can unfold.'[16]

The Bergers, in the same way as Parsons, depict the modern family as positively functional (or *eu*functional) in relation to economic structures and processes. In contrast, however, other writers have focused on what they see as its *dys*functions. As Michael Haralambos has reported:

> Fran Ansley translates Parsons's view, that the family functions to stablize adult personalities, into a Marxian framework. She sees the emotional support provided by the wife as a safety-valve for the frustration produced in the husband by working in the capitalist system. Rather than being turned against the system which produced it, this frustration is absorbed by the comforting wife. In this way the system is not threatened. In Ansley's words, 'when wives play their traditional role . . . they often absorb their husbands' legitimate anger and frustration at their own powerlessness and oppression. With every worker provided with a sponge to soak up his possibly revolutionary ire, the bosses rest more secure' (quoted in Bernard, 1976, p. 233). (Haralambos, 1980, p. 341)

From a Marxist perspective, modern family life may be functional in helping to maintain and promote prevailing economic structures and processes, but in that it is thereby eufunctional in relation to the interests of the capitalist class it is, at the same time, dysfunctional in relation to the working class's interests (which include the socialist revolution) and to women in their 'unliberated' role as 'traditional' wives. According to Marxists, there are a number of ways in which the modern family plays a major part in 'social reproduction' (Morgan, 1979) in relation to the

economy against the interests of the working class, by way of the reproduction of *labour power* not only *intra*-generationally but also *inter*-
generationally. Thus, David Cooper has argued that the modern family
is 'an ideological conditioning device in an exploitative society': within
it the 'child is in fact primarily taught not how to survive in society but
how to submit to it' (Cooper, 1972; see also Althusser, 1972).

The Marxist 'janus headed' view of the modern family's relationship
with economic structures and processes has been usefully summarised as
follows:

> Marxists have stressed . . . the functionality of the family for capitalism:
> it is a prime means of transmission of bourgeois ideology; its parti-
> cularism militates against the class universalism of the proletariat; it
> dampens discontent in the economic sphere by providing workers
> with a psychological outlet denied them in the labour process. (Harris,
> 1983, p. 179)[17]

As Harris points out, on the basis of their view of the modern family in
relation to the economy, Marxists in a way which is characteristic of
functionalist accounts tend to 'slip into a   teleological . . . mode of explanation of the family' (ibid, p. 193). In other words, they are prone to
identify the 'causes' of the modern family, its form and development, with
its consequences in meeting the needs and interests of the capitalist class
at the expense of the working class. Harris finds this kind of explanation
unacceptable (as do critics of functionalism in general: see Cohen, 1968).
But also, connectedly, both Marxists and functionalists as well as the
Bergers tend equally to concentrate on the 'satisfactory' as opposed to
the 'dark side' of modern family life (Morgan, 1975, ch. 3). It is to this
alternative, 'unsatisfactory', side that recent 'critical psychologists' have
drawn attention (for discussions see Morgan, 1975, ch. 4; Poster, 1978).
Most notably, R. D. Laing has made the generalisation that the experience,
demands and pressures of modern family life lend themselves to the
possibility of children and adolescents trying to escape by withdrawing
into themselves, in a way which is liable to attract the label 'schizophrenic'
(Laing, 1971). The character of family relationships within modern society
has then been linked specifically with the dominant conjugal family form,
as in a dramatic but memorable statement by Edmund Leach:

> Today the domestic household is isolated. The family looks inward
> upon itself; there is an intensification of emotional stress between
> husband and wife and parents and children. The strain is greater than

most of us can bear . . . The parents and children huddled together in their loneliness take too much out of each other. The parents fight; the children rebel. (Leach, 1967)

Chris Harris has adopted a poignant term to sum up the pressures of life within the conjugal family form while suggesting that they may be explained with reference to the character of surrounding society:

> The resultant concentration of creative and emotional energies within this small compass constitutes . . . the family's *implosion* or 'the bursting inward of a vessel by external pressure'. The notion of 'bursting' refers basically to the tensions created within the family by the attempt to realise within the family-household the creative potentials of its members which are denied expression elsewhere. (Harris, 1977, p. 79)

Here, Harris is alluding to the view of Parsons, the Bergers and Ansley of the pressures, tensions and dissatisfactions experienced within the economic sphere of modern society. For him, however, rather than being countered by a satisfactory family life, these features of surrounding society mould the family in their own image. The implosion of the conjugal family form means that the demands made upon it by its members cannot be met. A result may be the well-documented widespread occurrence of family conflict and violence (Dobash and Dobash, 1980; Johnson, 1981; Wilson; 1983) and adolescent 'rebellion' (Hall and Jefferson, 1976; Marsh *et al.*, 1978; Corrigan, 1979). Given its unsatisfactory character, the possibility arises of the modern family being dysfunctional for all its members and in consequence, moreover, for the rest of society. However, there is a plausible alternative possibility. By virtue of the dark side of family life, an outlet may be available for the potentially dysfunctional responses to, in particular, the economic sphere. The conjugal family form may be especially effective in this regard in so far as there is a cultural emphasis on 'the family' and its value as *the* area of society within which people can *or should* satisfy their emotional, affective and creative needs. Individuals will be ideologically persuaded to release their tensions through each other within the confines of the family, perhaps through conflict and violence, behind 'closed doors'. The modern conjugal family form may be dysfunctional 'at the level of the individual' (Morgan, 1975, p. 93), but it will be at the same time eufunctional in relation to economic structures and processes, and thereby the capitalist class.

One way of representing the simultaneous dysfunctional and eufunctional consequences of modern family life is with reference to the notion of 'contradiction'. The conjugal family form is both ideologically and structurally (by way of its articulation with the economy) 'affirmed', with the positive consequences this has *at the level of society* in the interests of the capitalist class. At the same time, in a contradictory manner, it is 'negated' by its internal character and the everyday experiences of its members, with the dysfunctional consequences this has at the level of the individual and for the working class (for relevant discussions, see Morgan, 1975, pp. 96–9; Harris, 1983, ch. 9; Sennett, 1970; Sennett and Cobb, 1977; Mitchell, 1971; Zaretsky, 1976)

As Morgan has noted about Parsons: 'Contradictions, or even serious dysfunctions, do not make an appearance in his work.'[18] Both Parsons and the Bergers portray the modern family in a somewhat idyllic fashion and as having only eufunctions in relation to the economy and for *society as a whole*. Nevertheless, the Bergers part company with Parsons when it comes to the issue of the significance of these functions for the explanation of the dominant conjugal family form. Parsons, in a teleological way, explains the modern family in terms of its consequences in meeting the needs of industrialisation, viewing it as an adaptation to industrial society and so as having major differences from the pre-industrial family. The Bergers argue that, on the contrary, the modern family appeared well before, and (by virtue of its functions) helps explain, the advent of industrialisation.

They claim that although the 'bourgeois' family's dominance can be traced to the eighteenth-century period of the Industrial Revolution, its origins are to be found in much earlier events. The modern family 'emerged in the West during the sixteenth and seventeenth centuries among the merchant and artisan strata of the towns', and 'in Western Europe in the sixteenth century if not earlier' (even as early as 'the high middle ages'). This leaves the Bergers in no doubt that its emergence was a *precondition* of industrialisation. Indeed, they go as far as to assert that 'modernity did not produce the nuclear family, but, on the contrary, the nuclear family produced modernity' (Berger and Berger, 1983, p. 91). The Bergers are led to the conclusion that the origins of the modern family lie in the pre-industrial development of capitalism:

The family and the economy changed in tandem. As early as the fourteenth century, in the very early stages of European capitalism, there emerged ... the separation of economic activities from family life ... Concomitantly, a distinctive private sphere began to come into being, separated from economic activity ... Also concomitantly, contractual relationships gained importance. (ibid, p. 96)[19]

In a similar way to Young and Willmott, the Bergers then single out for special attention those contractual relationships involving wage-labour:

> The rise of wage labor [*sic*], at the very beginnings of capitalism and prior to the coming of the industrial revolution, changed the relation of the household to economic production. Already in the late middle ages one can discern differences in family patterns between peasants and the classes out of which, later, the bourgeoisie was to emerge ... When industrialisation did come, of course, the nature of work changed fundamentally. Most important, productive work was progressively taken out of the household. The family changed from being a unit of production to being a unit of consumption. (ibid, p. 92)

This statement raises a number of questions not clearly answered by the Bergers. First, in that it would have been the (emergent) working class which was separated from the economy except for its supply of wage-labour, why wasn't it within this class (as Young and Willmott argue) rather than within the bourgeoisie that the modern family arose? Second, on what precise grounds can it be claimed that, on the one hand, there was a separation of the family from the economy (involving a change in its relationship to economic production) with the very emergence of capitalism, but that, on the other hand, families remained 'units of production' until industrialisation? Third, assuming that the destruction of families as units of production would constitute a fundamental alteration in the family's relationship with the economy, are the Bergers (in line with the implications of Young and Willmott's account and with the analysis of Parsons) inferring that, after all, the process of industrialisation is of crucial explanatory importance to the development of the modern family?

The agreement between Parsons, the Bergers, and Young and Willmott that industrialisation destroyed families as units of economic production would seem to rest on what are variously identified in their accounts as three connected consequences of industrialisation: first, the transfer of economic production to specialised agencies (Parsons); second, the transfer of this activity from households (the Bergers); and third, the participation of members of families in economic production as *individual* wage-earners (Young and Willmott). It is interesting to note that, in view of his stated theoretical principle that the family needs to be explained primarily in terms of its relationship with the dominant *mode* of production, Chris Harris argues likewise that it was left to these consequences of the Industrial Revolution (which, after all, in terms of Marxian categories represents merely a transformation of the *means* of production *within* the dominant

CMP) to have the fundamental effect on families of destroying them as units of economic production.

Harris proposes (in a way which is consistent with his theoretical principle) that 'the family under capitalism . . . is a "capitalist" family form' (Harris, 1983, p. 199). More specifically, he argues that within 'capitalist-industrial societies' the predominant family form is 'nuclear, "bourgeois" and "proletarian"' (ibid, p. 177). He clarifies his choice of labels by suggesting:

> within social formations characterised by the capitalist mode of pro-
> duction and industrial means of production . . . The vast majority
> of families are 'proletarian' in the sense that their members subsist
> by selling their labour power, or are dependent upon someone who
> does sell his/her labour power. Equally, they are all 'bourgeois' families
> in the sense of being 'closed domesticated nuclear families'. (ibid,
> p. 154)

Harris's use of the term 'capitalist-industrial' is significant. While, as we have already noted, he expresses doubts about the functionalist assumption that 'industrial society' constitutes a distinct theoretical type, he nevertheless proceeds to agree that 'modern' societies differ in a major way from earlier societies and that the dividing line between them can be located during the period of the adoption of the industrial means of production (ibid, p. x). That Harris does after all treat 'industrial society' as a distinct theoretical type becomes clear during his detailed account of the transformations which have occurred in the family from the early stages of capitalism through the Industrial Revolution to the present.

According to Harris, not all aspects of the modern dominant family form are peculiar to capitalist-industrial societies: some were established well before the Industrial Revolution. He notes in a Parsonian fashion that the nuclear family system is *functional* in relation to modern economic structures and processes:

> such a family system is consonant with social formations whose political
> and economic order requires that the society is seen as composed of a
> plurality of free, equal and independent individuals . . . unimpeded in
> their response to the operation of the market as they seek their indi-
> vidual interest and profit. [There is a] 'fit' between the 'nuclear family
> system'/'conjugal family form' and 'industrial society'/'capitalist social
> formations'. (ibid, pp. 93–4)

However, like the Bergers, he is in no doubt that the nuclear family system existed before the onset of industrialisation and that considerable importance needs to be attached to its pre-existence in any explanation of this process (ibid, p. 94). For supporting evidence, Harris refers to the findings of Peter Laslett and his colleagues on household composition in pre-industrial England, as well as to the work of Alan Macfarlane on the development of 'individualism' (Laslett, 1971; Laslett and Wall, 1972; Macfarlane, 1978). He then feels able not only to claim that this feature of the modern family pre-dated the Industrial Revolution by six centuries (Harris, 1983, p. 114), but also to accept the possibility that in England it even existed well before *the development of capitalism*. Thus, Harris does not rule out Alan Macfarlane's hypothesis that, unlike the rest of Europe, England did not witness a transition from the peasant mode of production to the CMP, 'for the very good reason that the peasant mode of production never established itself in England in the first place' (ibid, p. 111). Rather than the family form associated with the peasant mode of production, namely the 'collectivistic' family form represented by the (modified) 'classical extended family', for Harris it is probable that England always had the 'individualistic' family form represented by the 'smallholding family' (ibid, p. 117). He infers that the pre-existence of individualism and, connectedly, the nuclear family system helps explain why it was that capitalism arose *in England* instead of elsewhere. Although this may be a plausible argument, it begs the questions 'what is the source of the pre-capitalist nuclear family system which persists in modern society?'; 'if the modern nuclear family system is not explicable in terms of the CMP, does it represent some kind of exception to Harris's theoretical principle that the family, its forms and development, can only be explained primarily in terms of its relationship with the dominant mode of production?' If it is an exception, it would appear to be not the only one – at least, that is, if Harris's further analysis of the development of the modern dominant family form is anything to go by.

According to Harris, whatever the agrarian family form (or forms) which preceded capitalism, it was superseded by certain distinct family forms associated with transitional 'forms of production' specific to the period between medieval society and 'the rise of industrial society' (ibid, p. 116). That is,

> In contrast to [the] distinctively agrarian forms of production and family are those characteristics of 'protoindustrialisation', which term has been used to refer to the movement of manufacturing industry into the countryside during the seventeenth and eighteenth centuries.

This process was already underway in England at the beginning of the sixteenth century. (ibid, p. 118)

Harris offers an alternative way of locating the protoindustrial period: it occurred during the centuries between the 'feudal' period and the 'capitalist' period (ibid, p. 118). Here, he uses the label 'capitalist' to delineate the historical period since the CMP became dominant. To do so is conceptually respectable. However, the way in which he clearly identifies the advent of the 'capitalist' period with 'the rise of industrial society' is historically questionable. On unspecified grounds, Harris links 'the seventeenth century with the beginning of the rise of the capitalist mode of production and of the bourgeoisie' and the nineteenth century with 'the triumph of the bourgeoisie in which capitalism becomes the predominant mode of production' (ibid, p. x). This is somewhat later than others (as we shall see) have placed these events, at least in the case of England where they first occurred. But Harris goes further than merely *identifying* 'capitalist society' with 'industrial society'. He asserts that the accession of the CMP as the dominant mode of production was 'a victory to which the adoption of the industrial means of production was vital' (ibid, p. x). This clearly implies that the eventual predominance of the CMP and so of capitalist relations of production can only be explained by that transformation of the *means* of production within it which marks the Industrial Revolution. This is dubious in terms of Marxian theory: it is inconsistent with Harris's proclamation that the CMP (specified in terms of its distinctive relations of production) has greater theoretical value than merely the industrial means of production (than does the designation 'industrial society'). But it does suit his wish to identify 'industrial society' with 'capitalist society', and his approach *in practice* to the explanation of certain defining features of the modern dominant family form.

For Harris, the agrarian forms of production which preceded protoindustrialisation were associated with family forms in which families were units of economic production. However, protoindustrialisation was accompanied by the growth of a 'class of landless rural dwellers' who became caught up in the new form of production as a 'new class of cottage workers' (ibid, pp. 118–19). He argues that this development continued swiftly during the seventeenth century as feudal tenures were abolished and traditional landownership was undermined, culminating in the eighteenth-century Enclosure Acts when the smallholder was deprived of the use of common land. The landless provided a pool of wage-labour which to begin with was employed within the agrarian economy, but was gradually drawn into expanding 'rural manufacture' (ibid, pp. 123–4). It was then, in

England, that the dispossessed smallholding families and the families of agricultural labourers were 'modified, by market pressures, to approximate to the protoindustrial family' (ibid, p. 123).

Harris then makes the important claim that the protoindustrial family form was intermediary between the family as 'a property owning unit of production', based on ownership of or access to land, and the family as 'a unit of labour supply for capitalist production', that is the *proletarian* family (ibid, pp. 120, 124). Although, like the latter, the protoindustrial family depended totally or almost totally on wage-labour, it nevertheless 'combined the same functions as the propertyowning family' (ibid, p. 124) which had preceded it. In other words, 'protoindustrialisation preserved and did not dissolve the family-based forms of production which had pre-existed it' because it 'depended on the continued existence of families as productive units' (ibid, pp. 119–20).

Apart from the questionable (in the light of Harris's own doubts about the acceptability of functionalist teleological explanations) implication that families remained units of economic production *because of* their consequences in meeting the needs of protoindustrialisation, Harris's account so far raises the issue of 'in what sense can it be claimed that dispossessed, wage-dependent, families still constituted *units* of economic production?'. Harris provides a clear answer: 'protoindustrialisation threw up family forms which [were] still based on the family as an economic collectivity' (ibid, p. 120). The protoindustrial family may have depended on wage-labour, but it still operated as a 'labour collective'; its members did not sell their labour power in individual 'packets' to employers and were, therefore, unlike the members of the subsequent proletarian family.[20] In sum:

> The protoindustrial family, like the peasant family, constituted a self-regulating unity of labour, consumption and production. (ibid, p. 122).

According to Harris, although protoindustrialisation depended on and preserved families as units of economic production, it also established the conditions which resulted in their demise in this form. The class of cottage workers waned as 'it became possible to cut production costs . . . by the introduction of modern machinery into the productive process', and crucially by the introduction of the factory system of production (ibid, pp. 119–20). It was this latter development (in the last half of the eighteenth century) which finally destroyed families as units of economic production; which heralded the 'process of proletarianisation' with its accompanying distinctive family form (ibid, p. 125).[21]

For Harris, it is essential to an understanding of the emergent proletarian family to recognise that it differed from its predecessors in a
fundamental way: 'the family itself was not the unit of production'
because it had been displaced 'by the factory as the unit of production'
(ibid, p. 127). The process of proletarianisation and the rise of its family
form continued during the nineteenth century until eventually there was
a 'mature industrial economy' with a 'free' labour market on which a
proletariat made up of 'male individuals' competed for wages to support
the dependent members of their nuclear families (ibid, p. 127). By way of
its consequences for families as units of economic production, the process
of industrialisation:

> transformed the *character* of the domestic group, and the character
> of people's relations to their kinsfolk. This transformation came about
> as a result of the change in the mode of production which meant that
> employment, not family membership, became the precondition of adult
> existence; as a result of geographical mobility and the increase of
> settlement size [urbanisation] which diminished the efficiency of
> traditional controls over individual behaviour. (ibid, p. 130)

It becomes apparent that in the end, despite his declaration of support
for Marxian theory, Harris colludes with the reasoning which led Parsons,
the Bergers, and Young and Willmott to conclude that industrialisation
had the effect of destroying families as units of economic production, and
so of removing them from their integral place within the dominant mode
of production and their central location within society. In a manner consistent with *this* argument, Harris then implies that it was *industrialisation*,
rather than the prior development of capitalism, which undermined the
basis for nuclear families being subsumed within more inclusive family
groups – which brought about the 'relative structural isolation of the
conjugal family of procreation'.

Harris claims that the separation of *families* from economic production
is of vital importance to the task of understanding family forms following
the Industrial Revolution because:

> Once the transition to factory production has been made, we can no
> longer even make preliminary distinctions between family forms with
> reference to their productive activities . . . In other words . . . relation
> to the means of production [is no longer an] adequate criterion . . .
> for distinguishing the diversity of family forms which exist within a
> society with . . . a predominantly individualistic family type, and in

which, being capitalist in its basic structure, the majority of the population live by selling their individual labour power. (ibid, p. 133)

This statement *does* imply that the dominant family form in modern society can only be explained in terms of the relationships which families have (by way of the exchange of labour power for wages) with the CMP. But it nevertheless embodies an anomaly by explicitly departing from Marxian categories and theory. According to Harris, the Marxian notion of 'class' — used to denote a category of people with a distinct relationship to the means of production and which is thereby engaged in specific relations of production — has no value for 'the sociology of the family in capitalist-industrial societies' (ibid, p. 133). It would appear that as far as Harris is concerned 'class' ceased to have any theoretical relevance with and because of the Industrial Revolution. This is curious, because presumably the majority of the population still live by selling their labour power *to capitalists*, and will thereby be brought into *capitalist* relations of production (that is, class relationships in the Marxian sense) with the latter.

It is a central assumption of Marxian theory that 'class' divisions and relationships are integral to and inevitable under capitalism; that they are of primary explanatory importance in accounting for capitalist society *even in its industrial phase*. Hence Marx's 'class theory' of capitalist development towards the socialist revolution (Bottomore and Rubel, 1963; Fischer, 1973; Crompton and Gubbay, 1977; Giddens, 1981, ch. 1). For Marx, the particular relations of production which arose with the CMP were not transformed by that advance in the means of production which marks the Industrial Revolution: but, instead, they continue to be the distinguishing feature of the dominant mode of production in 'capitalist-industrial' society and so continue to have the same explanatory value.

Harris does not claim that there are no 'classes' in modern society. He *does* argue that in order to be able to account for the family since the Industrial Revolution 'we need to make distinctions in terms of the class situation . . . of the family'. However, what he has in mind here are distinctions 'between types of workers in terms of their labour-market situation, occupational history, relation to and type of community, and work and political orientation' (Harris, 1983, pp. 133–4). In other words, Harris favours the adoption of the Weberian definition of 'class' in terms of 'market situation' (Weber, 1966; Gerth and Mills, 1964), along with subsequent neo-Weberian modifications.[22] This suits his account of the development of the modern family because, as we have seen, he argues in effect that industrialisation destroyed families as units of economic production by way of its consequences for the labour market; for the 'market situation' or wage-labour. Whereas before industrialisation families exchanged labour power on the market as a 'collective unit', as a result of industrialisation family members exchanged their labour power as individuals.

However, in contrast to Weber's general notion of 'class' and Harris's application of this notion to capitalist-*industrial* societies, Marx and Marxists do not locate class divisions and relations at the level of the market. Marxists employ the term 'class' to denote those categories of people between which there are relationships characterised by inherent conflict and 'exploitation' due to their distinctive but mutually dependent relationships to the means of production. This is because *these* relationships have primary explanatory importance in the analysis of society and social change. These relationships underlie *and explain* market relationships and 'market situations'. As the Marxists Rosemary Crompton and Jon Gubbay (Crompton and Gubbay, 1977) have argued, under capitalism the purveyors of labour power on the market are not 'cheated', that is exploited, during the process of exchange; they receive the full 'exchange value', in the form of wages, for their commodity. But, the *fair* exchange which characterises market relationships represents merely 'surface processes' which serve to hide those underlying inequitable relations of production to which Marx's notion of 'class' draws attention (ibid, pp. 12–14).

For Marxists, market relationships have very limited explanatory value as far as the analysis of capitalist society is concerned (see Shaw, 1974). They themselves require explanation, and they can be explained in terms of capitalist relations of production. Class divisions and relationships in the Marxian sense explain what Weber and his followers take for granted, namely 'the market' and in particular the market in labour power. Thus, Crompton and Gubbay

raise the question of *why* skills and resources have assumed [a] marketable, commodity-like quality. [They answer] that these 'commodities' have emerged *as* commodities because of the development of capitalist relations of production. Such a mode of production requires freely transferable property and readily available labour. (Crompton and Gubbay, 1977, p. 17)

Labour power is a productive or creative capacity (Zeitlin, 1967, pt. II) and is, therefore, an ahistorical or universally applicable category. However, it takes on a particular form, that of a commodity, under capitalism because the development of the CMP requires and results in a dispossessed class which is available to exchange its labour power for wages.

If Harris were to be consistent with Marxian categories and theory, he would not offer an explanation of the modern family primarily in terms of market relationships (at any stage of capitalism) and changes which have occurred in them (including those associated with industrialisation). He would, instead, try to provide an explanation in terms of the advent, development and persistence of the more fundamental capitalist relations of production. His explanation would unequivocally locate the origins of the modern dominant conjugal family form in the very emergence of those relations of production which involve the employment and 'exploitation' of a class of producers by a class of owners of 'capital' for the purpose of profit and capital accumulation.

At points in his *actual* account. Harris gets close to the kind of explanation which would be consistent with his theoretical pretensions. He notes how the transition from feudalism to capitalism entailed the producers' dispossession of the means of production and resulting emergence as 'free' wage-labour to be employed by the capitalist class. They were employed initially in the 'agrarian economy', and then in rural, cottage-based, manufacture. Eventually they were transferred to urban, factory-based, machinofacture because, according to Harris, 'the needs of the capitalist [class] could no longer be met through rural manufacture' when the factory system of production became technically possible (Harris, 1983, p. 120). That is, the producers *could be* employed and transferred because they had been 'freed' from the means of production; or, to put it another way, they *were* employed and transferred because it was in the capitalist class's interests and *power* to do so. Their employment not only in successively different forms of production, but also as *families* and subsequently as *individuals* can be explained in this way.

It is historically general to the CMP that the capitalist class, by virtue of its possession of the means of production, can exercise control over the labour of those who are dependent on wages. Gordon Causer has noted the continuing importance in modern Britain of the possession of capital to the distribution of power and control (Causer, 1982). In the first place, private property in the means of production is highly concentrated, and far more so than other types of private property. Thus the richest 2.5 per cent of the population own over 25 per cent of all wealth in private hands, and about 70 per cent of the land and shareholdings included in this total (ibid, p. 131).[23] But, as Causer goes on to point out:

the significance of property lies ... not in its concentration alone, but in the relationships that are constituted by, and in their turn reproduce, the unequal distribution of wealth . . . Where property takes the form of land, or industrial or commercial capital, where its utilisation requires the use of the labour of others, a . . . set of rights involving the exercise of authority over labour . . . is entailed by the more general rights of control. (ibid, p. 131)

Causer argues that the institution of private property in the means of production and its associated authority and control relationships are of crucial importance to the class analysis of modern capitalist societies such as Britain (ibid, p. 131).[24]

The question arises: 'was there not a similar, if not greater, concentration of ownership and of authority and control prior to capitalism?' The answer to this can be found in a summary by John Scott of the particular form taken by feudal relations of production (Scott, 1982). In the feudal mode of production there was:

a set of underlying relations of production in which those who had *ultimate possession* of the land, as the basic means of production, were separated from those who actually worked the land . . . But the legal title to the land which the landlord held could not be directly translated into control over the conditions of production. The actual producers, the serfs, had *immediate possession* of the land. (ibid, p. 9)

Under feudalism, the lord may have owned the land but the serf as the producer had day-to-day, or *effective*, control over it as the means of production. The corollary to this control was that the producer, rather than the lord, also had effective control over the process of production, his or her labour, and the product of labour. This was the case despite the lord's intervention in the process of production by way of his demand for 'rent': that is, his appropriation of 'surplus product' and 'surplus labour' — the measure of his 'exploitation' of the producer.

According to Scott, during the twelfth century the feudal mode of production began to decline as the appropriation of surplus product and surplus labour became increasingly mediated by money and the market. The expansion of the market was in turn a reflection of the increasing influence of urban-based merchants as the incipient capitalist class. Under their guidance, the agrarian form of production became commercialised and capitalistic: hence the process 'often described as the "transition from feudalism to capitalism"' which 'resulted in a fundamental transformation of the pattern of stratification' (ibid, p. 12). The transition from feudalism culminated in the sixteenth-century victory of the CMP as the dominant mode of production. Capitalist relations of production became consolidated as producers lost their effective control of the land, due to the ending of serfdom and the enclosure movement, and so were finally separated from all possession in relation to the means of production. By the sixteenth century, the capitalist class and the wage-earning class opposed each other as the two principal classes in society (ibid, p. 19).

In that the process by which the producers became completely separated from possession of the means of production began with the advent of capitalism, the 'proletariat' in the Marxian sense emerged at the same historical moment. Having been dispossessed, producers were now totally dependent on wage-labour, on the sale of their labour power for wages to capitalists. After purchase, labour power like any other commodity is consumed — it is 'put to work' (Crompton and Gubbay, 1977, p. 13). Capitalists (and/or their agents) gain control over labour power; they co-ordinate and direct it within the process of production. During this process, the producers *labour*; they perform the practical activity of producing and creating value. The producers, labour power and labour are then controlled purely in the interests of capitalists, in the pursuit of profit and capital accumulation.

The transformation of labour power into a commodity is, as far as Marxists are concerned, of considerable significance for producers and the relations of production in which they are engaged under capitalism. As Crompton and Gubbay put it:

> capitalist relations of production involve the voluntary surrender of creative capacity, one result of which is the expropriation of surplus product in the form of surplus value. It is not simply that the worker has no [rights in the means of production and no] control over the product of his labour, but that the worker loses any control over labour itself. The surrender of creative capacity — labour power — is as much a part of capitalist relations of production as is the extraction of surplus value (product) through the application and utilisation of labour power. (ibid, pp. 31–2)

The sale of labour power by producers and the subsequent control of labour by capitalists means that the process of exploitation takes on a form which is specific to the capitalist mode of production. That is, under capitalism the extraction of surplus product and surplus labour is conducted by way of the creation of 'surplus value'. In this distinctive form, exploitation takes place *at the point of production*; or, under capitalism the process of production and the process of exploitation are 'fused together' (ibid, pp. 31–2). In contrast, under feudalism, these two processes are analytically distinct. The peasant has effective control over the means of production, his labour, and the product of labour, even though he *then* relinquishes a portion of the product to the lord as rent. Under capitalism, the capitalist having purchased labour power completely controls labour and its product. It is now the capitalist who 'relinquishes' a portion of this product, or more precisely of the value of this product, to the producer in the form of wages. The remaining value is 'surplus value', the source of profit and capital accumulation.

For Marxists, the producers' complete loss of control to capitalists over their labour has considerable significance for them as human beings. As Stolzman and Gamberg put it:

> If, following Marx, we understand that it is chiefly through *labour* that men (as a species) collectively construct their world, then we discover that the real significance of the wage contract under capitalism is that the producing class is structurally alienated from its world-shaping and history making powers. (Stolzman and Gamberg, 1974)

The necessary (albeit 'voluntary') surrender by producers of their labour power and the subsequent control of their labour by capitalists involves their structural (that is, 'objective') 'alienation' from, not merely the means of production and the product of their labour, but also their particular and unique 'species nature', themselves and each other (Fischer, 1973, ch. 3).[25] This kind of estrangement is distinctive *and general* to capitalism. It is the corollary to the capitalist class's specific but universal need and ability to completely control labour purely in the pursuit of profit and capital accumulation. *It therefore applies whether the producers under capitalism are employed in 'agrarian economy', in cottage-based manufacture, or in factory-based machinofacture; and whether they are employed individually, collectively, or as families.*

Essentially, in terms of Marxian categories and theory, feudal families were 'units of production' in the sense that they were unified around their *unity with* the means of production, the process of production or labour, and the product of labour. Families were then destroyed as units of production at the very moment when feudalism gave way to capitalism. It was at this historical juncture (not later as a result of the Industrial Revolution) that the family as such was separated from organised economic production, and that as a result the nuclear family was 'freed' from the previous family form.

Roberta Hamilton has noted that the feudal family had rested on the 'unity' between labour and the means of production, and that the separation of these two things means that families ceased to be units of economic production at the moment of transition from feudalism (Hamilton, 1978, p. 24). Therefore, she argues, the 'fundamental changes' in the family occurred 'not with industrialisation, but with capitalism' (ibid, p. 18). The transition to capitalism destroyed the basis of the feudal family form, giving rise to new forms – 'the bourgeois family and the proletarian family' (ibid, p. 23). Hamilton clarifies her argument in the following way:

> both the wage-earning family and the bourgeois family were well established long before the Industrial Revolution. The economic basis of this pre-industrial, but post-feudal family was the same as that of the industrial family: it was totally dependent either on . . . wage labour . . . or on capital . . . The peasant evicted from the land must turn to wage labour for sole support: the bourgeoisie lived not from the result of its own labour as did its predecessors . . . but off capital – the surplus value realised through the surplus or unpaid labour of the newly forming wage-earning class. (ibid, p. 18)

The freeing of producers from all possession in relation to the means of production and from all control over their labour, along with the concomitant liberation of the members of the emergent capitalist class from any dependency on their own and each other's labour, marks the origins of what has become the dominant family form:

> The nuclear family, as we still know it, emerged *with* capitalism. The nuclear family is one of the institutional developments of capitalism just as much as the corporation, the bank or the educational system. (ibid, p. 93)

At the same time as the genesis of capitalism released the nuclear family it provided the source of the various features associated with the conjugal family form. It undermined the cohesiveness which had existed among family members, and in particular between husbands and wives, based on their mutually dependent positions in the organisation of economic production. It led to 'the identification of family life with privacy, home, consumption, domesticity – and with women' (ibid, p. 19). With the separation of the family from economic production came 'the concurrent separations – really the same separation looked at in different ways –

between production and consumption, work and home, work and domestic [labour], public and private' (ibid, p. 27).

The occurrence of these separations are not merely matters of historical interest. Given that their origins are to be located in the emergence of capitalism, then their persistence needs to be explained primarily in terms of the development, eventual dominance and continuing predominance of the capitalist mode of production. The modern dominant conjugal family form is sustained largely by its 'articulation' with the dominant CMP in advanced industrial societies.[26] The modern family can be understood only secondarily in terms of the influence of the stage and progress of industrialisation (or the technical means of production), the political system, the state, the 'welfare system', the education system, and so on. This is not to say that these other institutional areas will not play any part in the shaping of the family (see, for instance, Donzelot, 1979), only that they will play a relatively minor, conditional and intermediary part.

It can be claimed that in modern society there is a *dominant* family form, the conjugal family form, on the grounds that this is the one which receives the greatest structural support from the dominant mode of production in conjunction with the other major institutional areas associated with capitalism. Concomitantly, it is the one which receives most support from the prevailing dominant culture or ideology. This cannot be claimed or, conversely, rejected simply on the grounds of the statistical frequency of different family types (not to say *household* types). The dominant conjugal family form will exhibit variations by, for instance, social class. There will be changes over time, perhaps involving a trend towards greater 'diversity', subject to developments in the CMP and its associated class structure and institutions (other than the family). There will be 'deviations'[27] from the conjugal family form, in part because the CMP may not be the only existing mode of production, but also because (in accordance with the principles of historical or dialectical materialism) the CMP does not 'determine' the family. The CMP merely 'conditions' the family in the sense that it places demands, constraints and limits on families in so far as they are dependent on wage-labour or, alternatively, the pursuit of profit and capital accumulation. However, such deviations will be subjected to structural and cultural strain towards conformity with the dominant conjugal family form. If they fail to conform (whether through an inability to do so or through choice and resistance against doing so) they may well have to face special 'problems' of the kind, for instance, which have been well documented in the case of single-parent families (Finer, 1974; Close, 1976; Dominican, 1982; Jackson, 1982; Popay, 1983) and 'family alternatives' (Abrams and McCulloch, 1976; Macklin, 1980; McCulloch, 1982).

The variations by social class (Pahl and Pahl, 1971; Young and Willmott, 1975; Rapoport *et al.*, 1978; Edgell, 1980; Harris, 1983, ch. 12) will reflect differences between families in the way they relate to the means of production and to each other through capitalist relations of production. The families of capitalists and their agents (managers of the means of production) will be conditioned by the legal ownership or immediate possession (effective control) of the means of production. They will be somewhat distinct from the families of the proletariat given that *their* relationship to the means of production is confined to the provision of wage-labour. The variations will be manifested in the content, or character, of family life. Chris Harris has equated the content of family life with its internal 'emotional structure', this being 'intimately tied to the differentiation of the [family] group in terms of age and sex' (Harris, 1983, p. 157). This structure will be strongly influenced by culture, and principally by those 'cultural meanings and prescriptions connected with age—sex categories, since these dimensions are the basic axes of differentiation of the biological [the nuclear family] group' (ibid, p. 159). Accordingly, David Morgan has suggested that the possible *dysfunctions* of the modern family *at the level of the individual* 'may be illustrated in terms of the two axes of family structure, generation and sex' (Morgan, 1975, p. 93). It is then interesting to note how Harris provides such an illustration through an assessment of parent—child relationships in modern society which implies recognition of the primary conditioning (and so explanatory) effects of relations to the means of production, and therefore recognition of variations in parent—child relationships by 'class' in the Marxian sense of the term. He argues that:

> The bourgeois family . . . is child-centred, and this child-centredness . . .
> appears to predate the industrialisation process. However . . . with pro-
> letarianisation, the family becomes the only creative sphere left to the
> parents and consequently children [come] to take on an entirely new
> significance. They signify not the continuation of their parents' identities
> [as in the case of the bourgeois family], but their parents' capacity for
> production. (Harris, 1983, pp. 175—6)

Harris points out that in the particular case of the proletarian family, where neither the family as such nor its individual members own or control the means of production, it can be claimed that 'capitalist societies are characterised by the absence of socially structured and sanctioned opportunities for self expression through creative activities' during the process of production. As a result, the content or emotional structure of proletarian families as far as parent—child relationships are concerned will be different from that of the families of capitalists and their agents. This is because capitalism involves 'depriving all but the owners of controllers of capital of the power even to influence events'. By virtue of their possession in relation to the means of production and or their control over wage-labour, capitalists and managers are that much more able to realise their creative capacities outside of the family and of parent—child relationships. They are the fortunate minority, because 'the majority of the population work under the direction of others' and find that 'work provides little or no creative outlet'. Hence, for the proletarian majority, the only thing left to create is children (ibid, p. 175).

As a result, proletarian parents tend to have an 'intense involvement' with their children, to place great demands on them, and to exercise strict control over them. But this may be stifling for children, and may involve the imposition of barriers to their autonomous development and self-realisation. It may be dysfunctional for them, and it may lead to conflict and rebellion, especially in a society in which there is a cultural emphasis on individualism and self-determination. At the same time, given these cultural prescriptions and the reactions children have to what is expected of them, proletarian parents tend to find that they are unable in practice to realise their creative potential even through their families.

While Harris appears to acknowledge the need to explain modern parent—child relationships largely in terms of the CMP, he explicitly rejects attempts to explain modern sex relationships in the same way. He notes and accepts claims 'from those working in the tradition of historical materialism [that] the domestic group under capitalism is not only the site of biological reproduction and of the production of subjectivities and ideologies, but the site of the reproduction of labour power, both daily and generationally'. He therefore concurs with the view that the family, or more precisely 'domestic labour', is functional in relation to the CMP. But, he argues, this does not explain *why* domestic labour is functional or why it is performed by *women* (ibid, pp. 185–6). Harris is wary of reverting to teleological explanations of these things, of translating their functional *consequences* into their *causes*. However, he is missing the point that it is not necessary for those operating with Marxian theory to rely on the kind of crude teleological explanations used by functionalists. Marxian theory directs attention to the explanatory effects of the practical activities of capitalists in the pursuit of profit and capital accumulation, and of the power and control exercised by capitalists over those who are dispossessed of the means of production. In this way it is possible to explain why it was, according to Roberta Hamilton, that (only) with the emergence of capitalism there occurred the separation of 'work' from 'domestic labour'. Hamilton argues that these 'concepts arose with capitalism', because under feudalism the 'family was engaged in providing a livelihood for its members. Domestic labour was embedded in the total productive process . . . Certain tasks of feudal family life can be labelled domestic but this reflects contemporary rather than feudal distinctions.' In other words, the term 'domestic labour' refers 'to the kind of work which we are *now* accustomed to women doing within the home' (Hamilton, 1978, p. 26).

In the pursuit of profit and capital accumulation, capitalists drew out tasks which had been embedded in the daily round of economic production performed by the feudal family. These tasks became the province and content of the now separate sphere of economic production, to be undertaken by emergent wage-labour. Left behind was a set of tasks which became the content of 'domestic labour': capitalists in effect created domestic labour where there had been none before. By extrapolating this argument we arrive at the general principle that ever since the emergence of capitalism the activities of capitalists in pursuit of their interests have conditioned the content of domestic labour; changes and variations in these activities will be of major explanatory importance to the analysis of any changes and variations (by social class) in the content of domestic labour.

Intimately tied to the creation under capitalism of domestic labour is the generation of a specific conjugal division pertaining to it. That is, in pursuit of their interests, capitalists left as the content of domestic labour that set of tasks which had been traditionally performed by women as wives and mothers. It was and it remains the activities of capitalists which provide a major source of *women's* identification with domestic labour, and a major source of the inequalities of opportunity (such as in relation to paid labour) and condition (such as with regard to the exercise of power within the family) they suffer (Burman, 1979; Edgell, 1980; Stacey and Price, 1981; Young *et al.*, 1981; Collins, this volume). These same activities will then be of considerable importance to an understanding of any changes over time and variations by social class in sex divisions and inequalities.

There is one final point which needs to be made. While capitalism, or the activities of capitalists, engendered and has since sustained women's identification with the domestic sphere, this does not mean that women have been divorced from any contribution under capitalism to economic production. They have, of course, participated in wage-labour (Land,

1976; Amsden, 1980; Lewenhak, 1980; Oakley, 1982, section III). But, in addition, there has been their contribution through their responsibilities for unpaid domestic labour.[28] After all, it is by way of domestic labour that the value of wages and wage-goods becomes transformed into the exchange value of labour power (the source of surplus value, profit and capital accumulation) both intra- and inter-generationally. In other words, the *content* of the domestic labour performed by women takes on (and will be conditioned by) a *form* in relation to the capitalist mode of production. Roberta Hamilton claims that while the 'modern family, even with its enthusiasm for pocket-size vegetable gardens, bread making or furniture finishing, is, economically speaking, a unit of consumption' – rather than a unit of production – nevertheless the 'capitalist family *does* produce labour power' (Hamilton, 1978, p. 25).

A possible implication here is that the family, or more precisely women's domestic labour, contributes to the *value* of labour power, and thereby to production *within the capitalist mode of production*. It has been argued elsewhere, for example, that domestic labour lowers the cost of labour power to capitalists, so enhancing the extraction of surplus value (Harrison, 1974). The possibility of domestic labour being productive within the CMP has been the theme of the Domestic Labour Debate (Hartmann, 1979; Smith, 1978; Harris, 1983, ch. 10; Close and Collins, 1983), conducted under the guidance of Marx's 'labour theory of value'. According to this theory, the value of wages, or the goods which can be purchased with wages, is equivalent to the (exchange) value of labour power. Hence the 'fair' exchange of labour power for wages which takes place at the level of the market under capitalism, and the point made by Rosemary Crompton and Jon Gubbay that labour power is a 'peculiar commodity' in that it is 'a source of more value than it itself possesses' (Crompton and Gubbay, 1977, p. 11). Therefore, as formulated by Marx, the labour theory of value does not allow *domestic* labour to make *any* contribution to the value of labour power (Middleton, 1974). It follows that any legitimate argument in favour of domestic labour making a contribution 'poses certain difficulties for Marxist theory' (Harris, 1983, p. 186).

However, as Harris reports, 'One of the few consensuses that seem to have emerged from the debate is that domestic labour does not produce *labour power*', that is any of the *value* of labour power. The family may be the 'site' of the production of labour power, but all that domestic labour 'produces are *use-values* which are consumed within the household. It transforms commodities purchased out of wages received by the household into consumable form and provides services to other household members' (ibid, p. 187). In other words, the performance of domestic labour in no way interferes with, adds to or subtracts from, the value of wage-goods during its transformation into the value of labour power. This conclusion conveniently salvages the Marxian labour theory of value, but it does so only after being arrived at on the basis of an interpretation of the form of domestic labour in relation to the CMP *in terms of* that theory. In other words, the usefulness or otherwise of Marx's theory to an understanding of domestic labour in modern society is judged *in its own terms*.

Chris Harris accepts that 'Domestic labour is functional for (that is, tends to maintain) social formations with capitalist modes of production', and that it is, therefore, 'an integral part of capitalist social formations'. But, he then argues, apparently on the grounds of the adequacy of Marxian theory in this instance, that nevertheless domestic labour 'is not part of the capitalist mode of production as such' (ibid, p. 190). For Harris, because domestic labour produces only use values and does not contribute to the value of labour power, *the family plays no direct part in economic production under capitalism*. In this way, Harris is able to support his argument that families are not units of economic production in modern society.

If domestic labour did contribute to the value of labour power, it would mean that families had constituted units of economic production every since and in spite of the Industrial Revolution *and* the advent of capitalism. It would establish families, and in particular women, as the main performers of domestic labour, firmly *within* the CMP and so at the centre of society as a whole (Kuhn and Wolpe, 1978, p. 199). The possibility that domestic labour *does* contribute to the value of labour power has not been finally dismissed, despite the consensuses which have evolved out of the Domestic Labour Debate. This debate has been able to conclude that domestic labour is not productive within the CMP, while recognising the *necessary* part it plays in converting the value of wage-goods into the value of labour power, only by either taking for granted the adequacy of Marxian theory *or* being unable to find a way of improving on this theory despite its apparent limitations.

The issue of whether Marxian theory is sufficient to explain the modern family is as yet unresolved. But the lesson of this chapter is that a framework largely informed by Marxian theory is essential for the purpose of understanding the modern dominant family form and assimilating the various features of its relationship with modern economic structures and processes.

NOTES

1. There are conceptual and empirical problems to do with the notion of families as 'groups' (Verdon, 1981). Nevertheless, families are regularly and conventionally described as *groups* in sociological and other works on the family, including the recent major text by Chris Harris to which this chapter pays a lot of attention (Harris, 1983).

2. Chris Harris equates 'family content' with the internal, culturally conditioned, emotional structure of families centred on 'age–sex categories' (Harris, 1983, p. 159).

3. Any decision to allocate a set of families to one family form rather than a plausible alternative on the grounds that it is 'dominant' will be a theoretical decision.

4. A more detailed clarification of this distinction is provided later.

5. Harris defines 'extended kinship relationships' as 'ties between members of overlapping elementary families' (Harris, 1983, p. 48).

6. Laslett's research on household composition in the past has led him to the conclusion that the conjugal family form was dominant *before* the Industrial Revolution (Laslett, 1971; Laslett and Wall, 1972; Laslett, 1977).

7. Several other recent writers have argued along similar lines and very much on the same grounds (Rimmer, 1981; Macklin, 1980). For a variation on the argument, see Bernardes in this volume.

8. The Rapoports provide very little direct evidence in support of their argument, and what they do refer to is highly ambiguous. They also adopt a remarkably crude approach to the definition of 'families', and one which displays important inconsistencies.

9. Parsons's description of the (necessary) conjugal division of labour is noticeably consistent with the view recently expressed that in modern society men tend to assume positions in the 'public' sphere to the exclusion of women, who as a result tend to occupy the 'private' sphere (Stacey, 1981).

10. Parsons's description, conceptualisation and explanation of conjugal roles and divisions has been variously criticised (Oakley, 1976; Edgell, 1980).

11. William Goode argues that industrialisation brings about the 'conjugal family' form *indirectly* through the somewhat independent intervention of ideologies surrounding the family *and* the mediating influence of a (universal) psychological predisposition towards *individualism* (Goode, 1963).

12. It also applies to the sociologically informed accounts which have been offered by a number of historians of the family (Ariès, 1973; Stone, 1977; Shorter, 1977).

13. The claims by Young and Willmott about modern conjugal relationships have been rejected by a number of writers, among whom are some of those who have also found Parsons's views unacceptable (Oakley, 1976; Edgell, 1980). The claims have been questioned on the basis of comparative evidence (Lupri and Symons, 1982).

14. Here, of course, the Bergers are going much further than Young and Willmott are prepared to do. For an analysis of middle-class couples which would seem to contradict the Bergers, see Edgell (1980), Harris (1983, ch. 12). For a more general assessment of male–female power relationships in modern society, see Barrett (1980).

15. This conclusion about the impact of household technology on domestic labour and women's performance of it needs to be treated with caution. See Thomas and Zmroczek in this volume.

16. This feature of modern family life and its 'functionality' in relation to the economic sphere has been detected in empirical studies, such as that by John Goldthorpe and his associates of 'affluent' manual workers in Britain (Goldthorpe *et al.*, 1969).

17. A useful summary and discussion of what Marxists have seen as the dysfunctional consequences of modern family life for the working class has been provided by Chris Middleton (Middleton, 1974). For more detail from Marxists themselves, see the series of articles in *Marxism Today* between December 1972 and April 1974.

18. Parsons on occasions does appear to show some recognition of these features of modern family life (Parsons, 1964c; Parsons and Fox, 1968). But he treats them as merely peripheral and 'deviant' to the main and normal features of modern family life.

19. It is interesting to note how for Marx the emergence of capitalistic contractual relationships had considerable significance, including for family relationships (Marx and Engels, 1968 [originally published 1848], pp. 33–4). For Marx, however, they signified mainly the emergence of a separate 'economic sphere' compared with the indistinctiveness of the economic and political spheres under feudalism (Giddens, 1981, p. 32). The corollary to the separation of the political from the economic would seem to be, following the Bergers, the separation of the familial from the economic.

20. According to Harris, in England the protoindustrial family's 'collective elements' were probably 'created by the conditions of protoindustrial production rather than being survivals from an earlier family form' (Harris, 1983, p. 125). This is a convenient assumption in view of Harris's support for the possibility that, at least in England, the protoindustrial family had not been preceded by the 'collectivistic' peasant family form.

21. The important point will be taken up later that in Marxian terms 'proletarianisation' refers to the process by which producers became dispossessed in relation to the means of production with the advent of capitalism. This means that producers will be dependent on wage-labour, but they will constitute the proletariat whether they sell their 'labour power' for wages individually *or* collectively.

22. Harris refers to the approach by David Lockwood (Lockwood, 1966). See also, Lockwood (1958); Parkin (1974); Parkin (1979); Giddens (1981).

23. For more detailed analyses, see Westergaard and Resler, (1976); Atkinson and Harrison (1978).

24. This remains the case in spite of a possible modification of the structure of authority and control relationships due to an increase in the managerial exercise 'of the functions of property ownership without participating formally in that ownership' (Causer, 1982, p. 138). This is because the possession and control by managers, *as managers*, merely symbolises 'their role as agents of capital' (ibid, p. 138; see Crompton and Gubbay, 1977, chs 5, 8 and 9). For a recent analysis of information relating to the 'managerial revolution thesis', see Scott (1979).

25. For Marx, producers suffered alienation under feudalism, but what they suffer

under capitalism in this respect is far more insidious. Moreover, under capitalism it is not only producers who are alienated; to a lesser degree so are capitalists, by virtue of not performing any labour and of their relationship to the means of production being limited to the pursuit of profits and capital accumulation.

26. Here, the issue arises of how the family in Western advanced industrial societies compares with the family in Eastern-bloc advanced industrial societies of the so-called 'state socialist' type. The available evidence (Buckley, 1981; Molyneux, 1981; Adams and Winston, 1980; Lapidus, 1982) indicates that while there tend to be some differences there are certain major areas of similarity (such as in the area of the division of domestic labour whereby women, as wives and mothers, still assume the major share of responsibility — despite their considerable participation in the paid labour force). Might this signify, as argued by Rosemary Crompton and Jon Gubbay (Crompton and Gubbay, 1977, ch. 7), that Eastern-bloc societies are 'state capitalist' societies?

27. This term is being used here strictly in the sense of behaviour, activities and arrangements which do not conform with what is *culturally* 'normal' and/or with what is *socially* 'dominant'. It is not being used with any moral or prescriptive connotations in mind.

28. For a useful account of the way in which women's domestic labour contributed to early capital accumulation, see Middleton (1982).

2 The Production of People and Domestic Labour Revisited

LINDA MURGATROYD

> According to the materialist conception, the determining factor in history is, in the last resort, the production and reproduction of immediate life. But this itself is of a twofold character. On the one hand, the production of the means of subsistence, of food, clothing and shelter and the tools requisite therefore; on the other, the production of human beings themselves, the propagation of the species. The social institutions under which men of a definite historical epoch and a definite country live are conditioned by both kinds of production. (Engels, 1972, p. 26)

In this chapter[1] I shall discuss some ways in which a primary concern with economics has dominated socialist analyses and policies. I shall argue that the analysis of the production process must be extended beyond the traditional boundaries of economics, and suggest some ways in which this can be done.

I discuss some ways in which a coherent conceptual basis for the analysis of non-economic aspects of production have been and might be constructed: for example 'the production of people', 'sex-gender systems', and the 'anthroponomic process'. A number of distinct dimensions of social relations of production are marginalised by the hegemony of economics within social science and policy. Like the economic process, these have their own internal dynamics and contradictions, as well as interacting with the economic and one another. Rather than consigning all those activities which are not 'productive' in the narrow economistic sense to the realm of 'reproduction' or any other single category, and thus assigning them a status secondary to, and defined in relation to, the 'economic', these should be analysed in their own right. Their influence on activities taking place within the economic sphere can then be considered, as well as those flowing in the opposite direction.

Political economists, since the days of Ricardo and Marx, have concentrated their analyses on a particular part of the system of production within industrial societies. They have focused on the manufacture of goods within the formal, market economy. Other kinds of social production have been defined in opposition to this. 'Services', for example, variously include the manipulation (as opposed to the physical production) of goods, the application of labour to people (as opposed to inanimate objects), or white-collar (as opposed to manual) jobs. Social and economic analyses of these have often been limited to discussions of the ways in which these areas of production and employment are similar to, or different from, archetypal models of factory production. Production in the domestic and informal economies within industrial society has been little discussed until recently, and has been hindered by similar considerations.

The need for economic analysis to be extended into, or take account of, a wider framework of the type I suggest is urgent for a number of reasons. Recent years have seen the flourishing of a plethora of groups concerned with the politics of gender, the environment, health and a host of other issues which have not traditionally been taken on board by socialist theories except very marginally. An increasing concern has developed among socialists (and others) with issues that are not directly related to economic production; and with aspects of production other than wages and profits. This trend is to be welcomed, since the subordination of other issues to economistic demands has for too long been a feature of labour politics in Britain. Through the narrow focus of British labour politics, a number of issues have been swept to one side and many dimensions of oppression have been perpetuated rather than challenged. However, while the diversity of autonomous groups is in many ways a strength of the oppositional 'fragments' (Rowbotham *et al.*, 1979; Wilson, 1980; Margolis, 1980), the lack of an overall perspective as to how these issues fit together is a weakness.

In addition, the long-term decline in manufacturing employment and in the formal economy (see, for example, Blackaby, 1978; Fröbel *et al.*, 1980; and Gershuny, 1978) also affects the relevance of economic theory in analysing the everyday productive relationships engaged in by the majority of the population, and in developing appropriate policies. The decline in traditional forms of employment in manufacturing industry has not only eroded and weakened the basis of trade unionism, but it also implies a shift in the type of production relations in which a majority of wage-workers are engaged. Classical models of capitalist factory production cannot throw much light on the social relationships involved in employment within, for example, the National Health Service. Neither can economic frameworks founded on assumptions of impersonal market systems be expected to deal adequately with production and distribution outside such markets.[2]

Furthermore, feminist insights have raised a number of specific problems for socialist theory and policy (Conference of Socialist Economists, Sex and Class Group, 1982; Ruehl, 1982). The latter must be redeveloped to take full account of gender, and to give adequate importance to the needs, perspectives and activities of women. This is necessary not only from a feminist point of view (although it is of crucial political importance in this respect) but also because any social, political or economic analysis which fails to take account of such a central element of social relationships must thereby be weakened. Whether or not a feminist stance is taken, analyses and policies which do not explicitly consider gender divisions are neglecting not only a crucial dimension of inequality, but also a set of social processes which affect most areas of life. In the context of a patriarchal society, in which the majority of social institutions are dominated by and operate in the interests of men as opposed to women (economic class notwithstanding), a lack of explicit consideration of gender is in itself likely to contribute to a perpetuation of women's oppression, both at an ideological level (denying it) and through the concrete policies developed and implemented.

Marx's analysis in *Capital* of the social relations of material production under capitalism was confined on the one hand to production of the means of subsistence, and on the other to production which took place within the impersonal relations of markets. His main concern was to demonstrate how the mediation of money served to camouflage the exploitative social relations of production and distribution under capitalism. It was an analysis of 'economic production'. It excluded, however, any analysis of the material production of 'human beings themselves', or of the social relations of non-market production within capitalist society.

Engels's project, in *The Origins*, was to complete Marx's unfinished task, that is the analysis of the production of human beings by applying his historical materialist method to the anthropological and historical data on family forms. The distinction between the production of the 'means of subsistence' and of 'people' (see quote at head of chapter) refers to the different kinds of objects to which human labour power can be applied. Broadly defined, 'production' refers to the application of human labour power to the natural environment and the appropriation of nature for human ends. This takes place at a physical level, where nature is transformed physically by the application of this labour power through a process of work, and objects are transformed by the use of tools, or are transported in space. It also takes place at the level of attaching social meanings to natural occurrences. 'Production', then, implies the cultivation of nature in both senses of the word; causing the world to develop in particular ways, and attaching cultural meaning to it. Now, just as production of the means of subsistence, of articles for human consumption (and for use in further production), involves the cultivation and the manipulation of the natural environment, so the production of people involves the cultivation of biological human animals. This happens through feeding and physically caring for them from birth (or conception) and also transforming their behaviour and biological urges into culturally meaningful (in a particular culture) and socially acceptable forms. The work involved in this set of activities may be said to be work done in the production of people, whereas that involved in the manipulation of the natural environment contributes to the production of goods. Marx's analysis is centred around his concern with the production and distribution of goods. The boundaries between these two kinds of production are hard to draw, and in practice many activities may at the same time be contributing to production of both kinds.[3] Indeed many difficulties are thrown up by the distinction. The labour process in the material production of objects cannot be divorced from the direct social relations among the people involved. Conversely, the physical manipulation of people cannot be completely divorced from the manipulation of objects. Nevertheless, it is useful to introduce the concept of the production of people, since it counterbalances the exclusive focus on the production of inanimate objects, and opens up the field for further investigation.

Another useful distinction in the analysis of the social organisation of production is the division between those activities which take place in the private, domestic sphere, and those taking place in the public realm of the market.[4]

Domestic labour is work, and it is work which takes up a considerable amount of human time and energy. Not only is it socially necessary, but its very structuring outside the wage-labour market is important in that this provides for flexibility in economic production under the unstable and ever-changing economic and political conditions. As the economic (and political) situation demands, areas of production can be transferred from the domestic sphere and back again, and in the short or long term. Domestic production of goods and services may be substituted either by 'pure' capitalist production (for example, convenience foods, canteens and restaurants may replace home cooking) or within the state sector (state education, health services and so on) (Gardiner, 1976; Weitbaum and Bridges, 1979).

While the relations of production and the organisation of production are different in domestic and market spheres, the fact remains that production of both people and of 'the means of subsistence' takes place in both contexts. These distinctions may be crudely represented in Figure 2.1. This figure does not encompass by any means all the relevant distinctions between different kinds of production, far less the different sets of productive relationships embodied in them. Instead, it demonstrates some of the distinctions which may usefully be made in order to further the analysis of production processes of different kinds.

Much of the literature (including Engels's study already mentioned) has tended to assume that the production of people was exclusively located in the domestic sphere, that is the family, and conversely that domestic production was entirely concerned with the production of people (or the reproduction of labour power). By distinguishing along different dimensions of production, we can begin to grasp some of the processes taking place within the family, consider differences among families and investigate shifts in production into and out of the domestic arena.[5] Briefly, under advanced industrial capitalism, box A is that defined by Marx as where value is produced, the sphere of 'economic production' (and physical distribution) of articles. Wage-labour in manufacturing, extraction, distribution and some services mostly contributes to production in this area. Some wage-work is more suitably located in box C; health work and teaching are good examples. Within the domestic domain, we might say that such activities broadly classed as housework, cooking,

FIGURE 2.1 *The locus and types of production in capitalist society*

Examples of production of each type:		LOCUS OF PRODUCTION	
A: Manufacturing industries (as defined for example, in the Standard Industrial Classification)			
B: Home cooking, dressmaking, etc.		Public Domain (wage labour)	Private Domain (domestic labour)
C: Hospital nursing, school teaching.			
D: Home-based caring work.			
PRODUCT	Objects/means of subsistence (economic production)	A	B
	People (anthroponomic production)	C	D

shopping, cleaning the house, gardening would be classed in box B, and childcare, education, care of the sick, and looking after other household members generally — both physically and psychologically — in box D. The difficulty of classifying some kinds of work is inherent in the continuity which ultimately exists between the production of people embodying labour power and the production of articles (later to be consumed in the production of people). Similar problems are often encountered with industrial classifications.

Production of 'the means of subsistence' continues to take place within both private and public spheres (boxes A and B) under advanced capitalism and state socialism, despite the expansion of capitalist (or state-organised) production. The snowballing expansion of capitalist production, driven by the need to make profits and accumulate capital, has both caused expansions in the amounts and kind of goods produced by society as a whole, and has eroded the share (and absolute amount) of total production done in the domestic sphere. A not insignificant amount of material production continues, however, to be performed within the domestic sphere despite the longstanding hegemony of the capitalist mode of production. Food is prepared, clothes and other objects are made, the contents of the domicile are cleaned. All these are tasks which are included in the production of the means of subsistence, involving the transformation of nature by means of the exercise of human labour.

The distinction between production for exchange and production for direct use cross-cut these others. Most household production is geared to the needs of household members, but the goods and services produced in the household also have an exchange value and may be sold in the market place. The household may be considered a unit of production, as well as the home being the locus of production. The relations of production and division of labour within the household may, in principle, be investigated just like those in the market. In practice, the investigation of production arrangements outside the formal economy is more difficult than within it, and such studies are in their infancy (see, for example, Young *et al.*, 1981). The mediation of markets means that information (for example, about how long people work, how much they produce, and what their rewards are) is the more easily available, and the conditions and relations of production have been open to closer investigation and scrutiny in this sphere than in others, as a result. The relations of production are also regulated (albeit imperfectly) by market forces. In comparison, the particular division of labour within private homes is often less clearly specified, being subject to continuous informal negotiations. Even if the relations of domestic production are regulated to some degree by the state, there are no contracts specifying hours to be worked and the rates of remuneration (see Barker, 1978; Delphy, 1977; Guillaumin, 1980, 1981).

Marx's discussion of social relations of production under capitalism, then, focused exclusively on production within the market. The labour theory of value, upon which his analysis is founded, in fact *defines* productive work as that which produces value *under capitalist relations*. It is predicated on a system of exchange through competitive markets.

The 'domestic labour debate' of the early 1970s[6] resulted from the recognition of the continued importance of domestic work in producing goods and services within an economy dominated by capitalism. The focus of that debate was whether Marxists should recognise domestic labour as 'productive' in the same sense that wage-labour is seen as productive. The protagonists of the 'Wages for Housework' position argued that domestic labour was productive and socially necessary, and that Marxists should therefore include it in their analysis of capitalism. Domestic workers (that is, housewives), they argue, were members of the working class by virtue of their domestic labour. The fallacy of this argument (Delphy, 1977) is that the relations of production under which domestic labour is performed are not identical with those of wage-labour production in the capitalist factory. The Marxist response to the suggestion that domestic labour is productive was to refer to Marx's definition of productive labour as being that which produced value and surplus value. The definition of 'value' in terms of the market production of commodities (Smith, 1978; Gardiner, 1976) means that domestic labour is *by definition* not 'productive' in this narrow sense. Marx's discussion of the value of labour power makes it clear that only wage-labour, or 'social labour', is considered pertinent. He implies that no expenditure of labour power is involved in the production of labour power itself, besides that which is involved in the production (in the market) of those commodities which the wage labourer buys for his (or her) own consumption (and that of their household).

> Labour power only exists as a capacity of the living individual; its production presupposes his existence; and therefore the production of labour power is dependent upon the worker's reproduction of himself, upon the worker's maintenance. Marx, 1974a, p. 158)

The worker is presumed to maintain himself (*sic*), given a wage which can provide the 'means of subsistence'. In fact this is merely a device used by Marx for defining the 'value of labour power' under capitalist production relations. Only that labour power sold by the 'free wage labourer', in fixed quantities, in exchange for a money wage, is considered within Marx's definition of 'labour power'. Labour power is thus a commodity which is needed for capitalist production. Marx is concerned with the market price of this commodity and the way in which the relations under which it is applied to production create profit, a surplus value, for the purchaser or capitalist. In so far as the production of working people embodying labour power takes place outside the capitalist market, Marx is not interested in it. His definition of production under capitalism is firmly in box A of the above diagram. He is interested in the amount of market-produced commodities which are necessary for the reproduction of labour power, but only in so far as this places a limitation on the degree to which workers can be exploited by their capitalist employers.

The transformation of wage-commodities into labour power requires, however, two distinct stages, both of which involve the expenditure of human time and energy:

(1) The transformation of wage-commodities (what Marx calls 'the means of subsistence') into people embodying labour power.
(2) The harnessing of their labour power, which includes:
   (a) ensuring that these people are prepared (and willing) to sell their labour power to capitalists;
   (b) and social control at the point of 'production' so that labour time is indeed effectively put to use.

A number of writers have attempted to develop an analysis of the non-economic by postulating another system, alongside the economic one, in which all non-economic activities and relationships are contained. This merely adds to the problems, developing a conceptual hierarchy of system analyses which are often functionalist, and do not allow for the dynamics of different relationships, for the autonomy of individuals or groups, or for historical 'accidents'.

Sex-gender systems. Hartmann (1979), for example, has postulated the existence of two separate but interconnected systems of patriarchy. Her conception of patriarchy is that of a specific form of 'sex-gender systems' (Hartmann, 1979, p. 12). According to Rubin (1975), sex-gender systems are the 'systematic ways' any society will 'deal with sex, gender and babies' (Rubin, 1975, p. 168), just as economic systems deal with the production of the means of subsistence. In other words, such a system consists of the 'set of arrangements' by which a society transforms biological sexuality into products of human activity and in which transformed sexual needs are satisfied' (Rubin, 1975, p. 159). Patriarchy, for Hartmann, is thus 'a set of social relations between men which have a material base and which, though hierarchical, establish or create interdependence and solidarity among men that enables them to dominate women' (Hartmann, 1979, p. 11). She argues that the material base upon which patriarchy rests is most fundamentally in men's control over women's labour power. Under capitalism, this takes place through denying women access to productive resources (for example well-paid jobs), and through controlling women's sexuality. Hartmann cites 'monogamous heterosexual marriage [as] one relatively recent and efficient form that allows men to control both these areas', but mentions that men's control over women's access to resources takes place outside of marriage also.

This analysis makes important points in demonstrating how non-economic social relations have influenced the development of capitalism: for example, how the opposed interests of men and women influenced the development of particular sexual hierarchies within the workplace, and of the 'family wage' system. However it can be criticised on many grounds.[7] A duality of systems implies that all social activities and relationships lie within one or other of the two spheres. In fact it is not at all clear why this should be so: for example, why should the relations of imperialism or racism be adequately encapsulated within such an analytical framework as Hartmann's, rather than having their own dynamics. The conflation of all non-economic relations into a 'sex-gender system' is incompatible with attempting to assign to such a 'system' the same tight internal logic as the capitalist economic has; the division between these two 'systems' is not symmetrical. The social relations of capital are based on 'economic production', and it is the boundaries of what is 'economic' and 'productive', under capitalism, that defines the boundaries of this system (see above); whereas the relations of patriarchy are between groups of people. By implication non-economic (by definition), the production of people comes under the aegis of 'sex-gender system' of which Hartmann's 'patriarchy' is a form. But again this tends to be conflated and confined to specific aspects of the production of people, namely domestic work done by women, as opposed to encompassing all those aspects of production which are not included within the scope of economic production (as defined by Marxists). 'Sex-gender system' can then be more usefully broken down into two constitutent parts: the social relations of gender, and the production of people. Together with other sets of social relationships, such an approach provides analytical tools with which to tackle particular empirical and social policy issues in a way that is critical and theoretically informed, and yet not hidebound by a narrow and functionalist determinism. Furthermore, as soon as a static 'systems' approach to social and economic investigation is dropped, room is immediately created for dimensions of space and time to be included in the analysis, or policy programme.

Anthroponomy and the production of people. I shall briefly illustrate this approach by discussing some aspects of a particular issue in further detail, namely some of the social relationships associated with the production of people. Daniel Bertaux has posited the existence of what he calls an 'anthroponomic process' which operates in parallel with the economic process (Bertaux, 1977). Through it the production of people is organised, as are their distribution to different 'places' in society, and their 'consumption', in the same way that economic goods are produced, distributed and consumed in the economic system. Bertaux is primarily concerned with the distributive aspects of the anthroponomic process, and especially discusses the formation of classes (at a macro-historical level) and the allocation of individuals to them. Through the process of anthroponomy, advantages and disadvantages are transmitted between generations. Bertaux argues that different strategies must be pursued by families according to the specific advantages they have over those least advantaged, in order to transmit whatever kind of capital they possess (be it finance, intellectual, business, land or cultural capital) in a form which is profitable to their descendants. The term 'class-family' (*famille de classe*) is coined to indicate the variation and specificity.

While his own analysis omits to consider the actual work of producing people in any detail, there is no reason why Bertaux's concepts of anthroponomy cannot be built upon, to incorporate a gender dimension, and an analysis of the social relations of anthroponomic production. The recognition that the production of people in a class society implies producing people embodying different characteristics according to their class of origin, may be combined with similar insights regarding the production of gendered individuals. Combining these insights with an understanding that the production of people involves work, we are well on the way to providing a conceptual framework within which to analyse the social relations of production and division of labour as a whole.

We may consider 'people-producing' work to be that which involves the direct manipulation of people in such a way that they embody more (or a different quality of) energy or productive capacity from that previously embodied. Those who nurture, procreate, feed, educate, give physical care (medical or otherwise) or manipulate others psychologically in such a way as to *increase the amount*, or *ameliorate* the quality of human energy and potential labour power embodied by directly manipulating people, are doing people-producing work. Those engaged purely in *harnessing* this labour power are not producing people. Managers engaged in directing workers' activities at the point of production of goods are contributing to economic production and to the consumption of labour power. Managers engaged in training others to become managers or to do some other work task are engaged in people-work; they are affecting the quality of the labour power embodied in the trainees. Although the purpose of their activity may ultimately be further production of objects, the direct result of their work is embodied in people, and it is only at a later stage that the trained workers may apply their labour power to the production of objects, whether directly or indirectly. This definition permits us to suggest how the social relations of the production of people might be analysed further, especially with regard to appropriation and control.

Medical sociologists and economists, for example, have made some progress in elucidating the social relationships in health care; these epitomise many of the relationships in the production of people more generally (Stacey and Price, 1981; Mackenzie, 1979; Carpenter, 1980). We need, however, to link an analysis of the production of people with an analysis of the relations of production in the production of objects, in order to understand the social relations of people-producing work. The link between these two is labour power. People-work (together with material objects, food, and so on) produces people who embody labour power of various kinds. This labour power *may* be put to productive use, either to produce more people, or to produce goods, but this will not necessarily happen. In so far as people have a certain degree of autonomy, they may choose to work or not to work, within a structured set of options constituted by social arrangements at a particular time. Even within advanced capitalist societies, the nature of tasks in people-producing work, the location of it, and the social relations involved in it can vary widely. Where it takes place in the private, domestic, sphere, it may be coupled with a certain degree of autonomy in relation to tasks done, within well-defined limits, and in addition, a certain degree of power over those to whom people-work is being done. Thus mothers gain influence over children, for example, and wives may be able to manipulate husbands, by the very processes of nurturing, servicing work that they do for them. At the same time, people-production in the home is subject to various controls. These may come from other members of the household, and their physical strength or the economic power they acquire by selling their labour power (or owning property), or they may come from outside, from the state, church or local community. Either way, though, the relationships are more personal, and of a different quality to those encountered in other spheres of production.

The importance of the influence of power relationships within the family on the psychological development of children and their learning of culturally appropriate behaviour patterns (as well as skills), and class and gender identities, has been widely demonstrated within the fields of psychoanalysis, child psychology and education. I am suggesting that these might be considered as part of the wider process of the production of people, and that the political dimensions of such processes should be more fully integrated into political priorities and policies.

Where it takes place in the public, market sphere, the division of labour may be more refined, and in particular the hierarchical forms of organisation produce concentrations of power and responsibility and relations of authority and deference among the workers, as well as between workers and work-object. The removal of people-producing work from the home into public spheres has been combined with changes in organisation and in technology. Capitalist or bureaucratic principles of organisations are introduced, and the nature of the work relations and the forms and standards of care alter accordingly. The relationship between worker and client/work-object also changes, and the amount of work done by the latter as well as the former may alter.

Some examples of the types of changes involved have been well documented in the literature on the medicalisation of various kinds of health care (Ehrenreich and English, 1979; Oakley, 1976a). In the management of childbirth, for example, the movement from community care in the home to medical and professional care, first in the home and increasingly in hospitals (which, in turn, have become increasingly centralised), has involved not only geographical concentration and 'rationalisation', but also shifts in power and control – away from both the mother and the person doing most work on her or to her (the neighbour/midwife/nurse). Technological changes and bureaucratic/capitalist forms of organisation of the process of birth management (a specific element in production of people) have transformed the mother from an active participant who puts a lot of work into the production process, with a certain amount of control over her own labour and the conditions and place of the birth, to a passive recipient of 'care', waiting in increasingly long queues for ante-natal care, the time and place of birth being dictated largely by the convenience of the medical staff, and with technology being used in such a way as to deprive her of control and to transform the experience of birth (presumably this has also some impact on the experience for the child being born). Such changes in the process of production of people mirrors changes in the production of objects; the organisation of work, the forms of technology used are similar, and the economic and other criteria which determine the form of production are essentially the same.

While the economic process has its own internal dynamics under capitalism, and influences the organisation of production elsewhere in society, this is not the only important dimension of the production system. Indeed, it is arguable that while capitalist production relations are becoming increasingly deep and concentrated, there is simultaneously a decline in Britain in the numbers of people directly involved in capitalist production relations (Urry, 1981).

The range of social relationships encompassed within the production system cannot be analysed solely through the prism of economics. Indeed, to do so means disregarding many aspects of the social organisation of production and relegating them to a separate and implicitly secondary area of policy. Thus, family policies and education, training, health, social services, housing, transport and so forth are all considered to be separate policy areas, between which there is relatively little co-ordination.

In political terms, these issues are increasingly coming to the fore. The number of jobs concerned with the production of people has grown considerably in the past few decades, and the threat to many of these jobs and consequently to the services provided by the state has produced a number of important recent confrontations precisely in these areas. I have discussed some of the ways in which non-economic dimensions of production might be analysed and some of the ways in which they are linked. Elsewhere[8] I have developed an analysis of certain aspects of the social division of labour in greater detail, building on the notions of the social relations of gender, the production of people within an anthroponomic process, and of the distinct relations of production within the family relationships. I hope that some of these concepts and arguments will be of use in developing a more sophisticated analysis of production relationships, and of the links between production and consumption of various kinds in the future.

NOTES

1. The material in this chapter first appeared in *Socialist Economic Review*, 1983.
2. Davidoff has argued that production in the household has been organised in such a way as to divide it off from the public domain. Economic and hygienic rationales are, she argues, subordinate to the need to separate the spheres by organising

them differently, according to different sets of values, traditions and relationships. See Davidoff (1976).

3. This point has parallels with Giddens's theory of the duality of structure. See Giddens (1979, 1981a).
4. By 'the public realm' I refer to both 'public' (state) and 'private' capitalist sectors of economic production. See Stacey and Price (1981, ch. 1) for further discussion.
5. See Murgatroyd (1982a) for further discussion.
6. See Kaluzynska (1980) for an overview of this debate.
7. See the subsequent essays in Sargent (1981) for further discussion of these.
8. See Murgatroyd (1981, 1982a, 1982b, 1983).

3 'Horses for Courses': Ideology and the Division of Domestic Labour

ROSEMARY COLLINS

Britain is a gender-divided society. Most women work in less well-paid jobs than men and are responsible for domestic labour at home. Most men earn more than women, have higher status at work and make a fairly minor domestic contribution. Few women hold influential public positions and few men choose to be house-husbands. This chapter examines why a division of labour along gender lines continues, despite the increasing employment of married women, the legal measures to establish equality between the sexes, a growing interest of fathers in childcare and an ethos of egalitarianism in marriage.

Data from research carried out in Middlesbrough[1] are presented which confirm that the division of domestic labour is assigned to the sexes in stereotyped ways. Women continue to do most of the work and retain responsibility for ensuring certain activities are always carried out. This responsibility, in itself, lends support to the common practice of women 'fitting in' paid employment around familial demands for domestic labour, and hinders many from achieving equal employment status with men. It is argued that the distinction between men 'helping with' and women 'being responsible for' domestic labour is reinforced by an ideology of gender. The results provide detailed evidence of the existence of forms of social consciousness, in which the position of women is thought of primarily in terms of home and children and the position of men is equated with wage-labour and social superiority. Three elements of the ideology are examined: service, motherhood, and the male breadwinner. It is concluded that an ideology of gender is integral to the practice of domestic labour and reinforces conventional sex-roles in the home and the wider society.

63

Domestic labour incorporates housework, related activities which produce utilities, childcare and more generalised care for family members. In the broadest sense, the different components of domestic labour are structured by the biological and culturally defined needs of families. They further derive from traditional patterns of domesticity; they include the adaptation of scientific knowledge to pre-existing domestic practices and complex domestic rituals, linked to cultural perceptions about what homes should be like. The caring component of domestic labour stems from physiological needs of families, socially accepted 'caring' practices and an ideology of care (see Ungerson, this volume). Domestic labour performed in particular families is more narrowly conditioned by family size, stage in the family life-cycle, type and location of home, income and resources.

When domestic labour takes place, a link is forged between families and the economic system. On the one hand, families help to perpetuate the process of capitalist production by consuming goods manufactured in the industrial sector. On the other hand, the utilities produced by domestic labour (such as meals, clean clothes, a comfortable environment and so on) renew labour power through the process of consumption. Caring, in the form of child socialisation, also plays a part in preparing children for their future role in the economy. In producing labour power, domestic labour is an aspect of social reproduction – the 'process by which all the main production relations in society are constantly reproduced and perpetuated' (Mackintosh, 1981, p. 10). Indeed, it has been suggested that domestic labour is beneficial and necessary to capitalism. Throughout the 1970s, in what came to be known as the Domestic Labour Debate, a range of arguments were presented showing how domestic labour is of 'the utmost productive importance to capitalism' (Middleton, 1974, pp. 197–8). The Debate concentrates on whether domestic labour makes a contribution to surplus value – the source of profits and capital accumulation. Drawing on Marxist categories, various alternative hypotheses have been put forward. John Harrison (1974, pp. 35–52) argues that domestic labour is a 'client' mode of production, operating alongside capitalism. Its principal function is to produce use values, which in turn 'reproduce' workers. Furthermore, by keeping housewives out of the labour market, domestic labour creates a reserve workforce, with the potential for weakening the bargaining power of male workers. Jean Gardiner (1976, p. 117) suggests that by keeping down the cost of reproducing labour power, domestic labour contributes towards profits. An alternative view from Wally Seccombe (1975, p. 89) argues that domestic labour creates value, embodied in the labour power sold to capital, but is divorced from surplus value production. More recently, Bonnie Fox (1980, p. 187) has pointed out that unpaid domestic services depress the value of labour power. If these services were not provided in homes, higher wages would have to be paid so that workers could buy equivalent services on the market.

These competing stances provide useful guidelines to what the economic functions of domestic labour might be.[2] Yet, as Paul Hirst points out:

> Theories of . . . modern family forms as necessary to capitalist reproduction attempt to place these questions within the confines of conventional socialist analysis, to subordinate them to a causality governed by the economic. (Hirst, 1979, p. 13)

Linked to this criticism, Maxine Molyneux makes the further points that the debate is unable to explain why domestic labour is *crucial* to capitalism, or why it is largely allocated to women (1979, pp. 20–21). The debate leaves unresolved the questions of how domestic labour reflects the level of economic development in society, how it is incorporated into the close emotional ties which characterise family relations, and how the division of domestic labour reflects and reinforces the social division of labour.

The division of domestic labour is historically connected to the way pre-capitalist gender divisions were incorporated into the structure of capitalist relations. Capitalism developed in conjunction with a 'cultural heritage of masculinity and femininity' (Rubin, 1975, p. 164); the concomitant development of women's economic and domestic roles has been well documented by, among others, Clark (1968), Pinchbeck (1977), Oakley (1976) and Hamilton (1978). Here I shall sketch key points in the process of the separation of home and workplace. Prior to industrialisation many women worked in economic partnership with their husbands. Roberta Hamilton has shown that in feudal society:

> The roles of husband and wife were integrated with the economy of their households, their labour directed towards filling the physical needs of themselves and their children. (Hamilton, 1978, p. 31)

Some of the earliest historical records reveal that recognition was given to the economic importance of wives, yet they were obliged by law and custom to provide domestic services for their husbands and to submit to their authority (Hall, 1980, pp. 48–50). As capitalism developed, men began to organise and control the new industries and professions. Women, on the whole, continued to do economically productive work at home. Chris Middleton, (1982, p. 13) has argued that the separation of men into the public world of work and women into the home developed out of the relations of male dominance and female subservience which existed in feudal society.

During the sixteenth and seventeenth centuries women lost some of their former economic independence, because their work became increasingly controlled by men (ibid, p. 14). They were more enclosed within the home, where their roles as wives and mothers were elevated by a paternalistic, public culture.

By the nineteenth century the separation of the public, male domain and the private, female domain had become complete for the middle classes. Middle-class women were now economically idle – their main role was to organise homes displaying their husbands' wealth. Working-class women continued to be economically active. Many worked as domestic servants, thereby lending support to the cultural practices of middle-class family life. Towards the end of the Victorian period, working-class women began to withdraw from industrial life into the home, where they tried to emulate the domestic life-styles of the wealthy. By the beginning of the twentieth century, most married women were at home doing or supervising housework and most men were earning wages or seeking employment.

Throughout the twentieth century, women have been shunted between the home and workplace in line with changing demands for wage labour (Davies, 1975). Most married women can now expect to work at some stage during their married lives (Land, 1975, p. 72). Their availability for work has been aided by methods of birth control, which give women the opportunity to choose when to have children. Women have achieved greater legal equality (enshrined in legislation like the Equal Pay Act (1975) and Sex Discrimination Act (1975)) and a larger share of the labour market. Parallel with these developments, men's role as the main economic provider has become vulnerable through widespread unemployment.

Young and Willmott (1975) argue that as employment increases among middle-class women, the traditional division of labour is being swept away. Egalitarianism is becoming the norm, husbands are taking on domestic work formerly reserved for wives and male power is becoming reduced. Young and Willmott's argument may apply to some middle-class families, but more recent studies suggest that the changes they observed are largely cosmetic. Stephen Edgell's (1980) research on middle-class couples, for example, shows people continue to associate the husband—provider role with decision-making and the housewife role with dependence. Ann Whitehead's (1981) review of the allocation of household resources shows that the husband's income is used for 'necessary expenditure' (bills, rent, heating and so on) and money the wife earns is used for 'extras' (holidays, clothes and so on). The way the wife's income is dealt with (necessary as it usually is to the household budget) supports an ideology of the greater importance of the male earner, compared with other earners in the home. Pauline Hunt's (1980) study reveals that when wives are working they still do most of the domestic labour; they try to provide 'good' services for their husbands, even when this entails little or no leisure time.

Sociological explanations for the persistence of the male–female division of labour have, until recently, concentrated on the issues of conjugal roles, marital equality and marital power (Bott, 1957; Pahl and Pahl, 1971; Rapoport and Rapoport, 1976; Edgell, 1980). This type of analysis reveals much about the inner structure of marriages, the way couples negotiate their relationships and the exercise of power through decision-making. Nevertheless, these explanations are limited in two ways. First, research into the division of domestic labour has been conducted with a wide range of operational definitions.[3] The available evidence has investigated division within different types and categories of domestic activities; consequently a 'typical' picture of conjugal roles is not readily available. Second, inequalities within marriage have not been situated within the context of the broader economic structure and social division of labour.

It has been left to Marxist and feminist writers to develop theories of the relationship between the division of domestic labour and the economy. Marxist analyses of the economic functions of domestic labour have already been commented on. Issues stemming from the Domestic Labour Debate have also become crucial areas of analytical inquiry. For example, the way capitalism utilises female domesticity to pay women low wages has been studied by Bruegel (1979) Anthias (1980) and Land (1980). The benefits to capital of an unequal distribution of power in the home has been tackled by Hartmann (1979), as has the possibility of a decline in male power alongside the development of corporatism (Smith, 1974; Easton, 1977). Furthermore, the role ideology plays in supporting cultural practices which are divisive for men and women has come to the fore of feminist analysis. One of the leading exponents, Michelle Barrett (1980), argues that the gender division of labour is connected to the different meanings which 'labour' has for men and women. Historically, women's involvement in production has been more variable than men's, either because they were directly or legally excluded from certain industries, or because their entry into employment was restricted by moral beliefs about 'a woman's place' and long periods of child-rearing. Women have been confined to the home, and:

> The consequences of the separation of the home and workplace for the family, and for gender relations, have been very marked . . . women have become dependent upon the male wage in capitalism and this mediated dependence on the wage is circumscribed by an ideology of emotional, psychical and 'moral' dependence. (Barrett, 1980, p. 179)

Through the family structure, men and women have achieved distinct relationships to wage-labour. For instance, although 64 per cent of married women are now in employment (*General Household Survey*, 1983) most of them are concentrated in low-paid and part-time jobs. In this sense they continue to be 'dependent' on the greater earnings of husbands. Unemployed married women are likely to be unpaid 'carers' for family members, relying on their husbands or the state for financial support. Within this context, the family nourishes, on an ideological level, the 'various themes' of 'romantic love, feminine nurturance, maternalism, self-sacrifice, masculine protection and financial support' (Barrett, 1980, p. 205). These notions characterise conceptions of gender and sexuality. Barrett argues that capitalism undoubtedly benefits from the way gender is socially constructed within an 'ideology of familism'. However, it would be simplistic to assume that an ideology of gender 'causes' women's generally low-paid position in employment or that 'capitalism creates an ideology of gender difference to legitimate the exploitation of women' (ibid, p. 211). The family, and its attendant division of labour does, however, provide an effective system for the reproduction of labour power and helps to stabilise the capitalist mode of production (ibid, p. 212). An ideology of gender is integrated within the practice of domestic labour and the employment structure, and perpetuates broad social definitions of male and female roles.

Recent research reveals the persistence of the ideology in a wide variety of social practices, both within and outside the family. For example, Sue Sharpe (1976) shows how socialisation plays a major part in constructing female identity. Spender and Sarah (1980) demonstrate how the education system encourages gender identities and a distinct male and female orientation to work. Looking at employment, Smith (1976) argues that male subcultures play a part in preventing women from gaining positions of power within the work hierarchy. There is no doubt that an ideology of gender prevails in social institutions, or that it is widely supported. As Mary Evans has remarked:

> So strong, and so limited, is the ideology of feminity in our culture that normal female existence — the hearth and the home — is expected

to furnish all that life might have to offer. (Evans and Ungerson, 1983, p. 10)

According to Barrett, 'ideology is a practice of representation, it is the way an individual lives his or her role in the social totality' (Barrett, 1980 p. 32). In other words, since ideology conveys existing social relations to individuals as being self-evident, natural, proper, and so on, ideology facilitates the continuance of society divided by class, race and gender. Moreover, people rationalise their behaviour and make sense of the world by drawing on such things as socialisation and conventional assumptions. Rationalisations are then confirmed by social behaviour and images of male and female relationships transmitted through socialising institutions (the media, for example). Within the family, an ideology of gender is reproduced through children learning from parents. If, for example, parents believe in the 'naturalness' of the gender division of labour, it is likely that these beliefs will be perpetuated generationally.

This chapter offers an exploratory analysis of some of the processes in which an ideology of gender is integrated within and reinforces the practice of domestic labour. The next section describes the dominant pattern of the division of domestic labour in Middlesbrough, variations in the pattern according to employment status and social class, and how the division is channelled through ideological conceptions about male and female roles.

Middlesbrough is a town which grew up around the Victorian iron and steel industries. It is now dominated by chemical production on sites adjacent to the River Tees. The town has limited opportunities for work, a low average income per household compared with the rest of Britain, and the widest gap between male and female wages in the country.[4] Unemployment is high – 21.9 per cent of men in Middlesbrough were registered unemployed at the time of the 1981 Census. Men have great difficulty in obtaining work, due to the decline of traditional industries and contraction in the newer industries. The proportion of married women working (50 per cent) is below the national average (64 per cent) but has risen by 10 per cent since 1971. On the basis of the Registrar General's categories of social class, the working class account for 69 per cent of the population: the relatively small middle class is inflated by professional men, recruited to industrial posts from outside the area.

I carried out fieldwork in the town in 1980 and 1981. The results are based on 338 replies to a postal survey and on interviews with a sub-sample of 31 couples drawn from the survey. Those who replied to the survey were broadly representative of the town's population; 60 per cent were working class; 40 per cent were middle class; 21 per cent of the working-class men were unemployed. The interview sub-sample consisted of middle- and working-class families at the child-rearing stage of the family life-cycle. Half of the women and most of the men were employed. The aim of the survey was to establish how couples divided domestic activities between themselves and whether attitudes about the roles of the sexes were predominantly 'traditional' or 'egalitarian'. The interviews explored in more detail the division of domestic labour and the ideological dimension of domesticity.

Domestic labour was divided into three categories for analytical purposes: the production of utilities; caring; and ideological reproduction (see below). The production of utilities was defined to include activities associated with laundry, food provision, cleaning, creating domestic order, maintenance and home improvement. Caring was defined in terms of the physical care and socialisation of children. The postal survey asked couples to study a list which included activities of the 'utility producing' and 'caring' kind, and to indicate whether they were performed by the wife usually, the husband usually, shared, not done at all or delegated to others. The interviews paid particular attention to men's domestic contribution and to the precise meaning of 'sharing'.

The results show that wives do most of the domestic labour and husbands give varying degrees of help. Laundry, food provision and cleaning attract the least amount of male involvement: 90 per cent of the women usually do the washing, ironing and mending; less than 10 per cent of men share these activities and less than 2 per cent usually do them; 70 per cent of women usually cook, wash floors and clean baths; 62 per cent usually do the shopping. Men do more in relation to maintenance, home improvement and creating order: 30 per cent usually do repairs (general, plumbing and electrical) and the same percentage usually decorate and do gardening; 42 per cent of men share tidying-up, 60 per cent share washing-up and 72 per cent go shopping with their wives for household goods. Men are highly involved with child socialisation: around 85 per cent play with their children and take them out regularly. Data on the physical care of children is more limited as only 20 per cent of respondents to the postal survey had babies and toddlers: 39 per cent of these fathers share changing nappies and 50 per cent share feeding the children.

The extent of men's domestic labour within the category of 'producing utilities' was measured with a scoring system, following the method used by Oakley (1974, p. 137). Like Oakley's sample, husbands were assessed as 'high', 'medium' or 'low' on their participation in cooking, decorating, shopping, gardening and so on. The criterion was similarly 'how much of a share the husband took in the total amount of domestic work' but, unlike Oakley, childcare was excluded from the scoring, because not all families replying to the postal survey had children still living at home. The assessments are relative – husbands with high scores do more than men with low scores but this does not necessarily imply a high standard of performance compared with the rest of men in Britain. Of the Middlesbrough men, 15 per cent gained a high score, 49 per cent a medium score and 36 per cent a low score. The finding that over a third of men do little or no 'utility production' and that only a sixth have high scores supports Oakley's claim that 'only a minority of husbands give the kind of help that assertions of equality in modern marriage imply' (1974, p. 138).

The interviews provided an opportunity to ask men why they do some domestic activities rather than others, and to assess whether sharing meant occasional help or taking an equal share of the labour. The example of laundry reveals the limits of male domestic assistance. Men typically replied that laundry was not 'their job', it was 'difficult', a 'mystery', or that they would 'mess the clothes up'. A postman said: 'Washing is a woman's job. I don't think any man would want to be lumbered with washing, although he could probably do it.'; and a lecturer asserted: 'Ironing is such a bind. If I were to iron a shirt, I would end up messing it up. It's a simple job to her, but to me it's so complicated.' Despite technological developments in methods for doing laundry, the task remains closely tied in with concepts of gender identity. Identifying women with specific domestic activities is evident in areas where men's contribution is higher than it is in laundry. For example, ten of the men interviewed state explicitly that washing up is a woman's job, although they often help. A laboratory assistant remarked: 'It's well known I do the pots on a Thursday night. I don't feel any need to do it. I do it because I think it will help her.'

When men share activities with their wives, the common pattern is to assist and work alongside them. This is evident in relation to cooking. All but one of the women interviewed usually cook the main meal of the day. Fourteen husbands often cook snacks (like beans on toast or bacon 'butties'). Six of them also cook the Sunday dinner. Seventeen of the husbands do no cooking at all and want to have wives who cook for them. A builder pointed out: 'I like to have a good meal cooked for me. There's three women in this house so there shouldn't be any complications.'; and a playgroup leader said of her husband: 'He's one of these fellows who won't have a wife and him do the cooking.' The division of cooking suggests that women remain largely responsible for providing meals. When men choose to cook they do not commonly take over the main meals, however competent they might be in the kitchen. Those who refuse to cook associate the task with the 'wifely duties' they believe to be implicit in the marriage contract.

Maintenance activities are traditionally regarded as the male contribution to domestic labour, but the interviews show that men's involvement in them is neither consistent nor regular. For instance, when repairing their homes, 10 men prefer to leave most of the work to tradesmen; 14 men sometimes do tasks like repairing broken windows and leaking taps; only 7 men work extensively on their homes, utilising skills acquired at work — joinery and plumbing, for example. A similar variable pattern of commitment is evident with respect to decorating and gardening.

The most popular side of domestic labour for men is childcare, commented on with much enthusiasm during the interviews. Most men are eager to have warm and loving relationships with their children. However, while they spend time playing with them and take them swimming, to judo classes, youth clubs and so on, most of the physical care is still left to their wives. Women are identified by men as the person in charge of managing the child's needs for food, clean clothes, being prepared for school and having a comfortable environment to come home to. A lecturer, for example, described how he would dress his son following his wife's instructions: 'I change his nappy. It's more likely to be at the weekend than during the week. She knows where everything is — where the baby clothes are kept.' The extent of men's sharing represents a relatively minor male contribution to the total domestic requirements of families. Despite some crossing of gender boundaries in activities like tidying, vacuuming, decorating and child socialisation, men and women in Middlesbrough continue to have gender-distinct relationships to domestic labour.

There is general agreement among sociologists that the division of domestic labour is modified when wives are employed (Blood and Wolfe, 1960; Fogarty, Rapoport and Rapoport, 1971; Young and Willmott, 1975; Hunt, 1980; Geerken and Gove, 1983). However, these accounts differ over the extent and implications of any modification. Young and Willmott, for example, argue that women's employment helps to erode 'traditional' sex roles (1975, p. 121). Less optimistically, Hunt notes that although husbands do more domestic labour when wives work, women still do most of it (1980, p. 112). Geerken and Gove confirm that men do more, but stress that there is no significant shift in women's domestic responsibilities (1983, p. 96).

The Middlesbrough data show minor changes in men's contribution in line with women's employment, but no changes in *responsibility* for domestic labour. The survey results demonstrates that men whose wives work do more of four domestic activities: cooking, washing-up, dusting and making beds. Furthermore, this increase occurs only at the level of 'sharing'. With the exception of cooking, these activities are straightforward and do not require advance planning. Even though men cook more if their wives work, women still have the same amount of shopping and clearing-up to do afterwards. Most dual-worker couples who were interviewed remarked on an increase in the husband's domestic labour after the wife re-entered employment. However, this assistance was not mandatory or consistent. Six working women, for example, had husbands with low domestic-labour scores, and they compressed their working and home lives into a seemingly unending sequence of 'jobs that have to be done'. All complained of permanent tiredness and 'minor' health problems like backache, headaches and muscular tension. The postal survey shows that a third of employed wives have husbands with low domestic-labour scores and only 12 per cent of employed women have husbands with high scores. This indicates that at least one in three women are disadvantaged by combining wage-labour and domestic-labour responsibilities. As long as men's domestic labour continues to be of the helping and variable kind, the roles of the sexes remain asymmetrical, even when wives work.

Variations in the division of domestic labour by social class is a further controversial issue among sociologists. Bott (1957), Young and Willmott (1975) and Oakley (1974) agree that middle-class men do more than working-class men. Conversely, Gavron (1966) found a higher level of working-class help. Pahl and Pahl (1971) and Edgell (1980) stress that professional middle-class men do very little domestically. The Middlesbrough results show no significant social class difference in the extent of women's domestic-labour responsibilities, but indicate a class difference at the sharing level. Middle-class men share more shopping, but working-class men share more cooking, tidying-up and cleaning. For example, 20 per cent more working-class men than middle-class men share cleaning the bath, 14 per cent more share washing the floor, and 12 per cent more share cooking. The difference in sharing points to a higher working-class male contribution. A fifth of the working-class men who replied to the postal survey were unemployed, and because they represent a significant fraction of the working class, the data were reanalysed to control for the unemployment variable. It was found that unemployed working-class men account for about half of the difference in sharing between middle-class and working-class men. Unemployed men therefore make a significant contribution to the greater domestic labour participation of working-class men as a whole.

The Middlesbrough data shows that when men do domestic labour, they are most often involved in the creation of an orderly environment, the improvement of the appearance of the home, and childcare. They are less willing to clean, cook, wash and iron clothes, and on the whole do maintenance jobs only if they already have the skills or find pleasure and leisure in doing them. The division of labour advantages men because they are able to choose whether to become involved or not. Women do not choose to do domestic labour. They are responsible for domestic activities within the categories of 'laundry', 'food provision', 'control of domestic dirt' and 'creating order' because they plan, organise and ensure that these activities are carried out effectively. For instance, the interviews reveal that women almost invariably decide what the family will eat, what the children will wear, what has to be bought from the shops, when the house has to be cleaned, what has to be done on particular days of the week, and so on. This pattern of responsibility is replicated by men in relation to repairs and decorating, but since women are responsible for the everyday, essential tasks they maintain overall a greater level of responsibility for domestic labour.

It has been suggested that men's avoidance of domestic labour is an outcome of inequalities in the relations between the sexes, where men dominate women. Heidi Hartmann (1979), for example, argues that:

> Men exercise their control in receiving personal service work from women, in not having to do housework or rear children, in having access to women's bodies for sex, and in feeling powerful and being powerful. (p. 14)

Hartmann equates male power over women with a particular pattern of domestic labour in which men do very little. Although her view of male power may well relate to those men in Middlesbrough with low domestic-labour scores, it does not tie in readily with the variation found in how much men do. Given that men do participate in domestic labour, Hartmann's notion of how power is exercised through the division of labour requires further elaboration.

Leonore Davidoff (1976, p. 125) has argued that it is men's ability to *delegate* domestic labour to women which places them in a position of power. She points out that the rewards of power include freedom from doing menial tasks. In support of Davidoff, there is empirical evidence which suggests that the activities men eschew are those women least like doing. Oakley's study of housework (1974, pp. 49–50) demonstrates that women most dislike ironing, cleaning and, to a lesser extent, washing. Oakley compares these activities with repetitive industrial jobs which 'tire specific muscles without engaging the attention of the mind or the concentrated energy of the whole body' (ibid, p. 50). When men refuse to do activities on the grounds they are 'women's work', they are refusing to participate in aspects of domestic labour which resemble the most monotonous and uninspiring features of work in industrial production.

In discussing who benefits from the division of domestic labour, Barrett offers another approach to the question of whether mere division of domestic activities is indicative of male power. She argues that it is women's dependence on men – arising from the division of domestic labour – which constitutes their subordinate position. Materially, women depend on men, and ideologically they are 'confined to a primary concern with domesticity and motherhood' (Barrett, 1980, p. 214). Men have perceived that the role of main wage-earner is more desirable than the role of dependent. Even though they are 'locked into' wage-labour, they still benefit from women doing domestic activities, caring for relatives and so on', and from the privileges associated with masculinity in a society which places a strong emphasis on achievement in the world of work.

The precise ways in which women are dependent on men ideologically can be illustrated from the Middlesbrough data. Although feminist arguments stress a close connection between an 'unequal' division of domestic labour and male power, it is also possible that inequalities in 'who does what' around the home might represent a 'cultural lag', where social practice has not yet shifted in line with changing norms about the marital partnership. As Oakley has remarked:

> Psychological intimacy between husband and wife, an intermingling of their social worlds and a more equitable division of power in marriage are undoubtedly areas in which marriage in general has changed. (1974, p. 164)

Attitudinal questions were included in the postal survey, to discover whether an ideology of equity is favoured in Middlesbrough, or conversely, whether an ideology which legitimates gender divisions along traditional lines is widespread. The replies confirm the continuance of traditional attitudes, especially in relation to housework. Only 18 per cent of the sample thought housework should be shared, for example. As few as 10 per cent thought husbands should do the same amount of domestic labour as their wives and 80 per cent thought working wives should spend most of their spare time catching up on housework. The dominant view of the sample identifies women with domesticity (although the minority who go against conventional wisdom may represent some degree of ideological change).

The interviews show that in spite of developments in the economy (reflected in Middlesbrough by more women entering the labour force and more men leaving it through unemployment), the idea that women should nurture the family and men should provide financial support still features highly in beliefs about marriage. A nurse spoke for many couples by saying:

> I think men should be the main breadwinner because it is in their making. We're more for the children, the food, the kitchen. But men, subconsciously, they take it on themselves. If he does this for you, you should jolly well look after him and give him a good meal and moral support.

Through socialisation in families and schools, women expect to spend their adult lives caring for others. As Sue Sharpe (1976, p. 206) has shown, marriage can be anticipated as an attractive and fulfilling option to employment, especially for girls with few educational qualifications and poor job prospects. Once married, domestic service can become a means for women to express their emotional commitment to their families. Moreover, women's overall lesser earnings than men and typical withdrawal from the labour market to have children confirms their material dependence.

The housewives interviewed were highly conscious of their lack of independent income. In general, they regarded their domestic labour as a service owed to their husbands in return for the standard of living provided by his earnings. A housewife said: 'I know if my husband is working and I am not, I am expected to do housework. I get paid and fed for doing that.' Women's belief that unpaid domestic services are fair exchange for wage-goods and security is a corollary of their dependent position. Paid employment allows greater independence and control over their lives, but, as was argued earlier, the division of domestic labour remains unequal for working women. The internalisation of an ideology of gender from an early age encourages working wives to feel that the home should come first. Providing good service is proof that women are not neglecting their families by working outside the home. One woman with a responsible full-time job said:

> I've all my housework done before I ever go out through that door to work. I think my husband realises that I am working full-time and I like my housework done. When he gets the opportunity, he'll muck in and help.

In contrast, men do not feel under any obligation to combine work with domestic labour. As an accountant said:

> I leave here at half past eight and I don't get home until half past five. You can't expect me, after working virtually solidly all that time, to come in and do housework.

The ideology of female service and its association with dependence becomes a convenient device which men can use to maintain a privileged position.

The idea that men, as financial providers, are more important than other wage-earners in the family and should be exempted from domestic labour still persists in Middlesbrough. Men's financial obligations towards their families were a recurrent theme in discussions of work with the men interviewed. As a rigger put it:

> To me, a man who turns round and says he'd rather be at home than at work, or he'd rather not work, I've no time for him. I believe it's a man's place to be at work, especially if he's married and got a family.

The ideology that men should be the main breadwinner is confirmed by social practice: the majority of the men interviewed provided the main source of family income. The extent to which men use their greater earnings as a rationale for not doing domestic labour varied. In general, husbands of non-working wives expect domestic services in return for their wages, although they would sometimes lend a helping hand. Men are less inclined to use their status as wage-earners to avoid domestic labour if their wives work. Nevertheless, in dual-worker families husbands continue to stress the primary importance of their jobs. In one case, the wife had managed a fish-and-chip shop for seventeen years, and even though her husband admitted borrowing money from her during hard times in the building trade, he still maintained that a 'woman's place is in the home' and 'a man should be making the main part of money in the home'. Expanding on this theme, he pointed out:

> It's horses for courses, that's what I believe in. I wouldn't get a joiner to do bricklaying. I'd get a bricklayer to do bricklaying and a joiner to do joinery. So I wouldn't expect a fellow to do the washing-up or get the dinner.

Here, the ideology that the man should be the chief wage-earner is upheld despite the practice of the couple involved. Hunt argues that:

> When people are unaware of the contradictions contained in their

situation, it becomes difficult for them to envisage things being other than they are; in this sense ideologies are inherently conservative. (1980, p. 180)

The social practice of wives working is not sufficient to dissolve servicing relations in the home nor attendant ideologies. The division of domestic labour reflects not only particular family circumstances, but also dominant images of masculinity and femininity. The culture of the workplace, for example, encourages the expression of particular masculine and feminine traits. Paul Willis (1979) illustrates this when arguing that men who work on the shopfloor are bound up with the machismo of manual work. Manual labour can be a form of masculine expressivity, with its emphasis on toughness and assertiveness. The wage packet is 'won in a masculine mode in confrontation with the "real" world which is too tough for the woman' (Willis, 1979, p. 197). Men who have internalised the culture of the workplace are unlikely to participate in the woman's world of domestic labour because it would threaten their masculine identity. While not all working-class men work in the collective atmosphere of factory life, the Middlesbrough research found instances of men who place an emphasis on the strength they deploy through working. These men were among those most likely to support traditional views about the sexes. A docker illustrated this attitude by saying:

Well, I look at it this way. I've got these jobs I'm telling you — them bags and drums on the dock. I'd like to see her come down and do them! Women's rights they say, but women can't do some of our jobs. Mind you, we can't do some of theirs. Housework — that's women's work, isn't it.

Women's employment is often an extension of the female domestic role. In providing services as home-helps, dinner-ladies, cleaners, nurses and shop-workers, women extend their identity as 'carers for others' beyond the family. As the identification of women with service is confirmed within employment, it becomes even more difficult for women to disengage themselves from the servicing role at home.

Middle-class men are not challenged to 'prove' their masculinity at work in the same way as working-class men. However, as Edgell (1980, p. 60) demonstrates, the prestige and status of the professional man gives him the power to legitimately avoid domestic activities he regards as onerous. Edgell's point is confirmed by managers in Middlesbrough who delegate most domestic labour to their wives:

> I basically see that a house is a woman's domain and a woman to look
> after that. It's not my job to change the baby or do the hoovering or
> the dusting. I've always felt that way.

On an ideological level, around a third of the male interviewees brought the culture of the public domain to bear on the division of domestic labour in such a way that it justified their self-exclusion from domestic chores. The other interviewees believed husbands should make a contribution, but only in the context of help, the husband remaining the main earner and the wife remaining the main carer.

It has been argued that concern with child socialisation dominates marriage to an extent unknown in previous centuries. Ariès (1973), for example, argues that as community structures have broken down, the modern family has become isolated, and obsessed with 'the physical, moral and sexual problems of childhood' (ibid, p. 395). The new importance attached to parenting is reflected in the replies to the postal survey questions on childcare, where 91 per cent of the sample thought *both* parents should be equally involved with the children. At the same time, women are still seen as the primary caretakers of small children — 63 per cent of the sample thought mothers of pre-school children should not take paid jobs, for example. In practice, low-paid jobs for women and patchy childminding services in Middlesbrough tend to discourage mothers from re-entering employment soon after the birth of their children. Since most mothers of babies do not work, their lack of employment helps to confirm their identification as primary carers.

The 15 full-time mothers interviewed were committed to being at home for the children's sake. Loving feelings towards their children were often tempered by regrets about a loss of public identity and a desire to demonstrate social utility outside the home. The 16 working mothers had all taken jobs which 'fitted in' with the family; 8 worked part-time and 8 full-time; 5 of the full-time workers were employed mornings and evenings, which maximised the time they had with their children; the other 3 full-time workers had teenage children who were able to assist with some of the domestic labour. Once women are established in jobs where it is possible to integrate childcare with working further ideological support is given to the primacy of motherhood over female employment.

All the fathers interviewed wanted their children cared for by the mothers (rather than, for instance, grandparents, nurseries or neighbours). Children's welfare is paramount in the modern, child-centred family (see

Qvortrup, this volume), and the most favoured form of childcare is defined by fathers as that provided by mothers. Moreover, male support for maternal care ties in with an ideology of the male breadwinner. If women are occupied at home as mothers, they are not competing with men for work within industrial production. Several Middlesbrough men revealed fears that their increasingly vulnerable position in the economy was being threatened not only by redundancies and lay-offs, but also by women. A salesman said:

> A mother's place is in the home with the children. I don't see why the housewife should go out to work which she could be taking from other breadwinners — taking food from their families.

When mothers are confined at home, men feel that they can assert more control over the world of work. At the same time, full-time motherhood helps to preserve an unequal division of domestic labour, however concerned fathers might be about their children's welfare. On one level, domestic labour done for children easily extends into domestic labour for the whole family — cooking and washing are good examples. On another level, women's acceptance of dependency encourages full-time mothers not to demand a high level of male housework.

Margaret Stacey and Marion Price have questioned why women continue to believe their place is in the home. They suggest that either women gain satisfaction from the wife—mother role which 'outweigh those that it is possible to gain in the public world', or that they are 'just trapped' in the family (1981, p. 101). Certain privileges accrue to women when they identify primarily with the home. They have more time with the children and more choice than husbands over participating in employment The positive aspects of child-rearing were repeatedly mentioned by the Middlesbrough women. Nevertheless, the evidence for women being trapped in the family is considerable. Few women enjoy domestic activities other than childcare, and some find housework an intolerable burden:

> I hate everything about it, especially windows and ironing. It's boring, dreary and nobody is good for it. You spend hours cleaning up and they all come in, shoes everywhere, papers everywhere, they sling their coats in that passage — definitely I hate it. I want to work because I'm sick of being in this house. He won't let me.

Men with low domestic-labour scores insisted that their wives' domestic load remained intact. They stubbornly refused to change their behaviour, intervened in wives' decisions about working and controlled the distribution of financial resources. Conflict emerged between couples during a number of interviews when the wife indicated she resented her domestic responsibilities. As one woman said:

> He won't help me and I get annoyed about that. We've come to the conclusion no matter how annoyed I get, he will not change. So I just do it, but I don't agree with it.

Men with medium domestic-labour scores were less inclined to assert power overtly, but still presented an unequal division of labour as a reasonable response to circumstance and colluded with statements which support the view that a woman's place is in the home.

The Middlesbrough sample's support for an ideology of gender does not rule out the possibility that prevailing beliefs might be modified. Ideologies derive from the material conditions in society, which change and develop over time. Hunt (1980, pp. 181–3) has argued that conventional ideologies can be undermined through a conscious choice not to subscribe to the ideology, as a result of widespread social practices which run contrary to the ideology, and through conflicting and competing forms of thought. In Middlesbrough, although most couples believe wives should be in charge of domestic labour, there are exceptions. One couple, for instance, hired domestic help so that the wife could work as a doctor's receptionist, study for an Open University degree, and attend to five children as well as a 90-year-old-mother-in-law. This woman maintained a caring role, but was freed from some of the constraints of domestic chores. Perhaps more important than occasional examples of women who do not identify primarily with domesticity are major developments in the economy, which may lead to disseminated ideological changes. The ideology of the male breadwinner, for instance, draws its strength from equating male earnings with social superiority. As unemployment tightens its grip in Middlesbrough, increasing numbers of men are losing the status which is associated with working. The working-class men interviewed all feared unemployment and were in agreement that they would expect to do more domestic labour if they lost their jobs. Male unemployment may be the catalyst which will weaken the identification of women with domesticity in the future.

In conclusion, the data confirm that domestic labour remains divided along gender lines. The social context in which domestic labour is carried out supports men sharing, but not taking over, domestic responsibilities. Men's relatively low commitment is reinforced by an ideology which identifies men primarily with earning and women with caring. Men are in a position to exercise power as a result of the division of domestic labour, because women are materially and ideologically dependent upon them. The advantaged male position is manifested in a variety of ways in the home which include self-exclusion from disliked domestic activities, expectations that wives will automatically provide services like meals and clean clothes, a relationship to employment which is not built around stages in the family life-cycle, and freedom from having to fulfil both employment responsibilities and daily domestic responsibilities. Since men continue to expect women to do most of the domestic labour, women are hampered in their choice of employment, often opting for jobs which 'fit in' with the family but which are badly paid, poorly protected and offer little opportunity for advancement (see Chaney, this volume).

An ideology of gender reinforces a division of domestic labour in which women are mainly responsible for the reproduction of labour power. Stacey and Price (1981, p. 187) argue that the element of the ideology which draws on 'love, service and loyalty' has 'twin and contradictory consequences' for women. On the one hand, it places women in a subservient role within their families. On the other hand, it makes 'valued and warm social relations' possible. Extending this argument, an ideology of gender grants men power over their wives but does little to foster male expressivity. That many men desire greater closeness in personal relationships is evident in studies of fatherhood (for example, McKee and O'Brien, 1982). At present, the relationship between the economy and the family imprisons women and men in conventional roles, and what remains is to find a way of developing alternative gender roles which are mutually beneficial to both sexes.

NOTES

1. A more detailed discussion of the research summarised in this chapter will appear in my PhD thesis entitled 'The Division of Domestic Labour among Families in Middlesbrough' (currently in preparation).
2. For a further discussion of the limitations of the Domestic Labour Debate, see Close and Collins (1983, pp. 48–64).
3. For example, Berk and Berk (1979) investigate the division of domestic labour in over 600 domestic activities, while Gavron (1966) examines domestic divisions in only eleven activities.
4. CSO Regional Statistics, 1981.

4 Gender Divisions and Power Relationships in the Australian Family

LOIS BRYSON

'Diary of a Mad Househusband' was the title of an article which was reprinted in the Sydney *Morning Herald* (31 March 1983), having appeared earlier in *The Guardian*. It began with the observation that 'more men are taking over house and children while their wives go out to work', and proceeded to list the tribulations of a househusband involved in what would have once been called a 'role reversal' situation. Today, sociologists tend to avoid this term because it implies that the traditional male and female roles are somehow fixed and given, whereas there is no reason to assume that childcare is a female occupation, which males only undertake through taking on a female role.

That the article originally appeared in *The Guardian* indicates the generality of popular interest in men's role in the domestic division of labour in advanced capitalist societies, and one could cite many examples of this public discussion of the issue of housework and childcare in particular. As well, we have a developing literature in the social sciences which explicitly focuses on fathers and their role within the family. In Britain, for example, in 1982 an edited collection entitled *The Father Figure* (McKee and O'Brien), was published, and in Australia, Russell has written on *The Changing Role of Fathers?* (1983).

The issue of who does what in the family has received the attention of sociologists over many years but this interest has recently taken on greater force, as part of an attempt to understand and theorise gender inequality. Feminists see the issue of childcare as a crucial basis of the subordination of women. Firestone (1971) probably represents the most extreme position on this topic, defining child production as the cause of women's oppression, but almost all writers on the issue of gender inequality see childcare as being of key importance.

Within the popular media the underlying theme is that change is ocurring and that this has led, or is leading to, greater equality. The acacemic literature is also concerned with change but is likely to be much less sanguine about how much change has occurred and how we should interpret current trends.

Here I shall be concerned with the division of labour between wives and husbands within the Australian family over the last thirty to forty years. The ultimate purpose of such a review is to analyse the nature of any changes and to see whether they should be interpreted as contributing to greater gender equality.

In undertaking an examination of life within Australian families, it is fortunate that one of the few threads of continuity in family research has involved the internal division of labour. This is a crucial area for understanding power distribution, but more practically the interest may be explained by the apparent ease with which the topic can be investigated and the fact that it was studied in the 1940s, which provided later researchers with an obvious impetus. The availability of systematically collected data spanning more than a thirty-year period offers a welcome opportunity for historical analysis, something which is certainly rare within Australian sociology. The research can be conveniently considered in two time-periods, with the earlier research being carried out in the late 1940s and 1950s and a second wave during the 1970s — which gives every indication of continuing into the 1980s.

Between 1947 and 1950 one of Australia's most extensive family studies was carried out by the Department of Psychology at the University of Melbourne (Oeser and Hammond, 1954). As part of this study, Herbst developed the 'Day at Home' questionnaire, a research technique which in its original or somewhat modified form has been used widely for family research in Australia and elsewhere. The technique involves giving schoolchildren a questionnaire which asks them who carries out, and decides about, a range of family activities. Herbst divided these activities into four broad areas: housework, child control, economic activities, and social activities. An additional question tapped the amount of disagreement between husband and wife about 'when and how [something] is done' (Oeser and Hammond, 1954, chs 9–12). The 33-item questionnaire was administered to eighty-five 12-year-old children at school, and follow-up interviews with the families were conducted. It was found that housework tasks fell into three categories: some were virtually exclusively the mother's (for example, ironing, cooking, washing); some were predominantly the father's (for example, household repairs, mowing lawns); and in a third area both tended to participate (for example, shopping, doing dishes).

Both parents participated in childcare activities, though these were 'predominantly controlled by the mother'. Social activities were said to be 'generally engaged in and decided about by both husband and wife', as were economic activities (ibid, pp. 120–1). However, in terms of sheer numbers, wives clearly made most decisions and carried out most activities. Tension within the family was greatest in the relatively infrequent cases of family management designated 'husband dominance'. Herbst identified three other family patterns. Husband and wife acting independently of each other ('autonomic') was the most common, followed by 'wife dominance', and then a 'syncratic co-operative' pattern in which both partners decided and acted. This pattern was said to be associated with the least family tension (ibid, p. 167).

The next study of family activity in Australia was undertaken by Fallding (1957). He carried out a particularly intensive study of thirty-eight families in Sydney chosen mainly in terms of their willingness to devote a considerable amount of time to the research. Each family had at least two children and they were visited from four to seven times for a full evening on each occasion. Interviews were conducted with each member and with the family as a group. Fallding came to the conclusion that:

> Husbands and wives divided authority or family control between them in the traditional way, accepting the customary responsibilities of bread winner and homemaker respectively. (Fallding, 1957, p. 60)

While the division of labour within the family was quite uniform and almost always along traditional lines (that is, with the wife taking key responsibility within the home), there was greater variety 'in matters of family management'. Fallding found that in 55 per cent of families, mostly with the father in a skilled occupation, 'the fathers could be said to be in effective control', in 11 per cent the 'mothers were in effective control', and in 34 per cent there was 'partnership in management'. In a majority of cases in which the husband was in control, the patriarchal situation was considered 'rightful' by both husband and wife, but in no case was mother control seen in this way. In the few cases where the mother 'had control' this was seen to have occurred by default. In the vast majority of cases of 'partnership' (and these were found mainly in families in which the father had a professional occupation), this arrangement was seen as the right and proper way to deal with family affairs (Fallding, 1957, pp. 60–6).

In 1957–8, Adler (1965) carried out a study using a modified version of Herbst's 'Day at Home' questionnaire, in which 1,525 12-year-old schoolchildren from five different States participated. Adler, like Herbst, found that mothers were active in all areas except for 'traditional male household duties'. He found the mother's action role to be 'only a little less developed than her decision role' and both were pervasive. This led him to coin the term 'matriduxy' to denote the mother's powerful leadership functions within the home. He eschewed the use of the term 'matriarchy' because the basis of the Australian mother's power is 'not a function of inheritance, legal structure or formal organisation'. Comparison of the Australian family patterns with data Adler had collected for Mexico and the United States highlighted the role of the Australian mother. In Mexico fathers were quite clearly major decision-makers, while in the United States Adler had found greater co-operation. The Australian figures showed that mothers, on their own, made 50 per cent of the decisions and carried out 40 per cent of the forty-four questionnaire items, figures similar to those of Herbst which were 50 per cent and 30 per cent respectively (Adler, 1965, pp. 149–55).

The Herbst and Fallding studies were largely restricted to families in which the women were not working outside the home, but Adler's sample included 29 per cent of women who were. In these cases husbands' participation was greater and there was more disagreement about the activities, leading him to conclude that 'apparently matriduxy is the acceptable way of family life in Australia and that alteration in the mother's role accompanied by increasing father participation tends to be disruptive and tension producing' (Adler, 1965, p. 155). This conclusion is broadly in line with the Herbst finding, that greatest tension was associated with husband-dominant families.

The outstanding finding of these three studies is the key role of women in family decisions and activities and the generally traditional division of labour along sex lines, a finding also supported by a number of other studies undertaken in the 1950s (for example, Taft, 1957). Most of the women in the studies were not in paid employment, as would be expected, because the proportion of married women between 30 and 40 years of age who were in the workforce in 1954 was only 13 per cent. Adler's high figure of 29 per cent working is due to the fact that he chose his sample from areas with high migrant populations, and rates of employment of married women have been higher in these groups. Adler's findings showed that husband participation increased when the wife was employed, though the amount by which it increased was not great. This relative rigidity of the sexual division of labour was also demonstrated in a study carried out in Melbourne in 1959, comparing fifty-two families in which the mother worked outside the home with a matched-pair sample in which she did not. Husband participation was found to be greater where the wife was in paid employment, though the husband's contribution almost never came close to the wife's. However, the increase in husband participation only occurred when the wife intended to work temporarily. If she intended to work permanently then the husband's contribution was only equivalent to that of husbands of non-employed wives (Sharp and Bryson, 1965). Such a finding adds additional weight to those studies which establish the traditionality of the sexual division of labour within the family in the 1940s and 1950s, and points to a possible dimension which does not seem to have been pursued in recent studies.

How do we account for the fact that Herbst found a mixture of family types, Fallding found patriarchy being challenged by 'partnership in management', while Adler pronounced the Australian family a matriduxy? All take a more or less traditional methodological approach, and it is clear that a feminist approach would suggest that both similarities and discrepancies in interpretation result from this. However, the evidence is straightforward enough: the women in all the studies were very active within the household. This is not surprising given that the vast majority were not employed outside the home. Questions about the findings arise only when the researcher's judgement seems to impute some more generalised notion of female power, as occurs with Adler's term 'matriduxy', Fallding's term 'partnership', and to a lesser extent Herbst's 'syncratic co-operative'. Matriduxy, in fact, was claimed by Adler to have a restricted meaning but its semantic associations inevitably result in broader connections being made. Also, Adler questions why women should be more powerful within the Australian family than their counterparts in Mexico or the United States. Without going into the possible reasons for such a finding, one could counterpose: why wasn't Adler surprised that men in the other countries had more power within the family than he found them to have in Australia? Fallding's term 'partnership' is also equivocal, as it suggests equality without sufficient consideration of the effect of the male's economic role on the marital relationship. The same can be said of the term 'syncratic co-operative', though the choice of words makes the meaning relatively obscure (and was perhaps intended to be cautious).

A more perspicacious comment on the overall situation was offered by Encel in a later general commentary on the Australian family. He pointed out that 'the strongly masculine texture of "public" social relations is balanced by the dominance of the mother in "private" social life within the family' (Encel, 1970, p. 283). Even here we must question the use of the word 'balanced', because only by suggesting that the private sphere is accepted as equal in importance to the public sphere could one come to a general conclusion about 'balance', or 'partnership', or make sense of a term such as 'matriduxy'. Also, none of the studies paid attention to the relative importance of the decisions made by husbands and wives, yet a number of studies since that time (cf. Edgell, 1980, p. 58), demonstrate the predictable point, the husbands' decision-making may be infrequent but does pre-empt major issues.

Williams, in her recent study of families in a Queensland mining town, offers a fundamental criticism of family studies like those of Herbst, Fallding and Adler, by pointing to the importance of ideology. The studies all worked from the premise that a form of equal sharing could be achieved within families, but Williams points out that:

> a 'companionship' ethos in the midst of a patriarchal institution in a patriarchal society is part of the capitalist hegemony by which the oppression of women is maintained. (Williams, 1981, p. 133)

In her own study, Williams suggests that women in unhappy marriages displayed greater consciousness of inequalities, and tensions in the marriage often resulted from this. Her work certainly throws into doubt the interpretations made in these studies of tension as being largely deviant or dysfunctional. It could be suggested that the tension found by Herbst associated with husband-dominated families, and the increased tension found by Adler when husbands participated more in household tasks, may have resulted from women resisting reductions in their already limited powers. Adler comes close to recognising this, though he does so in terms of a breach of norms, rather than an issue of power and inequality.

Since the workforce participation rate for married women in the 1940s and 1950s was low, a traditional division of labour within the home is what one might expect. What do studies of the 1970s find when more women had entered the workforce?

The more recent studies do suggest that some changes have occurred and that a somewhat greater range of options is open to men and women. The number of married women working outside the home is today more than 40 per cent, and some other changes can be demonstrated in the realm of childcare. In 1977 the government's Supporting Mothers' Benefit was extended to males and became the Supporting Parents' Benefit, making it financially possible for a single father to take on a full-time parenting role (though of course with the same difficulty as the female supporting-parent beneficiary). There seems to be a greater acceptance of more extensive fathering in two-parent families as well, and a range of 'shared care' options are emerging.

Harper and Richards's *Mothers and Working Mothers* (1979) reports the findings of two detailed studies that considered the orientation of Melbourne husbands and wives to family roles, in which 195 wives were asked about the contributions of each spouse to household tasks and childcare. The findings confirm that where wives are in waged work (half the sample mothers were employed outside the home), husbands do take a greater share of the housework and childcare. The tasks that husbands participate in most are similar to those found by Herbst and Adler, and the figures also confirm that husbands almost *never* contribute as much as wives. When wives are working part-time, husbands' contributions to childcare are marginally greater than when wives are home full-time, but their participation in housework remains the same. (Thomas and Shannon, 1982, in fact found that in some cases husbands with wives working part-time made reduced contributions to housework.) What is achieved, however, is some form of rationalisation of household tasks, because the wives employed part-time had lower housework scores than those at home full-time, though their childcare scores were the same. A similar rationalisation is accomplished by those employed full-time outside the home, since their husbands' increased participation does not make up for the entire reduction in the wives' housework and childcare scores (Harper and Richards, 1979, p. 294). This was not accomplished by buying in domestic services, though other studies do demonstrate this to be an option for wealthier families. As Thomas and Shannon's evidence shows, this rationalisation process is quite a general phenomenon, as is the fact that in most cases women still carry a heavier total burden of work (an overload) in terms of daily and weekly hours than their husbands (cf. Vanek, 1980; Hartmann, 1981). From a summary of a number of US studies, Pleck and Rustad establish that this 'overload' can be estimated to be between 1.2 and 2.8 hours per day (Pleck and Rustad, 1980, p. 4). Thomas and Shannon's findings are broadly in line with this though they find the overload to be somewhat less. Unfortunately the data are not available to make such a precise estimate for Australian mothers, but the trend is in general agreement.

Harper and Richards's evidence is broadly supported by a study carried out by Russell in 1978 of 275 families living in Sydney and two New South Wales country towns. He found a range of levels of participation among fathers but in the vast majority of cases their contribution was far less than that of the mother (Russell, 1979, p. 62). He was concerned with childcare and not with household talks; none the less, because it is well established that childcare is more likely to be a shared activity than housework, we might assume fathers' contributions to be generously treated if we use childcare as a gauge for the division of labour. We need, however, to exercise some caution since Harper and Richards discovered men's contribution to childcare was greater than their contributions to housework, but also found this activity was not as much affected by the mothers' employment status. (Husbands with wives in full-time employment were one third more active in childcare than the husbands of women at home full-time, but were twice as active in housework (Harper and Richards, 1979, p. 294).) Russell similarly found somewhat higher levels of involvement of fathers in childcare when the mother was employed.

Harper and Richards point out that there is great variety in patterns of family activity, with husbands of professional workers (mostly themselves professionals) on the whole doing more housework than the husbands of non-professional workers, whether or not their wives were employed at the time (ibid, p. 191). This may reflect the importance of the wife's educational level, which Russell found to be significantly related to the husband's contribution to childcare (Russell, 1981, p. 4). Despite this trend, however, Harper and Richards found wide discrepancies even among the professional workers. The husband's contribution ranged from an almost 50 per cent share to virtually no share at all, prompting the researchers to suggest that 'it would seem that broad class differences in approaches to marriage disguise a confusion of norms in all classes' (Harper and Richards, 1979, p. 191). A similarly broad range of styles was reported by Russell. He found 20 per cent of fathers from 'traditional' two-parent families had only 'a very minor involvement' in childcare while 14 per cent of 'traditional' fathers were involved in all the aspects investigated (Russell, 1981, p. 3). Both studies support the general contention that, 'sharing with child tasks [is] much less class based than sharing the chores' (Harper and Richards, 1979, p. 191).

The variety of patterns found in the 1970s is not dissimilar to the earlier studies and the pre-eminence of the mother's activity has been maintained. With more women in paid employment more 'help' is probably being offered by fathers, but Harper and Richards conclude that:

> whatever the social group, it could generally be said that when the wife worked it was more or less taken for granted that she would carry out what came to be called in the first studies of working women in the 1950s, the 'dual role'. (1979, p. 192)

The broad picture presented by the major Australian studies is one of resilience of traditional patterns. This is highly consistent with the findings of recent British studies (cf. Oakley, 1974; Pahl and Pahl, 1971;

Edgell, 1980; Thomas and Shannon, 1982). Only Young and Willmott's (1975) invocation of 'the symmetrical family' sounds a dissonant note and it seems clear that their interpretation, like that of Fallding's earlier Australian study, is more strongly influenced by what they hoped to find than by truly perturbatory information. Edgell's conclusion, in respect of his British *Middle Class Couples*, that despite 'an extensive feminist and women's liberationist literature, public debate and agitation in recent years, little change was evident even in the consciousness of the couples studied' (1980, p. 112), is applicable to the Australian research.

In 1976, Curthoys had suggested that a 'quiet revolution' was occurring, with Australian men taking greater responsibility for childcare (Curthoys, 1976). By 1979, Russell was moved to comment that 'if there is a revolution, as Curthoys suggests, then it appears not to be very widespread, or else it is very quiet' (Russell, 1979, p. 62). However, a few years later, after further investigation, he was of the opinion that:

a small but nevertheless significant cultural shift has occurred with fathers increasing their levels of participation in both child care and play. (Russell, 1981, p. 2)

During his research he discovered a number of families in which 'fathers did share all aspects of childcare'. He refers to these as 'shared care' families and has undertaken a separate study of this group (Russell, 1983). Harper too has developed research along similar lines and presents this in her book *Fathers at Home* (1980).

Curthoy's comment and Russell's revised opinion reflect a fairly general belief, not always supported by the research, that changes are occurring which may result in a change to the patriarchal nature of the family. It is worth, therefore, considering directly how such views can be reconciled with a variety of evidence. What certainly seems to have occurred is that women have received greater encouragement from employers as well as from husbands to take paid work. The rigidity of sex divisions with regard to home and employment has been blurred, and, as in the past, husbands seem to 'help' more when their wife is employed outside the home. This may well be a key to understanding the common belief about greater equality between husband and wife.

There is almost certainly greater approval by husbands of wives working than there was earlier. The 1959 Melbourne study of working and non-working mothers found a significant proportion of families in which the husband disapproved of his wife working (Bryson *et al.*, 1965), and a similar finding was recorded in the *Australian Newtown* study, a study of a working-class suburb of Melbourne carried out in 1966. In Newtown it was found that 21 per cent of wives reported that their husbands disapproved of them working, 36 per cent approved conditionally, and 43 per cent approved unconditionally (Bryson and Thompson, 1972, p.75). Harper and Richards, on the other hand, report that 90 per cent of their 195 husbands agreed when their wives went to work and had continued to agree. Almost as high a percentage (83 per cent) were happy with the wife's decision when she had chosen to stay at home (Harper and Richards, 1979, p. 90). Harper and Richards's sample spanned a range of socio-economic levels, so 'working-class' husbands must have accepted married women's employment. Harper and Richards's Melbourne data probably can be taken as reasonably representative of urban Australia (and therefore of the population generally). Greater approval of women working outside the home can be seen as one important strand in what appears to be a relaxation of rigid sex stereotyping.

We find evidence as well of a few families in which the traditional sex division of labour is altered fairly radically. Such families tend to receive a disproportionate amount of media attention so we must be careful not to exaggerate the extent of this trend. Harper and Richards report five families from their sample who had negotiated what they term 'new contracts', which 'in its pure form involves equal sharing by husband and wife within the home and usually, therefore, in work outside' (Harper and Richards, 1979, pp. 198–202). They also found one couple who had 'reversed roles', though it is interesting to note that the 1959 Melbourne study of working and non-working mothers also included *one* case out of fifty-two (Bryson *et al*, 1965). The 'new contract' families were made up of tertiary qualified women and their husbands, so again we see the importance of women's education.

Russell too found a group where husband and wife 'shared' childcare, and since his earlier research has undertaken an additional study of seventy-one such families.

As already pointed out, it is difficult to judge exactly how Russell's shared-childcare families relate overall to an equal division of labour within the home, since childcare has always been an area in which fathers are more likely to take part, and Russell does not give systematic information about household tasks. None the less, childcare is certainly a critical issue because of the extent and constancy of the demands on parents, and his sample of seventy-one families probably does represent an important and innovative group. This is seen in the total working hours of the parents. The mothers on average were outside the home for employment purposes for thirty-five hours per week, while the fathers averaged thirty-four hours. Fathers' contribution overall to childcare in hours actually exceeded the mothers', but not sufficiently to make the combined number of work-plus-childcare hours equal. These women apparently still suffer somewhat from the 'overload' noted in other research, even though the fathers' participation is well above average (Russell, 1983, p. 29).

Another interesting remnant of the traditional division in these 'shared care' families is that mothers still undertook a greater share of the basic-care chores such as feeding, changing nappies, bathing and dressing. Fathers' contributions were, however, greater in the category of general interaction with the child and play (Russell, 1983, p. 37).

Russell's shared-childcare families showed greater diversity than Harper and Richards found in their 'new contract' families and were 'not simply members of the professional middle class', nor were they 'simply a group of people who had rejected traditional career and work values' (Russell, 1983, p. 25). The involvement of fathers in shared roles was connected with several factors, including:

> flexibility of hours (a major contributing factor in about 60 per cent of families); rejection of traditional work values; rejection of traditional family roles; a strong belief that parenting should be shared; and economic factors (e.g. a father being retrenched or a mother able to earn money). (Russell, 1980, p. 136)

Russell was able to estimate that shared-care families make up between 1 and 2 per cent of families, but it seems we should consider these arrangements as impermanent ones (possibly similar to mothers' working patterns). A follow-up two years later of eighteen of the sample of shared-care families found a reversion to traditional patterns in nine cases, and in only four cases were the arrangements the same as when the first interview was conducted (Russell, 1980, pp. 136–7). Thus, as Russell indicates, the phenomenon needs to be treated with caution: old patterns clearly die hard. Key institutional supports in society push towards traditional patriarchal family arrangements. This can be seen in two of the cases of reversion, described as originally 'the most committed families', which were better-off financially after the decision to return to a more traditional lifestyle. Such are the effects of the segmentation of the workforce on the choices of individual families.

Without adequate historical evidence one must be particularly careful about declaring change to have occurred. It is difficult to know just *how* different shared-care families are. It may be that they have just been ignored in the past. The notion of fathers 'helping out' in an emergency has been well established, and the classic case where parents work different shifts can be seen to have at least some of the characteristics of 'shared care' arrangements. In *Australian Newtown*, 19 per cent of pre-school and 14 per cent of school-age childcare was provided by fathers during the mothers' absence at work (Bryson and Thompson, 1972, p. 71). The 1959 Melbourne study presented a similar picture. This pattern is obviously not new although the reasons why fathers might be available for 'shared childcare' might be different. Certainly Russell's few un-employed fathers are victims of their time. A key difference with Russell's families is the extent to which fathers seem to have voluntarily relinquished the traditional male breadwinner role in favour of shared childcare, a tendency also recognised by Harper (Harper and Richards, 1979, ch. 12). It is interesting that Harper, like Russell, drummed up some more instances and undertook a study of fifteen 'fathers at home', which was published in 1980. The fathers, like the majority of Russell's, had consciously challenged the father—breadwinner, mother—housewife tradition. They were a somewhat less diverse group than Russell's, being 'all young, middle-class, urban living' (Harper, 1980, p. 15), though this is explained by the fact that the group was located by direct and indirect acquaintance.

The problem of generalising is thrown into high relief by Williams's study of *Open Cut*. She found an almost universal, traditional division of labour, with men employed in classic masculine mining jobs, women full-time at home (apparently because of lack of opportunities for employ-ment) coupled with male disapproval of women's paid work (Williams, 1981, ch. 7). The relationships between the sexes have almost caricature qualities of the working-class village situation, with many men eschewing close relationships with their wives that involve discussion of work prob-lems, spending leisure time with the male mates, and having minimal participation in the home (Williams, 1981, pp. 308, 382). Another study, this time of a farming area and its associated township in New South Wales, also uncovered extremely negative attitudes within the farming com-munity towards women working outside the home. Both men and women believed women's work had a negative effect on the husband—wife re-lationship and on the children. The townspeople similarly deplored the effects on children but were much less likely to predict negative effects on the marital relationship. Even so, Poiner points out:

> beliefs that a woman's outside employment would have no effect assumed that it would not interfere with the execution of her house-hold responsibilities. (Poiner, 1982, p. 262)

Another 1979 study of families of far wealthier workers, in this case airline pilots, provides something of an 'up-market' version of this attitude.

Here the exacting demands of the father's occupation form the pivot of family life. The wife stays at home full-time, not from lack of opportunity, or general disapproval of employment, but because of the perceived need to cater to the husband's erratic hours of work and minister to the peculiar health requirements caused by the stresses of his job. For many of the wives of these international pilots the role they are forced into, as wives, is quite tyrannical, though there are the obvious compensations of high income and high derived status (Quicler Davies, 1981).

These later studies suggest that there remains a great variety in orientation to women's work roles despite the increase in the proportion of women working. The distribution of domestic tasks between husbands and wives does not appear to have altered radically over the thirty-to-forty-year period, though men are more active today and a greater variety of patterns of activities are detectable. This change is largely connected with women's greater involvement in the labour force, and to an extent just expands the tendency, noted in the earlier studies, for husbands to participate more in domestic labour when their wives go out to work full-time. Although men have increased their participation in household tasks, their contribution rarely comes close to that of their wives: a conclusion in line with the evidence from other countries, as writers such as Stacey and Price (1981) and Collins (this volume) have shown for the United Kingdom, and Hartmann (1981) for the United States.

The second trend which is established with less clarity by the research, but which does seem supportable, is that fathers, or at least some fathers, are taking a more active role in parenting. This conclusion can be drawn from Russell's shared-care families and Harper's *Fathers at Home*. Because of a lack of earlier studies looking explicitly for this phenomenon, though, we must remain cautious in pronouncing it new. None the less, the number of single fathers or fathers in blended families who take a significant responsibility for their children seems almost certainly to be growing, as the divorce rate increases, and this contributes to the trend.

A third conclusion we can tentatively draw from the evidence is that women with higher levels of education are more successful at extracting contributions from their husbands than are those with lower levels of education. This does not come through strongly in the studies but would be worth pursuing as it suggests a dynamic that may be involved at the interpersonal level. However it is a conclusion which should be treated circumspectly as it is not clearly supported. It may be that researchers with tertiary education are apt to notice this factor but ignore others which may be of greater significance, particularly to working-class women. A clue to other factors is provided by Williams's work, where she finds marital dissatisfaction and conflict to be indicators of embryonic feminist consciousness (1981, p. 133).

This analysis has focused on a narrow range of activities within families and has not considered the contextual social structure, nor questions of ideology which are obviously crucial for a detailed understanding of the situation. None the less, the evidence does allow the raising of some broader issues about whether this will presage greater gender equality. I will now attempt a commentary on the evidence.

Quite simply, as will already be obvious, the evidence is far from persuasive that changes over the last thirty years have significantly altered relationships between the sexes. More important, we must be aware that any changes that have occurred have the potential to weaken as much as strengthen the power position of women unless they are accompanied by certain other changes. A similar point was made recently by McKee and O'Brien. They suggested we could speculate that an increased involvement of men in fathering 'might be an expression of the move towards women's equality' (1982, p. 5). But:

> Alternatively, it could represent a backlash against women, where men, facing competition from women at work, are attempting to compete with women in the home and to appropriate an area in which women were previously autonomous. (1982), p. 5

The earlier Australian studies established that there was a relatively autonomous, though still subordinate, domestic role for women in Australian families. Historically this was more than counterbalanced by women's restricted power in the public domain, but the tensions which were associated with an increased husband involvement seem to suggest that women may well have guarded their territory, be it ever so humble, quite spiritedly and resisted the greater potential for exercising power which husbands' increased activity would have represented. The classic writers on the US family, such as Goode (1963) and Blood and Wolfe (1960), did point to the increase in husband-power associated with greater participation in domestic activities.

It is as plausible to suggest that greater husband involvement in domestic tasks represents a net loss in power for women, as it is to suggest a net gain. I am not suggesting that it is not advantageous to women to have the burden of domestic work lightened. Clearly it is, and so help with or sharing of housework may improve women's immediate quality of life (assuming the assistance is effective and not more trouble than it is worth). However, the question of relative power is a separate one. We can conceptualise the position in much the same way as the issue of welfare benefits. The quality of life of the working class has improved through available income support systems and general welfare services, but at the same time the provision by the state of benefits and services inevitably extends its realm of control over individuals. Similarly within the home, women may gain benefits from a reduction in the amount of dreary chores and demanding organisational and childcare work they are required to do, but inevitably forfeit some control they previously had and indeed become more subject to control by their spouse.

Since the domestic realm does not have high status generally we might ask does it matter if one loses power there? The answer to that question would certainly be 'no' if the loss of power in the home was compensated by a gain in power within the public realm, so I shall now turn to consider women's relationship to the public realm.

Married women are much more strongly represented in the labour force than they were during the 1940s and 1950s and the significance of this must be evaluated. For our purposes though, we need only note that their position in the labour force remains overwhelmingly in the lower status and worst-paid jobs and that security of employment is problematic. Part-time work for women is increasingly prevalent and part-time work must be recognised as allowing far greater potential exploitation – not only in the workplace but also in the home, since, as we have seen, husbands rarely increase their contribution to domestic work when their wives work part-time. In moving into the workforce, women may well be adding another dimension of patriarchal control to their lives or, at best, swapping private patriarchal control for public, in those rare cases that private patriarchy may be rejected on an individual family basis. This hypothetical situation clarifies the inadequacy of conceptualising the problem of gender inequality as an individual one, and highlights the almost inevitable lack of long-term success of voluntaristic efforts (as in Russell's shared-care families) to restructure the power distribution from *within* families alone.

The issue of parenting and the father's role, is also raised by the research. Russell is critical of fathers' traditional lack of involvement in childcare and is obviously committed to a more active participation, as are a number of recent researchers (cf. Lynn, 1974; McKee and O'Brien, 1982). The evidence over the last thirty-year period suggests that some fathers are becoming more active, but this is linked with a wide range of changes. These include notions about good parenting. If justice were to be done, a discussion would need to take into account such factors as the development of the bourgeois family and its associated ideology (Poster, 1978;

Shorter, 1977), fewer children, increase in expectations about physical care, consumption and comfort, changes in the structure of work and working hours and changes in 'expert' views about child development. While it is not unreasonable to accept that fathers are doing more fathering and of a different kind, it is less certain how this links to gender equality. The traditional male role has always included a fathering component and mothers are also subject to changes in views about appropriate parenting. They may well be doing more and different mothering. None the less, direct evidence suggests that within the notion of parenting, the traditional 'ideology of motherhood' remains fit and well even among those involved with feminist causes (cf. Wearing, 1981). Richards (1978) did find changes in the specifications for the 'new good mother', who is likely to be in paid employment, *vis-à-vis* the 'old good mother', but found overwhelming support for the idea that ultimate responsibility for childcare and running the household was the mother's, a finding supported by virtually all the studies on parenting.

If, though, we assume that there has been a genuine increase in fathers' participation in parenting then we must assess the implications for the distribution of power between spouses. As with the arena of housework we can interpret this as having as much potential to diminish women's power as to increase it, though hypothetically it leaves women freer to take up opportunities to exercise power elsewhere. As Ruddick has put it:

> as long as a mother is not effective publicly and self-respecting privately, male presence can be harmful as well as beneficial. It does a woman no good to have the power of the Symbolic Father brought right into the nursery, often despite the deep, affectionate equalitarianism of an individual man. (1982, p. 90)

Other consequences follow from a greater interest by men in fathering. Brown makes a case for a shift in the importance of private patriarchy, where men dominate clearly within their individual families, to public patriarchy, where, within the economic system and the state, men and men's interests take precedence. She explains that this shift has occurred because children are no longer an economic benefit to the family but a cost (Brown, 1981, p. 246). She points to the way in which fathers in the United States have increased their capacity to gain custody of children from the mother even in cases of illegitimacy and over the objection of the mother. Her point, though, is not simply based on the fact that fathers may be awarded custody but on the degree of choice they retain:

> If the father wants the children for the social pleasures of this . . . he is increasingly able to get them. If he does not want them, and most do not, then he need not have them. The *freedom* is his. (Brown, 1981, p. 258)

The situation in Australia is probably similar, although to my knowledge no one has done similar research. It must be stressed that, as with shared housework, shared parenthood is something most of us would welcome eagerly for practical and ideological reasons. My point is, once again, that the consequences of changes are rarely simple, and that for women this trend may also result in a net loss of power and control. For men, increased involvement in parenting has the disadvantages of curtailing discretionary time and entailing tasks and activities which can be tiring, stressing and not always intellectually stimulating. Yet parenting clearly has the rewards involved in closer relationships with one's children, and it seems likely to lead to a greater development of nurturing capacities which should result in a 'more rounded' person than the traditional male role prescribes, as well as offering increasing power within the domestic realm.

A number of writers are also pointing to the contradictions involved in the current trends – trends which feminists have themselves often urged. It is worthwhile considering these trends as a strengthening of public patriarchy at the same time as there may be a weakening of private patriarchy. Stacey and Price have, for example, pointed out that historically the pattern of changes often designated 'loss of functions of the family' can be seen as the removal of activities from the 'private female domain into the public male domain' (Stacey and Price, 1981, p. 128). Within this private domain women formerly had 'considerable power and authority' over such activities as the health and education of family members, food production and so on. The sphere of childbirth provides a notable illustration of an activity which has been 'expropriated from the private domain of women' (ibid, p. 129).

Poster has suggested that 'when men share housework and child care with women, important mechanisms of patriarchy are threatened' (1978, p. 199). Such a statement implies an independence of the domestic sphere, while the evidence scrutinised here makes it clear that we cannot adequately theorise the nature of patriarchy except in terms of the relationships between the private domain of the family and the public domain largely centred as it is on the economy.

NOTE

I would like to thank Jackie Worley and Gloria Pinto for typing the draft of this chapter and to Graham Russell for his very helpful comments on an earlier draft and his continuing generous co-operation in providing copies of his work prior to publication.

5 Household Technology: The 'Liberation' of Women from the Home?

GRAHAM THOMAS and CHRISTINE ZMROCZEK[1]

'Every time you open a can you save a little bit of your life.'

'Zanussi — the appliance of science.'

'Take on a butler. Or get yourself a Teasmade.'

'Who's built a Turbo for women drivers? Hoover, who better? With the new Turbopower cleaner, technology has moved into the home in a big way.'

'As for the washday workload, the new Lavamats take it almost entirely off your hands.'

'[Our dishwashers will] save you hundreds of hours of miserable toil.'

'The Liberators. Front loading automatics.'

'They all want to eat when it suits them. Not the cook. So if mum isn't organised as a catering corps, she's in trouble. Unless she's got a Sanyo microwave oven.'

Despite its lack of systematic exposition in current social science literature,[2] there does exist a 'conventional wisdom' on the subject of how technology affects household work. This wisdom can be found very easily by turning the pages of popular women's magazines; all the above quotes except the first were collected in a single morning from a pile of periodicals in the foyer of our office building. The message from advertising and marketing is that new household technology will remove most of the sheer drudgery from housework tasks, improve standards of performance and save a substantial amount of time in the process.

Behind these 'direct' claims there are others of equal importance in the selling strategies, for instance the implied conferring of certain kinds of social status upon the buyer ('They'll think you spent years in India and hours in the kitchen', says an advert for a curry mix), or the suggestion that only by purchasing a particular product can the housewife be seen to be caring *properly* for her family. Here we will be concentrating on the direct effects of household technology which, it is implicitly claimed, have reduced the burden of household work so much that women are being 'liberated' from the home and 'freed' for other activities such as taking up paid employment.

Evidence for this last 'result' of the application of household technology certainly exists. Despite some recent reverses brought about by the general rise in unemployment and despite worries for the future as a combination of new technology and a changing international division of labour affects many paid jobs in the West, there is no doubt that women's employment has greatly expanded in industrial countries like the United Kingdom in the past few decades,[3] but whether this has been a cause or an effect of developments in technology remains an open question. The claim that technology has 'liberated' or can liberate women from the home is even more problematic. What is meant by 'liberation' in this context? It appears to mean freedom from the burden of household work commonly borne by women, but it does not appear to challenge the assumption that this work is primarily women's responsibility. The disadvantages of having to service and care for other household members are in effect to be overcome by means of a 'technical fix', as the time and effort involved in performing the necessary tasks are reduced to insignificance. Yet it is not clear that technology does save time and effort on housework overall. In particular, the conclusions of Joann Vanek have been widely quoted. She states that there has apparently been no significant fall in the number of hours American housewives have spent doing housework over the last fifty years (Vanek, 1980). Yet despite this and other attempts to revise the conventional wisdom,[4] it is obvious that women in the United Kingdom today do not have the same kinds of domestic burdens as their grandmothers. So what has been the effect of domestic technology on the household and the work done within it?

Before we can answer this question we must clarify what we mean when we talk of domestic technology, household work and the different ways in which they interact. That both the 'conventional wisdom' and the attacks upon it seem to have some validity, while neither seems to be wholly adequate as a definitive explanation, is due at least in part to the fact that they both deal with a range of technologies and their relationships to different sorts of household work, and that different combinations of these produce different results. We can see this clearly when we start to disentangle the issues.

Any classification of technologies is bound to be arbitrary to some extent, but we have found the following breakdown of technologies which directly affect the household to be useful. First, there are the *utilities* such as water, gas and electricity provision, as well as sewage systems, rubbish collection and other infrastructural amenities generally provided through publicly owned organisations.[5] Second, there are the household *appliances*, tools and machines such as washing machines, food mixers, vacuum cleaners and drills. These are the things most commonly associated with the term 'household technology' and because of their diverse nature they are often divided further into subgroups of large/small, manual/electrical, durable/non-durable (and so on) appliances. Closely related to the second category is that of *materials* in the broadest sense, encompassing such items as new detergents and fabrics, cleaning agents, convenience foods, wipe-clear surfaces, stainless-steel cutlery and a host of other things. Finally there are the new *services* and facilities which affect the content and amount of household work, such as supermarkets, launderettes and fast-food restaurants, and which may in the future include new information-technology-based services such as teleshopping and home banking. Clearly we are now moving away from what is conventionally regarded as household technology – though the point is really that no technology can be properly understood in isolation from the social organisation in which it is situated – but this classification is heuristic rather than definitive and its main purpose is simply to illustrate the variety of technologies which, directly and less directly, impinge on domestic work.

Up to now we have used the terms 'housework', 'domestic work' and 'household work' loosely and more or less interchangeably. Normally 'housework' is thought of as a subset of the other two, consisting mainly of various cleaning and tidying activities but sometimes being taken to include washing, cooking and other routine household work. Domestic work usually includes housework and other activities traditionally done by women such as childcare and mending clothes. Household work has connotations of the full range of economic activities performed within the household, and consequently includes traditionally 'male' activities like DIY and car maintenance as well as vegetable-growing, home brewing and winemaking and other work which would probably have to be paid for if it were done by someone outside the household. Sometimes household work is used to describe all the work, both paid and unpaid, done by members of the household; this is the way it is used in the term 'household work strategies'.

Like the classification of technology above, this is not definitive. However, the very vagueness of the different ways in which work in the household can be described highlights a very important point – work carried out in the household does not consist of an immutably fixed series of tasks, but will vary with changes in social organisation and in technology. People's needs can be satisfied in different ways and through different social institutions. At any given time, in Western industrialised societies at least, people will buy some of the goods and services they need (or rather can afford) in the marketplace — that is, they will buy the products of wage-labour — and will do other things themselves or will have other household members do things for them without entering into a wage relation. In the latter case their labour, or that of the household members who are working for them, may be combined with goods bought outside the household to produce the ultimate 'final service'.[6]

This rather abstract dichotomy is more readily understandable when it is put in terms of some everyday examples. Thus people need a regular supply of clean clothes, which they can get (once they have the clothes in the first place) either through a commercial laundry or through washing done in the household, probably with the aid of bought goods such as washing machines, detergents, clothes lines and pegs, and the utilities for heating the water and powering the machines. Food can be bought at a restaurant or canteen or it can be cooked at home. These two examples also have 'intermediate' options such as launderettes and takeaway fast foods. Transport needs can be satisfied either by using public and private transport services or buying goods like cars, bicycles, and so on and transporting oneself. The combination of these different 'modes of provision' of the services ultimately provided is crucial in determining how much work, of what kind, gets done within the household. This leads on to questions such as: which members of the household do how much of which sorts of household work?; what makes different households 'choose' different modes of provision for their final services?; how does the resulting distribution of household work affect the well-being of women and women's position relative to men?; and how is the distribution of these modes of provision throughout the economy related to household and other technologies?

Keeping the preceding discussion in mind we can see how different technologies might affect household work, and household work organisation, in different ways. A change in technology might:

— take work *out* of the household, as happened with a wide variety of economic activities during the industrial revolution
— put work *into* the household: for instance, the spread of car ownership and the related decline of public transport has meant that many children are now 'chauffered' to school each day by their parents
— reduce the time needed to perform specific tasks: as, for example,

the introduction of piped water eliminated the need to make journeys
to the well
- ease the burden and drudgery of specific tasks – the above is also a
good example of this
- increase the frequency with which tasks are done: so, for instance,
as washing clothes became easier it could be done more often
- bring in new, associated tasks: as, for instance, the increase in appliance
ownership has meant an increase in dealing with (and waiting for)
suppliers and maintenance engineers
- raise standards of expectation: when washing clothes or cleaning floors
becomes easier it is not only possible to do these things more often, it
becomes expected that they will be done frequently
- reallocate tasks among household members: for instance, children might
be expected to put clothes into a spin-dryer when they would have
been forbidden to touch a dangerous mangle.

We should of course bear in mind that these 'effects' are not a one-way
process, and that the technologies which are developed and the form
they take are a reflection of the social organisation and values in which
they arise.

So how have the different forms of technical change affected household work over time? As we said at the beginning, the picture is not a
simple one. There are many possible, often conflicting, effects on a
number of areas of work, and there is certainly no one indicator which
will provide us with evidence for an overall conclusion. Perhaps, then, the
best initial approach is to use a series of partial indicators, which will
each shed light on a different aspect of the problem. We can divide these
indicators into three types: aggregate trends and statistics, examinations
of the changes in provision of specific final services, and analysis of individual household work strategies. The first would cover employment
figures, broken down by industry, occupation and gender, which can be
used to show the formal economic balance of goods and services as well
as to highlight the specific areas where women's employment has been
rising and falling. It would cover alternative ways of assessing the balance
of goods and services, such as figures on industrial output and, closer to
home, family expenditure statistics and figures on the spread of ownership of consumer durables. This area would also include studies of household time-use, which can to some extent capture the balance of formal
and informal economic activity, of work done inside and outside the
household, and can give an indication of whether household goods are not
only bought but also *used*. The second type involves detailed case studies

of particular 'final service functions', more or less broadly defined (such as food and drink, transport and communications, shelter, clothing), and itself brings many different approaches to bear on a particular area. The third type — analysis of individual strategies — requires detailed interviews with individuals and households in specific social and/or geographical localities. In this chapter we do not propose to cover all the components of the three types of indicator but will concentrate on the first two, paying particular attention to changes in the amount of time spent in household work and the associated household division of labour, and using washing and laundry as an example of changes which have taken place in the mode of provision of a particular 'final service', clean clothes.

A look at how people spend time both in and out of the household ought to be one of the better ways to gauge the impact of technology on the work patterns of household members. If, as is claimed, the application of new technology in the home saves labour, then it might be expected that at least time spent in housework, if not time spent in domestic work as a whole, will decline. Alternatively, if labour is being saved on some tasks only for other tasks to be added to the domestic workload, then this should be reflected in the balance of time devoted to different activities. If time saved simply results in a particular task being done more often, this will not be shown using aggregate time statistics, but if the data can be ordered in a different way and the *number* of discrete occurrences of each activity recorded, the presence or absence of this effect, too, might be shown, though this way of working requires a more detailed coding of activities than we have at our disposal. An analysis of people's time-use patterns will also help to determine what changes, if any, have taken place in the distribution of household labour among household members, particularly between women and men.

Time-budget research has been used in a more or less systematic fashion by social scientists since around the turn of the century, and some researchers have examined time-use surveys from this period onwards in order to assess long-term societal changes. However, they have generally been frustrated by the key problem of comparability, for survey designs, samples, methods, coding schemes and a host of other details have varied widely. More recently, however, serious attempts have been made to achieve comparability between surveys in different countries and at different times. A large-scale multinational study was carried out in the mid-1960s,[7] and in America and Japan national studies have been replicated in different years. In Britain the BBC's Audience Research Department has carried out national time-use studies since the 1930s, and their 1961 and

1974/5 surveys have now been recoded for comparability with each other and the American and multinational studies. A survey carried out for the Countryside Commission for Scotland in 1981 was similarly designed and coded, as was a major survey funded by the ESRC in 1983/4, the results of which are not available at the time of writing. In this chapter we will be mainly using the BBC surveys of 1961 and 1974/5, and drawing on the Scottish data where appropriate.

A detailed description of the methodology used in the BBC surveys can be found in Gershuny and Thomas (1980). Here we should note that the surveys were not originally conducted with our purposes in mind — understandably the BBC was most concerned with people's availability to watch television or listen to the radio. Paid work activities, mainly done outside the home, were less well described than domestic activities, and this has probably led to a relative overestimation of the former as paid work time not only includes travel to and from the workplace but also, in many cases, breaks in the working day which were not recorded separately. This means that in practice men's work is overestimated relative to women's. Also, because respondents entered their *main* activity for each half-hour throughout the day, very short activities and secondary or concurrent activities are not taken into consideration. Given the fragmentary nature of many people's domestic work routines and the way many people do several things at once, it could again be argued that domestic work is probably underestimated relative to paid work. This problem of simultaneous activities may be of special relevance to discussions of new technology, for the advent of the automatic washing machine, to take just one example, makes it possible to do other things while clothes are being cleaned. If these other activities are also domestic work activities then there is no problem about recording total time spent in domestic work, but the distribution of tasks within domestic work would be misrepresented and the questions of productivity and intensity of work would not be answered at all.

With these reservations in mind, let us see what can be gleaned from our time-budget surveys. First, how much domestic work is done overall and what changes took place between 1961 and 1974/5 (from now on abbreviated to 1975)? From Table 5.1 it can be seen that on an 'average day' — simply the total weekly time divided by seven — the population as a whole each did 3 hours 28 minutes of domestic work[8] in 1961 and that this declined by 12 per cent to 3 hours 3 minutes by 1975. This represents an average decrease in domestic work time for the whole week of nearly 3 hours, which is a significant though not startling amount.

TABLE 5.1 *Participation and time spent in paid and domestic work, UK 1961 and 1974/5 (Time: hours and minutes per average day. Participation: per cent participating during week)*

	All				Men				Women			
	Paid Work		Domestic Work		Paid Work		Domestic Work		Paid Work		Domestic Work	
	61 (1873)	75 (2306)	61 (1873)	75 (2306)	61 (888)	75 (1104)	61 (888)	75 (1104)	61 (985)	75 (1202)	61 (985)	75 (1202)
Population average time (hrs mins)	4.22	4.06	3.28	3.03	6.24	5.39	1.37	1.34	2.24	2.29	5.15	4.30
Participation rate	66	72	95	97	91	89	91	94	44	58	99	99
Participants' time (hrs mins)	6.37	5.42	3.39	3.09	7.02	6.21	1.47	1.40	5.05	4.16	5.18	4.33

Contrast this with the equivalent figures for paid work, which fell from 4 hours 22 minutes to 4 hours 6 minutes, a smaller decline of just over 6 per cent.

These figures are in themselves interesting, for they tell us something about the amount of work done in the society as a whole, but they still leave many questions unanswered. It is equally as useful to know what proportion of the population actually did any paid or domestic work and how long the people actually engaged in the activities spent on them. Also we need to know how these figures break down between the sexes and whether men and women are converging or drawing apart in their time-use patterns. And it is also interesting to move from the time patterns of *individuals* to the investigation of *household* strategies where the time-use of one person influences and is in turn influenced by that of other household members.

Participation in domestic work (generously defined as a person recording at least one half-hour during the week on at least one domestic work task) is almost universal in both years, so the activity times of those who participate in the activity are very similar to those of the population as a whole. In comparison, participation in paid work went up from 66 to 72 per cent of the population over the period, and time spent in paid work by those who actually did some dropped 14 per cent from 60 hours 37 minutes to 5 hours 42 minutes, a decline caused by both a general reduction of working hours and the entry of many women into part-time employment.

When we look at gender differences we find that in 1961 women on average did 5 hours 15 minutes domestic work per day, or just under 37 hours per week which, though certainly an underestimation for the reasons mentioned above, is nevertheless a large amount compared with men's 1 hour 37 minutes per day, equivalent to 11 hours 19 minutes per week. By 1975 this had fallen by 14 per cent to 4 hours 30 minutes for women, whereas the men's figures had declined by only 3 minutes. The inequality is still large, but the difference is decreasing. One reason for this, not hard to guess, is the relative increase in time spent by women in paid work. In 1961 women spent an average of 2 hours 24 minutes in paid work compared with men's 6 hours 24 minutes, but by 1975 women's paid work time had slightly *increased* to 2 hours 29 minutes, in contrast to the 12 per cent decline in men's paid working time to 5 hours 39 minutes. These aggregate changes are of course the product of changes in the proportions of men and women participating and changes in the time spent by participants. Participation of women in paid work increased from 44 per cent in 1961 to 58 per cent in 1975, while the time spent in paid work by employed women dropped 16 per cent from 5 hours 5 minutes per day to 4 hours 16 minutes.

At first sight we appear to be presented with a fairly optimistic picture, with both paid and domestic work time in general declining and with women working relatively less in the home and more in paid employment. Glaring differences in time-use remain, but women's time-use does appear to be very slowly converging with men's.[9] Is this because of the 'liberating' influence of household technology? During the period in question there was certainly an increase in the amount and power of the technology available to households; for instance, according to the Family Expenditure Survey, ownership of refrigerators went up from 21 per cent of British households to 87 per cent between 1960 and 1976, and that of washing machines from 38 to 72 per cent. So the circumstantial evidence is in favour of the argument. The only negative feature to show itself so far is the slight increase in women's total (paid plus unpaid) work time compared with men's, creeping up from 95 per cent of men's total work time in 1961 to 97 per cent in 1975. However, this increase is small and may well be due to chance variations in the sample.

This optimistic picture is in marked contrast to the results of some earlier attempts at cross-time and cross-cultural comparison. In an article where he assesses the effects of household technology on women's domestic labour time in America, John Robinson (1980) notes that a 1966 publication found that households owning more appliances estimated that they spent more hours on housework than those with fewer appliances. He also quotes figures showing that employed American women in the mid-1960s did only slightly less domestic work than their counterparts in Yugoslavia and Poland and *more* than those in Bulgaria and Peru, all societies where it may be safely assumed that the benefits of household technology are less generally diffused than in the United States. Both Walker (1969) and Vanek (1980) found that virtually the same amount of time was spent on housework by American housewives in the 1920s as in the 1960s, though they point out that the surveys they were comparing were not designed for comparability.

Robinson, however, drawing on evidence from a comparison of Americans' time-use in 1965 and 1975, then goes on to claim that this alleged constancy of time devoted to housework – this 'homeostatic mechanism', as he calls it – may no longer exist. He notes a decline in housework time which 'occurred during a decade of remarkable diffusion of household technology' (Robinson, 1980, p. 55). He charts increases during that decade in the American household ownership of washing machines (from 57 to 70 per cent), dryers (26 to 58 per cent), dishwashers

(13 to 38 per cent), garbage disposal units (14 to 39 per cent) and freezers (27 to 44 per cent), but then continues by noting that, in 1975 at least, ownership of these appliances did not significantly – or in some cases even at all – reduce time spent either on the tasks for which they were designed or on domestic work in general. He cites the decline in the birthrate and the increased entry of women into the labour market as the factors most influencing the decline in housework time, and his opinion is that, while time devoted to housework will continue to fall and technology will be increasingly diffused throughout the population, nevertheless 'the two trends will occur largely independently of one another' (Robinson, 1980, p. 65).

How real, then, is the decline in women's domestic work time which is shown by the BBC's surveys? In the previous figures we compared the domestic work time of men and women *as a whole*, and it can be argued that we have not really been comparing like with like, that the greater participation of women in the paid labour force in 1975 distorts the comparison. We therefore need to compare domestic and paid work done by people in different employment categories, and in addition to compare the distribution of work among the members of various types of household.

In doing these sorts of comparisons we were restricted by a lack of information in the 1961 survey on the normal working hours of respondents. We therefore had to divide the samples according to *actual* hours worked in the survey week, declaring people of working age who did less than five hours paid work during the week to be 'not employed', people who did between five and thirty hours to be 'part-time employed', and people who did more than thirty hours to be 'full-time employed'. Comparing the 1975 distribution thus obtained with the information we had on people's normal working hours, we not surprisingly found many more men in the 'part-time' and 'not employed' categories when actual hours worked was the measure (there were 98 men in the 'part-time' group according to hours worked whereas only 6 men officially worked part-time, and the equivalent figures for men who were not employed were 68 according to actual hours and 37 according to normal hours worked). The women's figures remained much more stable.

Men who in a particular week spend fewer hours in paid work than normal may do so for a number of reasons, for instance because they are sick, or on holiday, or are taking time off to do some particular domestic task like decorating the house. While the 1961 and 1975 surveys took place outside the main holiday season, the 1981 survey was carried out in the summer, and for this year we were able to exclude people on holiday. For 1975 we were able to ascertain that part-time and non-employed men according to actual hours worked did *less* non-routine household work such as decorating and odd jobs than their 'official' equivalents, so the risk of grossly overestimating the amount of domestic work done by men in these categories seems to be minimal.

The breakdown of work by employment category shown in Table 5.2 is interesting for a number of reasons. Whereas, taken as a whole, women apparently do slightly less total work than men – although we should again bear in mind the probable underestimation of domestic work described above – for each employment group taken separately women work longer hours than men. Not only that, but *proportionally* the amount of domestic work done by women in the various employment groups is generally increasing. Part-time employed women, for instance, did 2.09 times as much domestic work as part-time employed men in 1961, 2.28 times as much in 1975, and 2.33 times as much in 1981. The exception to this trend is the full-time employed group, where women did 2.14 times as much domestic work as men in 1961, 2.29 times as much in 1975, but just 1.71 times as much in the 1981 survey.

Comparing the more detailed categories of domestic work in the three surveys is made more difficult by slight variations in the coding scheme of the Scottish survey and by the fact that the survey of one particular region, at a different time of year, is anyway not directly comparable with the national surveys. Any of the detailed comparisons involving the 1981 survey should therefore be treated with some caution. Nevertheless there are some trends shown in Table 5.2 which are worth pointing out. The amount of domestic work done by full-time employed women, for example, has remained remarkably stable, though the 1981 survey shows a shift towards what we have called 'non-routine' domestic work. We would not wish to put forward any hypothesis about an irreducible minimum of housework time, but it does appear that women who have taken up full-time employment have reduced their domestic work time to a level which cannot drop much further without a significant contribution in that area by other household members.

There is much in Table 5.2 to provoke speculation on the changes which have taken place in the composition of domestic work. For instance, full-time employed men appear to be increasing the amount of routine domestic work they do, with the clearest increase being in the amount of shopping – perhaps a reflection of a trend towards households doing more of their shopping in a 'lump' towards the end of the week, outside the hours of paid employment at times when men are likely to be more available.[10] Knitting, sewing and gardening declines for most groups between 1961 and 1975, but made something of a comeback in the 1981

TABLE 5.2 Paid and domestic work times of men and women aged under 65, by employment status*. Great Britain 1961 and 1974/5, Scotland 1981

| | Employed Full-Time | | | | | | Employed Part-Time | | | | | | Not Employed | | | | | |
| | Men | | | Women | | | Men | | | Women | | | Men | | | Women | | |
(Sample size)	61 (732)	75 (891)	81 (244)	61 (312)	75 (392)	81 (130)	61 (38)	75 (98)	81 (31)	61 (110)	75 (293)	81 (79)	61 (47)	75 (68)	81 (71)	61 (469)	75 (487)	81 (200)
Paid Work	465	428	439	402	371	381	170	182	176	151	159	170	1	2	5	1	2	3
Domestic Work	71	66	87	152	151	149	174	133	146	365	303	340	226	186	195	458	380	413
Total	536	494	526	554	521	530	344	315	322	516	462	510	227	188	200	459	382	416
Domestic Work:																		
routine	22	27	35	125	126	112	75	60	73	319	257	264	157	90	91	399	327	336
non-routine	48	39	52	27	25	38	99	73	73	45	46	75	69	95	103	59	54	77
Routine:																		
cooking/washing-up	7	8	6	56	56	35	22	14	18	138	114	92	56	25	23	163	131	111
cleaning/washing	5	4	9	47	43	50	35	8	19	123	88	101	50	24	24	141	111	129
shopping	7	10	14	19	23	23	12	28	25	40	38	42	39	35	36	53	45	45
childcare	3	5	6	3	4	4	6	10	10	18	18	28	12	6	8	41	40	51
Non Routine:																		
odd jobs/decorating	22	26	24	10	9	8	63	51	36	12	14	11	21	63	44	16	16	16
gardening	24	7	18	4	2	5	30	11	27	10	4	11	42	24	35	13	6	12
domestic travel	1	6	7	1	6	11	4	10	11	1	13	24	2	8	18	1	14	25
knitting/sewing**	–	–	3	13	8	13	1	0	–	23	14	29	5	–	7	28	18	24

* Employment status defined by actual, not normal, hours worked. Less than 5 hours of paid work per week = not employed. 5–30 hours = 'part-time'. Over 30 hours = 'full-time'. ** Includes other 'hobbies' in 1981 survey.

survey. No clear trends emerge from the figures on men's time spent in odd jobs and decorating (which include car cleaning and maintenance), though it does not seem that the time devoted by women to this activity has been increasing. The most obvious decline in a major activity is in time spent on meal preparation and washing-up, especially women's time. The 1981 survey shows an increase in the amount of time women who are not employed full-time spend on childcare, though this activity is notoriously difficult to capture in time-budget surveys, as much of it goes on concurrently with other activities.

All these figures, however interesting, conceal changes which might be taking place within the employment groups, and are subject to certain 'fallacies of aggregation' where like is perhaps not being compared with like. For instance, are women who are not in paid work in the later surveys more likely to be only those who have young children? This might account for the increase in time spent on childcare. Are men with full-time paid jobs more likely to have employed wives in the later years, and does this account for the longer time they spend on routine housework? The numbers presented in Table 5.2 cannot give us more than a few clues about the ways in which actual households distribute their work and how they respond to changes such as the introduction of new household appliances or the decision of a woman to take up full-time or part-time employment. For the answers to these sorts of questions we need, at the very least, time-use data on complete households.

Unfortunately, both the 1961 and the 1981 surveys sampled individuals rather than households and so we cannot compare household time distribution across the whole period. However, we can indicate the sort of comparison which would have to be made, in greater detail, in order to assess technology-related changes in the amount and structure of household domestic work. From our 1975 data we selected couples living together (almost always husband and wife) and treated the couple rather than the individuals as the case for analysis.

Table 5.3 shows the differences in paid and domestic work times in those households where women have paid employment and those where they do not, holding men's employment constant. It can be seen that when women go out to work they do indeed reduce time spent on household tasks, especially the routine housework tasks, but not by enough to compensate for the extra time spent in paid work. The total amount of work done in the household, both paid and unpaid, increases when the woman is in employment, but the bulk of this increase is made up by a lengthening of the *woman's* working day.

Men also work longer when their wives go out to work, but very little

TABLE 5.3 *Paid and domestic work times of couples by employment status of wife, 1974/5. Men working full-time, women under 60. (Minutes per average day)*

	Wife Employed Full-time		Wife Employed Part-time		Wife not Employed	
	Men (155)	Women	Men (193)	Women	Men (280)	Women
Paid Work	387	320	404	178	375	7
Domestic Work	100	204	82	299	95	405
Total Work	487	524	486	477	470	412
Domestic Work:						
Routine	39	173	35	260	39	349
Non-Routine	61	31	47	39	57	55
Routine:						
Cooking/ Washing-up	14	77	11	112	9	134
Cleaning/ Washing	7	62	4	94	5	117
Shopping	15	27	14	36	14	47
Childcare	3	6	6	17	11	51
Non-routine:						
Odd jobs/ decorating	39	10	29	11	38	20
Gardening	12	3	11	4	12	7
Domestic travel	9	7	7	13	7	15
Knitting/Sewing	–	11	0	12	–	14
Total Household Paid Work	707		582		382	
Total Domestic Work	304		381		500	
Total Household Work	1011		963		882	

of this increase is in domestic work. In fact, men whose wives work part-time actually do less domestic work than those whose wives have full-time paid employment, although most of this difference is accounted for by their doing fewer odd jobs rather than by differences in the amount of routine housework. The most remarkable feature of husbands' domestic work time is how little it changes, even in quite detailed activities, in response to changes in wives' working patterns, with the only notable increase in any domestic work activity being in time spent cooking and/or washing-up by men with full-time employed wives. Of course, as the amount of domestic work done by women decreases when paid work is taken up, the *proportion* of household domestic work done by men rises.

Women in the different employment groups are likely to be at different stages of the life-cycle and will therefore not have the same amounts of the various sorts of domestic work tasks to do. In particular, young children are not present to the same extent in the three groups. Women without paid jobs are much more likely to have children who need constant care and attention, and indeed time spent on childcare is one of the major components of the larger amount of time non-employed women spend on domestic work. It is interesting, though, that time spent on other routine household tasks varies by no more than five minutes between non-employed women with and without children in the home (not shown in the table).

As with Table 5.2, the figures from Table 5.3 cannot by themselves provide adequate answers to the most important questions concerning changes in domestic work over time and the contribution of household technology to those changes. Although time-budget research has already made a useful contribution in this area — for instance by showing the sheer amount of domestic work done in this society and by refuting claims that men are now doing significantly more of it than they were twenty years ago — there is some way to go before its full potential is realised. To say something more precise about the relationship of technology and household labour we would need the sort of data presented in Table 5.3 for several points in time over a long period. We would need to examine domestic and other work activities in more detail and we would need to relate household time-use directly to ownership and use of household 'capital goods'.

Some of these things have already been done in separate studies. Berk and Berk (1979) carried out a careful time-use study on some very detailed domestic work activities, though they treated husbands and wives separately and looked not at overall time spent on activities but at the sequential order of domestic work tasks. They hoped to find what they called 'feasibility' and 'efficiency' relationships between different tasks, but finally confessed themselves disappointed that the complexity and variety of women's household work patterns prevented them getting very far in their analyses of 'household production functions'. As part of an intensive study of an area in South London, Gershuny (1982) analysed the results of questions about which members of households 'normally used' a range of household consumer durables. His results show broad agreement with our data on the distribution of domestic work between men and women and the way this changes very little when the woman takes up paid employment. In that study he was not able to relate these figures to households' use of time, but it is hoped that this can be done when the data from the 1983/4 Economic and Social Research Council study become available.

Even so, the contribution which time-use research can make towards answering questions on the effects of household technology will remain limited, as it cannot assess the qualitative effect it has on household work. To gain information about this, we will need to do work in the other two areas previously mentioned, work on specific 'final service functions' and on individual household work strategies. Here we will look at one household 'need' in particular: clean laundry.[11]

Washing in the 1930s was described as 'at all times and in all circumstances arduous' (Spring Rice, 1939, p. 100). It involved long hours of hard work and physical exertion for women in all classes except the very rich who could afford to pay someone else to do it all. As well as the washing for their own household many women did laundry as paid work, either at home, in an employer's home or in the public washhouse, although this was often discouraged by a rising scale of hourly charges. Women were also the majority of employees in commercial laundries.

Most women washed at home, usually in cramped and inconvenient conditions which added to the unpleasantness and general enervation of the tasks themselves. Most clothing and household linen was made of cotton which had to be boiled to get it really clean. Boiling the wash took place either in pans on the stove or in the copper or boiler installed in many kitchens for that purpose. The copper often had a fire beneath it to heat the water and this had to be kept going. Coppers were frequently not connected to a water supply so had to be filled and emptied manually several times for the different loads of wash. The clothes had to be constantly stirred to keep them from discolouring during boiling and then lifted and wrung out between washes and after the final rinsing. Then they were put through a mangle or wringer if one was available and hung out to dry, involving much bending and lifting and carrying heavy wet washing.

Some women without access to adequate facilities in their homes used the communal washhouse in their block or street, others used the public washhouse if there was one available. Public washhouses usually offered amenities not necessarily available at home; hot water, boilers, mangles, wringers, perhaps washing machines and dryers and space to sort and fold. However, public washhouses were never provided in sufficient numbers to meet the demand for them. They were a charge on the rates and rarely seen in towns with under 10,000 inhabitants. Even in such a densely populated area as Bolton in the 1930s there were only two. They were by no means uniform in either conditions or facilities – one of the Bolton washhouses had no equipment for boiling for instance – they were frequently crowded which meant a long wait before even beginning to do the 'wash, there were no creche facilities, and their scarcity meant that women often had to come from quite a distance to use them, carrying the heavy and cumbersome laundry load and perhaps bringing along children too small to be left at home alone.

Another way to get the washing done was to use commercial laundries. They offered a variety of services. The wash could be fully finished, including ironing, or semi-finished which meant that some items were ironed, or partly ironed like the fronts of shirts for example. It could be returned un-ironed but passed through a mangle to smooth out creases in large items like sheets or tablecloths; it could be returned damp or dry, folded or not. It could be collected and delivered to the customer's door or she could take it into the laundry office herself. Despite the costs involved, surveys in the 1930s and 1940s showed that women of all classes and incomes used commercial laundry services if they were available, although there were many complaints about damaged and lost items (Institute of British Launderers, 1945; Kemsley and Ginsburg, 1949).

The most basic requirement for washing is a supply of water, followed by the means for heating it. Improvements in the provision of public *utilities* means that all dwellings, almost without exception, have a supply of water and gas and/or electricity. Consequently, piped hot water has become the norm: whereas in 1947 44 per cent of households had no piped water, 7 per cent had no water supply at all and 4 per cent were without either gas or electricity (Gray, 1947).

The manufacture of domestic *appliances* accelerated in the late 1940s at the end of wartime restrictions. In the mid-1950s, leading manufacturers began to concentrate on the market for domestic washing machines. Technical developments led to improvements in the design and efficiency of the machines and increased factory productivity. Costs could be lowered and a wider market reached. In 1945 only one in twenty-two households had a washing machine of any kind, by 1963 this figure had jumped up to 50 per cent of all British households, and it has increased steadily to the 1982 levels of 80 per cent.

In the 1930s and 1940s washing machines were very basic, consisting usually of a drum on legs with mechanical parts exposed underneath, in which the wash was agitated or tumbled. They did not go through their cycles automatically nor did they spin-dry but had to be stopped and started and have soap and other additives put in at appropriate moments, and be filled and drained by attaching pipes. Even if they had an attached mangle or wringer the clothes had to be put through manually. So it was unlikely that much time was saved overall although the physical exertion was somewhat reduced.

Washing-machine construction remained essentially similar until the twin-tub was introduced in 1957. It consisted of one tub for washing and one for spin-drying in the same cabinet. The washing had to be transferred manually between the tubs and it was still necessary to guide the machine through the steps of its operation. It was not only the construction of the machines, however, but the selling methods of some manufacturers which captured a far more widespread consumer market at this time. Leading manufacturers instigated huge advertising campaigns and began to use market research for the first time to determine what 'the housewife' wanted. They concentrated on quality and aimed at the middle-class market that could afford to pay for it. Other newer entrepreneurs stepped in to secure the lower-priced end of the market, using direct selling methods — that is, having salespersons call at the home in response to filling out a form in the newspaper. The removal of government restrictions on hire purchase was also a contributing factor in the rapid increase in home ownership of washing machines in the 1950s and early 1960s.

The next major development in washing-machine manufacture was the mass production of automatic washers which wash, rinse and spin in one consecutive operation. Speed change and timing mechanisms necessary for this process were first constructed in 1939 in the United States, but did not come into use in the United Kingdom until the early 1960s. Automatics were extremely expensive at first, and often unreliable — flooding, vibrating and occasionally catching fire. By the mid-1960s, cost-effective designs had been developed, and their market share increased steadily from 5 per cent in 1969 to 40 per cent in 1981.

Automatic washer/dryers, which take the washing right through to the ready-for-ironing stage in just one operation, are a recent innovation which, according to a recent market research are 'fast growing in popularity' (Read, 1982, p. 2). This may represent a new trend towards clothes-dryers in the United Kingdom which up to now have proved far less popular here than elsewhere despite the vagaries of British weather.

In the 1950s many women continued to use a wringer or mangle to remove excess water from the wash, although spin-dryers began to be popular. By 1972, 30 per cent of households owned a spin-dryer, but this figure declined by almost half over the next ten years, due no doubt to their incorporation in the washing machine itself. Ownership of tumbler-dryers has increased in the last decade but still only 20 per cent of households owned one by 1981.

There have been significant changes in the *materials* used in washing, both in terms of the clothes themselves and the substances with which they are washed. The development of synthetic fibres began to be successful in the late 1940s and has resulted in a proliferation of fabrics such as nylon, polyester, acrylic and a range of mixtures with natural fibres, all of which need different treatment from traditional natural fibres. In the 1930s, hard soap which was grated or melted for washing clothes was still the most popular detergent. Soap powder and soap flakes were also available although they were considered expensive by many women (Mass-Observation, 1939). Synthetic detergents were developed which had some advantages over soap in, for example, dissolving and stain removal and they became popular in the 1950s. There have been continual adaptations of both soaps and synthetic detergents to make them compatible with the requirements of both the new fabrics and domestic washing machines. For example, powders with a very low level of sudsing have been specially formulated for use with newer models of washing machine.

Services have been affected by all these developments. The final service in this case is the provision of clean clothes, and on the whole it has been and continues to be women's work to provide this service, sometimes as paid work but usually unpaid. A woman has at *her* service a range of methods, equipment and services, any combination of which she may use, although this is by no means a 'free' choice, but governed by factors like expense, availability of equipment and services, how accessible they are, and what options actually are being developed for the market.

In the case of commercial laundries, for example, both high costs and the lack of a sufficient number of laundries meeting the demand for high-quality, cost-effective services contributed to their decline. This coincided with the appearance of launderettes, which spread rapidly, and the gradual disappearance of public washhouses. Many women first became used to using a washing machine in the launderette and quickly recognised the convenience of having one at home, prompted by the extensive advertising of domestic washing machines.

There seems little doubt that having a washing machine at home is the most convenient way to deal with the wash, given present social structures based on privatised nuclear-family housekeeping. But it is far from the case that even (front-loading) automatic washing machines 'liberate' women from washing. There is still plenty of time-consuming work to do both before and after pushing the button to activate the wash-cycle. The wash has to be gathered together, from all over the house if household members do not or cannot co-operate in putting it all in one place. It has to be sorted into items and fabrics suitable for washing together, put into the machine, and detergent has to be added. Then the button can be pressed, but if the washer is *not* an automatic — and only 40 per cent of British households owning a washing machine in 1981 owned a fully automatic model, that is only about one-third of the households in the country — then there will be several parts of the process to be gone through manually. Once the load is washed, it may have to be spun-dry separately and then hung out to dry. If a tumble-dryer is used a little less effort is required, but the clothes still have to be sorted, folded and some of them ironed, according to the requirements of the woman herself or those imposed on her by the wishes of individual household members.

Requirements and standards regarding clothing and cleanliness have risen considerably in the last few decades. Writers such as Ruth Schwartz Cowan, Susan Strasser and Joann Vanek have charted the rise of house-keeping standards in general in the United States and pointed to the turn-of-the-century theorists of domestic economy who advocated the use of technology to this end. Similar developments have taken place in the United Kingdom. It can be seen, for example, that in comparison with the 1930s, people in general own far more clothes, due in part to cheaper materials and manufacturing processes, and in part to the overall rise in the standard of living including wages and the payment of some means of subsistence to the unemployed by the state. We not only own more clothes than before but expect to have them cleaned more often. These expectations have been fostered by advertising which suggests that we must have clean clothes every day, and perhaps change them several times a day depending on our activities. Somehow a connection has been made between providing clean clothes and a woman's love for her children — their shirts must be whiter than white or she is not a good mother. It would be most interesting to carry out an investigation of the part played by advertising in raising standards of laundry-work; the point here, however, is to suggest that whatever the reason for these higher expectations, women have to meet them. So the introduction of more and more technology in the home may merely make it possible to do this without necessarily reducing the time spent on housework. With domestic appliances available the work involved is often made invisible. A recent survey reports that on average a fully automatic washing machine is used for four-and-a-half wash-loads a week, comprising some seventy-seven articles, and this increases substantially when young children are present in the household and even more if they are babies. How can this be called 'liberation' from housework?

From this discussion we have gained some insight into the social processes at work in one particular area of domestic work (and its related non-domestic work). But clearly we are still some way from being able to specify the relationships between household technology and household work strategies. This will not change later in the chapter, but the very · complexity of the issues leads us to emphasise an extremely important point: if there is no easy answer to the question of whether technology has 'liberated' or could liberate women from the home, then there is also no quick 'technical fix' that can achieve liberation for domestic workers. Admittedly there is evidence that a lot of the sheer drudgery has been removed from a broad range of tasks, in this case from washing, but equally there is evidence that the standards of expectation for the performance of domestic work have been raised as technical advances have made possible increases in efficiency and productivity.

We have said that there is a choice to be made between the various modes of provision of final services for households, and that this choice determines the balance of paid and unpaid work done by the different household members. But what exactly do we mean by 'choice'? How free are we — women and men — to choose the work we do, to determine the balance of bought services and 'self-services'? We would argue that in general the opportunity for choice has been severely constrained by the economic and social environment in which the household functions.

It is generally accepted that the industrial revolution and the spread of the factory system took some kinds of work out of the household, and that despite income inequalities, urban/rural differences, and so on, most households were before long buying certain basic goods such as clothes, soap and candles instead of producing them in the home. Later on, the advent of municipal piped-water provision and the introduction of first gas, then electricity, made possible a reduction of both time and labour necessary for certain household tasks. However, these innovations also made it possible for the domestic burden of some women to be increased. The industrial revolution took household members out of the home into paid employment, leaving — at least in working-class households — fewer hands around the house to do the work. New forms of lighting extended the time available to do housework into the evening hours.

Because it was *possible* to increase the burden of domestic work tasks it does not mean that this necessarily had to happen. In general, it is not hard to see that, over time, the higher rate of increase in the productivity of manufactured goods as opposed to marketed services (in the absence of a comparable decrease in service wages), will cheapen goods in relation to services and make it more attractive for households to buy goods for use in household production rather than to pay for household services. But this overlooks the problem of why these particular sorts of goods should be developed in the first place. In the early part of this century, when household goods like refrigerators and washing machines started to come onto the market both in the United States and in the United Kingdom there was an undercurrent of debate about the industrialisation and/or socialisation of domestic work.[12]

When the achievements of industry were compared to those of domestic labour, it was not infrequently pointed out that industry's achievements stemmed from a new organisation of work, the principal features of which were centralisation and the division of labour. These allowed for the increased use of technology embodied in machines, the development of skills and talents suited to particular tasks, and the elimination of inefficiencies associated with the constant switching from one task to another. Charlotte Perkins Gilman concluded that the absence of such features of industrial practice from domestic work confined it to 'the level of universal average' and retarded the development of women, children and the family in general. She therefore advocated the transfer of food preparation, laundry and certain aspects of childcare from the home into 'professional hands' (Gilman, 1980). In Britain at the end of the First World War, women in the Labour Party urged the setting up of co-operative kitchens, washhouses and nurseries, of communal central-heating and kindergartens. And in the newly formed Soviet Union, Alexandra Kollontai declared that 'the individual household is dying. It is giving way in our society to collective housekeeping . . . Thus the four categories of housework (cleaning, cooking, washing, and mending) are doomed to extinction with the victory of Communism' (Kollontai, 1977, p. 255).

While we might be more than a little uneasy at the naive acceptance of the ideology of industrialisation shown by Charlotte Gilman, and some of the other reformers mentioned in Dolores Hayden's (1981) book, the important point is that the socialisation, or at least the transfer into the sphere of paid work, of much domestic work was seen as a real possibility. In fact the very espousal of industrialism shown in these writings indicates that the creation of domestic work services was looked upon as an opportunity for entrepreneurs, as a means of making not inconsiderable profit. From our present perspective, where such debate and the voicing of such opinions has an air of unreality, where the socialisation of domestic work is seen as the province of dreamers, it is difficult to realise that such change was viewed as a real possibility.

Why, then, was this path not taken? Why, then, do we still have the situation which Charlotte Gilman complained of, where, to quote Ruth Schwartz Cowan, 'Several million American women cook supper each night in several million separate homes over several million separate stoves — a spectacle which should be sufficient to drive any rational technocrat into the loony bin'? (Cowan, 1979a, p. 223). She notes that all the major new devices, appliances, foodstuffs and so on offered to American households in the 1920s were made and marketed by large companies with considerable amounts of capital investment. Was it therefore simply the case that there was more profit to be had in selling millions of appliances to millions of households than in investing in and rationalising services? This would seem to make sense only if the inefficiencies attached to the domestic labour of separate households do not matter in (capitalist) economic terms; if, in other words, there is no danger of a company manufacturing domestic appliances losing its market to the more efficient production methods of an extensive service industry.

This can be seen as a realistic assumption only if it is also assumed that domestic work, and that means basically *women's* work, is a factor which does not have to be taken into account in economic calculations. We would argue that, while this is not the whole story, women's work was indeed seen in this way, in economic terms as a 'free good', and that this tipped the balance of eonomic calculation. Given this background of privatised domestic work done unpaid by women, developing individual household appliances not only became the obvious 'choice', their introduction into the home had little effect on the division of domestic labour. Thrall makes the point that, while the technology embodied in household appliances allows the possibility for both considerable savings of domestic labour time and to some extent a renegotiation of the domestic division of labour, this has not generally been the case. After studying the work patterns and appliance ownership of ninety-nine families living in Boston, he concludes 'Rather than break down the traditional role-assignments, modern household equipment seems to reinforce them by making it easier for those who are stereotyped as doing particular tasks to do them without help from others' (Thrall, 1982, p. 192).

To sum up, the introduction of the various types of household technology over the years has indeed had profound effects on domestic work. Chiefly these have involved the saving of time on specific tasks combined with an increase in the frequency and (in some cases) the number of different tasks to be performed, a raising of the standards of domestic work, the elimination of some of the drudgery of certain household tasks and, at least until quite recently, the devolving of a greater proportion of domestic work onto wives.[13] The development of the technology itself, though, has been constrained and directed by the social and economic environment in which it was developed and introduced.

What, then, of the future? As far as we can see there is no new technology lurking just around the corner which is radically going to transform domestic work. The Information Revolution may mean an increase in the number of microprocessors and sensors around the house but, at least until the advent of exceedingly 'smart' robots, most of the manual tasks of domestic work — cleaning and tidying especially — are going to remain much as they are. This is not to say that there will be no change. There is the possibility of new information-based services such as teleshopping, telebanking and computerised medical and advice services, which may have an effect on the amount of domestic travel undertaken. New catering services may further cut the amount of time which the average household spends on meal preparation. And changes in the structure of formal employment, whether in terms of the overall size of the labour force or of changes in modes of working which could lead to more home-based work via computer terminals, will probably have far-reaching effects on domestic life. But none of these in themselves will necessarily lead to revolutionary changes in the division of domestic labour.

This is not, however, a reason for fatalism. The point is that different futures are possible and that social and political choices can be made which will make these different futures more or less likely. To be sure, these choices are themselves constrained by present conditions and social forces, and are not to be understood as choices which can be freely made by individuals, but nevertheless we can examine some of the possibilities and consider the implications of going in particular directions. Here we will sketch out just two alternative paths of development, although we recognise that neither of these paths is likely to be followed exclusively. One is the path of continued or increasing privatisation of domestic work, perhaps as a consequence of government policy on reducing state expenditure; the other follows from a commitment to improving women's social and economic situation and achieving a fair distribution of responsibility for all types of household work.

There are already signs that one of the likely responses of the state to the current economic recession will be to encourage the 'return' of women to the home. This is in part because of the general worsening of employment opportunities and the specific threat posed by information technology to industries and occupations where a high proportion of women are employed, and in part a result of a desire to devolve many of the state's current financial responsibilities, especially in the field of health care. The latter has led to plans to take much of the care of the old and infirm out of the hands of paid workers and place more of the responsibility in the hands of the 'community', which in practice means women in the community.

The reduction in women's paid work opportunities generally might in the future be complemented by the introduction of new work patterns for those still in employment, with an attempt being made to promote the combination of paid and unpaid work in the home by arranging for paid work to be done via home-based computer terminals. This may have some advantages in terms of flexibility, so that more women with young children may therefore find it *possible* to take up such paid employment (and remember that, in this scenario creche and nursery places will become at least relatively, if not absolutely, scarcer), but it will bring with it all the disadvantages of not being able to go 'out' to work: isolation, confinement within the family circle and lack of an identity separate from it, constant interruption of paid work by the demands of childcare and domestic work, the feeling of always being 'on call'.[14]

These developments would lead to women's responsibility for domestic work becoming even further entrenched, and their opportunities for broadening the scope of women's paid work becoming even more limited than they are now. Women would continue to be excluded from technical jobs, and opportunities to influence the general direction and design of technology would remain minimal, even domestic technology of which women are the primary users. This course of development would also discourage the seeking of alternatives to the nuclear family; legal barriers to different household forms would not be removed, and houses would still be designed along the 'two adults plus children' format.

What might be involved in the alternative course, of making a serious commitment to an equitable shareout of responsibility for all forms of work? First, household work must be recognised as socially essential labour, and here feminist research has already made a great contribution. Then the interlocking nature of paid and unpaid work must be seen, and steps taken to reorganise *both* so that everyone can do a fair share of both. This is all, of course, easier said than done, for the vast majority of paid employment in our society operates on the assumption that the employee has someone else to look after most of their household's domestic work. This can only change through such measures as a general reduction and more flexible timing of working hours, encouragement of job-sharing which does not simply involve employers getting a cheaper workforce, more communal and workplace provision for childcare, the enforcement of anti-discrimination practices in employment and the encouragement, backed by adequate training, of women to enter 'non-traditional' jobs.

Changes in the organisation of paid work would have to be accompanied by changes in that of unpaid work.[15] No doubt household appliances would still be used, perhaps increasingly so, but the need for a much greater user input into their design would be recognised.[16] Also, there would have to be some attention given to ways of organising household work other than by concentrating it within the nuclear family. Already this household type is less dominant, but the consequences of this in terms of the organisation of domestic work and the balance of goods and services such 'non-standard' households require have not been given serious attention. At the very least there should be changes in housing-tenure law and home financing in order to make living in non-nuclear households easier, and more experimentation in housing design should be encouraged in order to produce flexible-sized housing units. One aspect of such housing design could be the possibility of several households sharing certain items of household 'capital equipment', while keeping open options to choose not to do so.

These are only elements of the sorts of changes which would be needed, and it would take far more than our space or abilities to think through all the interactions and consequences of these and other components of change. The point once again is that there are no quick 'technical fixes' to the problem of women's overwhelming responsibility for domestic work. Only by the efforts and commitment of many people can the changes outlined in the second scenario be brought about. One small part of this effort will involve thinking about the restrictions and possibilities of present and future technologies and work organisation, and assessing their worth from the perspective of ensuring an equitable distribution of socially necessary work.

NOTES

1. No order of seniority implied. We would like to thank our colleagues at the Science Policy Research Unit and the sponsors of the research programme on which our work is based, in particular the Joseph Rowntree Memorial Trust and the Countryside Commission for Scotland.
2. Bose (1979) suggests that perhaps the clearest presentation is to be found in Ogburn and Nimkoff (1955).
3. For detailed figures on the increases in women's employment in the UK see SPRU Women and Technology Studies (1982). For the effects of technology on the international division of labour see Huws (1982).
4. See also Meissner *et al.* (1975).
5. However, as the current disputes over the privatisation of state-run services show, this cannot be taken for granted.
6. This is an extremely condensed version of an argument presented more fully in Gershuny (1983) and Gershuny and Miles (1983).
7. For details of this study see Szalai (1972).
8. Domestic work is here taken to include meal preparation and washing-up, house cleaning, washing clothes, 'odd jobs' and home decorating, gardening, car care and maintenance, shopping, childcare, knitting and sewing and domestic

travel. Obviously the distinction between work and leisure with some of these activities is not hard and fast.

9. This is also the conclusion of Stafford (1980), who compared data from American surveys in 1965 and 1975.

10. This can of course be a mixed blessing, as men may then assume much more control over day-to-day household spending. See Pahl (1982).

11. The historical material which follows is based on information obtained from the Mass-Observation Archive at the University of Sussex, an invaluable source for the 1930s and 1940s in particular.

12. This is dealt with much more fully in Hayden (1981) and Malos (1980).

13. This last point has been particularly argued by Cowan (1979b), who sees technology as a means by which middle-class households came to be managed without servants.

14. For a discussion of the value of employment outside the home, see Jahoda (1979). Ferree (1980) discusses satisfaction, or otherwise, with housework.

15. Dare we suggest that if men had to do more domestic work these changes would not be long in coming? When male SPRU researchers started taking their turn at serving tea and coffee there was a sudden upsurge in mental effort on how to make the work easier and more efficient.

16. For a fuller treatment of the issues involved here see Goodall (1983).

6 Placing Children in the Division of Labour

JENS QVORTRUP

About 40 per cent of the world's population are children under the age of 15, and within a few years there will be more than two billion children. By far the greatest proportion of them (maybe 80 per cent) live in less-well-developed areas of the world. Nearly sixty million of these children are registered as economically active in one way or another, but this figure is probably the tip of the iceberg. In most countries the gainful employment of children is against the law, the introduction of compulsory schooling being the main factor which triggered its illegalisation. Yet despite prohibitive laws childwork is still practised wherever it is felt to be advantageous.

Historically, children have always been subjected to the authority of adults. During certain periods of development, parents demanded children's labour in order that they and their families could survive. During other periods, the community has demanded schoolwork from children to meet the needs of society. The demands we put on children *and* their socialisation cannot be separated.

The way we perceive children and concomitantly our attitudes towards them depend very much on how we interpret their activities; in other words, on the meaning we assign to their activities. When children's main activities are thought to be play, our attitudes are different from those when they are thought to be work. Work is generally defined as 'instrumental', belonging to that category of activities which we label 'organised'. Play, on the other hand, is classified as 'affective', belonging to the category of spontaneous activities. It is beyond doubt that children generally are viewed in terms of the spontaneous category. This is illustrated when we derogatively speak of 'childish' adults and, more appreciatively, use the phrase 'childlike'. There is a plethora of these denigrating expressions, which unfortunately are unwittingly supported by the scientific treatment of childhood. But we need not deny children their affective traits to understand that they also perform instrumental functions in and for society, and we need not jettison psychological wisdom to hold the view that children have important *sociological* attributes.

In this chapter I intend to examine sociological approaches to children and childhood. I will ask questions about the character of children's most important activities and the extent to which childhood is regarded as being part of organised society. I will argue that the form and content of children's activities depend on the mode of production, but despite the contribution made by children to the production of the labour force they are deprived of rights accorded to other groups in society. I will propose that the inconsistency between children's economic importance and their lack of societal recognition contributes to an explanation of the 'problems' of childhood.

Sociology as a discipline has historically evolved with, and revolved around, the world of work. Sociology originated with nascent industrialism, at the time when the modern family emerged. The evolving division of labour demanded only the husband as an industrial worker, and because women were not gainfully employed they were not, until recently, a focus for sociology. Also 'primitive' societies were largely excluded from sociology on the grounds that they allegedly lack the complexities of labour to be found in the modern world (Furfey, 1940).

Children are thought to represent *both* 'negative' elements: they are not gainfully working, and they are — even if the word 'primitive' is not used — immature and irresponsible. According to Parsons and other modernisation theorists, adolescence is 'the point in the life-cycle when particularistic identities were dissolved and universalistic habits and values assimilated' (Gillis, 1981, p. 215). In terms of Parsons's pattern variables, children would be categorised as affective, particularistic, diffuse, and so on. Parsons's analysis in this respect has antecedents in classical sociology. Although children were not specifically mentioned (since they were not an issue), they would have ascriptive rather than achievement status according to Linton's categorisations; their relations would be of the status type, not of the contractual in Maine's terms; for Durkheim their solidarity would have been mechanic, not organic; and for Tönnies they would belong to *Gemeinschaft*, not to *Gesellschaft*.

Underlying such conceptualisations is an implicit value judgement about what is most important for the modern world and thus for sociology. For example, Inkeles *de*values childhood in the following way:

It seems obvious . . . that of the various later stages which *socialisation looks forward to*, it is the personally enduring and *socially important adult stage* which is the critical one to consider. (MacKay, 1973, pp. 28–9) (my emphasis)

Likewise, over forty years ago Kingsley Davis said:

An individual's most important functions for society are performed when he is fully adult, not when he is immature. Hence society's treatment of the child is chiefly preparatory and the evaluation of him mainly anticipatory (like a savings account). Any doctrine which views the child's needs as paramount and those of organized society as secondary is a sociological anomaly. (Davis, 1940, p. 217)

If Inkeles's and Davis's statements are accepted, then childhood is merely preparation for adulthood; children are nothing but an investment in the future – a raw material in the socialisation process; they do not belong to the organised society of adulthood. In so far as such statements represent a general attitude to children, they then contribute to how children perceive *themselves* and childhood. The possibility arises that a self-fulfilling prophecy will be contained in these statements in that they will have demotivating consequences for children.

These views have assumed in an uncritical way the vocabulary of psychology. Within psychology, the child, according to Skolnick, is 'defined by a place on a staircase of development – the child of ages and stages' (Skolnick, 1978, p. 305). The child gradually becomes more mature and complex until he or she reaches adulthood. Some writers have gone so far as to question whether children are 'human' before they are socialised and domesticated (Rafky, 1973, p. 62). This developmental approach to childhood used by psychologists has limited sociological worth.

When sociologists have not borrowed the vocabulary of psychologists, they have often fled into a role-analysis of children. Family sociologists have analysed the roles of children as sons or daughters within kinship, their roles as incumbents of positions within childcare institutions (in relation to one another and their guardians), their roles in relation to each other and to teachers within the education system, and so on.

Role-analysis has the limitation of losing sight of children as whole beings and the danger of hiding them behind the analysis of institutions. There can be no doubt that a sociology of childhood must draw heavily on detailed research about the roles of children, but it is equally obvious that we must go further. Role-analysis constitutes a barrier to appreciating the common characteristics of children in their ensemble of role capacities.

The alternative is to establish children as a sociological category *per se* along with such other social categories as peasants, blacks, the elderly, women, and so on.

The limited interest which sociologists have shown in childhood *in itself* reflects the assumption that children are not part of organised society. They have been marginalised and residualised — kept in a waiting position until they can be classified as 'adults', living and competing in adult society. *Children are not human 'beings' in sociological literature, but only human 'becomings'.*

The conceptualisation of childhood is more complex and uncertain than might appear at first sight. A number of stages have been listed: infancy, early childhood, young childhood, early adolescence, and so on. There is, however, no unanimity as to exactly when an individual passes from one of the stages to another. Childhood is conceptualised by *psychologists* in terms of chronological age. Any individual is seen as passing through a number of phases, each of which carries certain physiological and personality traits. We are told that individuals remain children until they are able to think abstractly (Piaget) or until they are sexually mature (Freud). Many other developmental schemes have been elaborated, and the idea of presenting childhood chronologically has been influential not only in the scientific study of childhood itself but also in everyday perceptions.

There are other approaches. According to the law, for instance, the age at which children become adults differs from one area of activity to another. Adulthood variously begins when an individual reaches the age of majority or the voting age; the division may be the legal age of marriage or the minimum criminal age. It may also be regarded as the age for completing compulsory schooling and for entering paid employment. These 'ages' differ over time and between cultures and are not necessarily dependent on psychological age and development. If, for instance, voting age somehow indicated maturity, then a century ago childhood would have been a very long period. Psychological age shows a high degree of stability, but the legal divisions are far more important *sociologically* since they are socially defined and determined.

Administrative statistics are very instructive about the social variabilities of childhood. Early statistics placed the age limit of childhood at about 14 years, but this has been gradually increased in many countries to about 20 years and even more (a normal classification in Denmark, for instance, is 'families with children under 26 years of age'). Cross-culturally, there are wide differences between countries at different stages of development in their statistical delineation of childhood.

The historical and cross-cultural variations in 'official' definitions of childhood are then supportive of the sociological argument that childhood (Ariès, 1973) and adolescence (Gillis, 1981) are fairly recent discoveries or social constructs. While biologically and psychologically childhood and adolescence have always existed, sociologically they have not. However, the sociological approach, although useful, is not without dangers: the 'liberation' of childhood from age determination might lead back to a quasi-psychological conception whereby childhood is equated with incompetence. This is something which an adequate sociological conception should explicitly avoid.

Childhood *does* need to be specified in terms of the descriptive categories of age. A child is an individual in the first part of the life-cycle. Childhood *is* an age-span, but its limits are culturally and historically determined. Those individuals who at a given moment belong to the *age-span* 'childhood' constitute the *age-group* 'children'. Whereas psychology stresses individual development and regards children as a transitional phase, sociology views children with reference to 'determining' social factors. From a dynamic point of view, it is not the individual's passage through childhood into adulthood which calls for attention, but the changes and continuities of a persistent age-group. To whatever extent the size of the age-group may contract or expand, its presence is permanent. The age-group of children therefore represents a 'stable' structural category which nevertheless is subject to a massive inflow and outflow, to a process of 'demographic metabolism' (Ryder, 1965, p. 843).

The concept of children as an age-group which at one and the same time exhibits continuity and constant replacement helps clarify the concepts of 'cohort' and 'generation'. A cohort constitutes in aggregate terms a temporal dimension of an age-group, but it is also a transient phenomenon without replacement. On the other hand, a generation may experience replacement but is in principle without age-limits (cf. Abrams, 1970; Mannheim, 1952). This conceptualisation does not require a precise and universal age limit being placed on childhood. While its starting-point is the newborn child, its completion depends on the social determinants surrounding children's activities, authority relationships, degree of organisation, and so on. There is no *theoretical* contradiction between this conceptualisation and those of psychology or role-analysis. Neither the view of childhood as a developmental and transient phase nor the relational perspective of childhood as a period for role-internalisation is invalidated by an approach which focuses on the societal, or macro-sociological level of analysis. None the less, the latter represents a necessary alternative for the purposes of achieving a balanced perspective.

Industrialisation, in eroding traditional habits and values, resulted in cultural uncertainty and confusion. The crucial event here was the massive expansion of the division of labour connected to the development of the market. It was no mere coincidence that 'work' came to be the main sociological concern. There is considerable agreement about the penetrating influence of the increasing division of labour, but various interpretations as to its significance. Functionalists claim that of paramount importance was the process of specialisation which resulted in functional differentiation and accompanying inequality of remuneration. Marxists, however, single out the importance of the divisions and relationships between capital and labour. They argue that the progress of capitalism has resulted in an asymmetrical power relationship between these conflicting classes; in other words, specialisation has involved an expansion of the proletariat, the dispossessed who are forced to depend on the sale of their labour power. For instance, whereas in 1780 80 per cent of white American men were self-employed, in 1969 the figure was only 9.2 per cent (Philipson, 1981. See Tilly, 1981).

The world of work has also had a major influence on parallel developments in the family — the most pertinent institution for children. It has been argued, for instance, that there have been major changes in the functions of the family. Industrialisation left its imprint by first of all drawing the father out of the home to become a wage-earner in specialised industry, and later the mother was similarly affected. However, the issue remains 'what has been the place of children in this major social transformation?' There are few clues in the available literature. At best, children have been treated residually within institutional analyses of family and school. At worst, they have been viewed as having no more than nuisance value. Between these extremes, family research has viewed children as emotionally indispensable, but very costly in economic terms. I wish to argue that there is an alternative: that of according children a major part in the development and transformation of society, notably in the processes of specialisation, the expanding division of labour and proletarianisation.

Children did not simply *exist* in past society, they actively contributed towards historical development. There is no historical period in which their activities have been separated from economic and societal changes even though this has been seldom recognised, and their roles have been determined by forces outside their control. On the surface, it might appear that these external forces lie abstractly in the 'external world'. But, more concretely, adults have always exercised power over children. Under the pretext of the necessity of socialisation for adulthood, children have been both assigned a number of tasks and denied societal rights. The subtle mechanisms governing these child—adult relationships have attained almost 'natural' forms, which make it difficult to perceive the underlying material forces.

If, as claimed, children have had an active historical role, it is necessary to account for the continually changing position of children within society as it develops. The process of socialisation is a point of departure, because whatever children's duties are they will nevertheless remain an integral part of socialisation. Learning is not a one-way process: teaching and socialisation depend on those who are taught being receptive and responsive. Children have never been merely passive recipients of education: they have actively taken part in and elaborated upon what has been 'given' them. The key to understanding the role of children in history and society thus lies in the constructive, even productive, societal activities they perform.

If it can be demonstrated that this view of children's position in society is sound, a number of further questions are raised. Does the sociological, or the psychological, conceptualisation of children have the stronger explanatory power? Are children ontologically, but not sociologically, different from adults? Will it be necessary to define 'work' to include children's activities?

In pre-capitalist societies, children[1] were an essential part of the community in which they lived. As soon as it was physically possible, they took part in those activities which were necessary for making a living. Children's welfare was not a focus of concern and many died before coming of age. Socialisation took place in the course of everyday community life (Ariès, 1973; Stone, 1979; Shorter, 1977). Schooling did not exist because it was not necessary. Children had to learn about local community tasks, since they could anticipate spending their adult lives following the occupations of their parents or neighbours. They were also expected to care for their parents in old age, although only a few people achieved longevity. Thus, available evidence *does* point to the economic importance of children in pre-capitalist societies in these respects (Ladurie, 1980, p. 250).

As capitalism developed, the foundation for productive work in the family was eroded. The 'self employed' became wage-labourers and many had to migrate to the towns and cities. At this time, the prototype of the nuclear family emerged, where fathers became primarily earners and mothers began to assume primarily a caring role. Children became 'visible' as the basis for home production was displaced by the eventual process of industrialisation.

This short historical sketch omits an analysis of differences between the classes. The period was characterised by crude class divisions (Gillis,

1981) in that occupational differentiation involved a process of proletarianisation (Olsson, 1980, p. 18). The material basis for making a living was destroyed for a large part of the population and, as a consequence, children could not remain idle. Child labour became widespread and schooling on a massive scale began to appear.

Child labour was not novel to industrialisation, but children now performed both wage-labour as well as other activities. For example, some undertook domestic duties to enable adults to be more heavily engaged in production. Child labour was a necessary part of the family income: Gillis reports that as late as 1914 'ten per cent of the families in some English communities had no other source of income but their children', and that in 'the poor districts of London, fathers earned less than fifty percent of the family income' (Gillis, 1981, p. 124). Olsson reports that in Sweden in 1875 children constituted up to 20 per cent of the labour force in factories producing glass, matches and tobacco (Olsson, 1980, p. 50). In Germany, a study of a glass factory in Silesia showed that 12 per cent of the workers started their jobs before the age of 8, and almost a third before the age of 10 (Kuczynski, 1958, p. 169). Like Gillis, Kuczynski also shows the indispensability of child labour for the survival of a worker's family.

The story of child labour is a very gloomy one. This aside, my purpose here is to establish the involvement of children in a range of organised societal undertakings: for example, children often participated in industrial and agricultural labour (with or without remuneration), begging, and domestic duties. There are illustrations of the importance of children for the economy of many families. For instance, Zelizer writes about the insurance taken out on the lives of children in the United States before the turn of the century:

> Against objection that child insurance was an illegal wager, 19th century American courts ruled that the right of parents to the services and earnings of minor children gave them an insurable interest in their lives. Judicial approval then rested entirely in the pecuniary bond between parent and child. (Zelizer, 1981, p. 1046)

Recently, Lewis has shown that the increase in nineteenth-century US savings rates by one-quarter can be attributed to a decline in the dependency rate — an indirect indication of children being economic assets (Lewis, 1983).

The emergence of compulsory schooling in the nineteenth century reflects the growing dominance of the division of labour and the demands of specialised labour. During this period, there was a continuous struggle between the state and the progressive labour movement on the one hand, and employers and poor workers on the other hand, over keeping children at school. This struggle was not terminated until recently in Western societies and is still a feature of many less-well-developed countries (Hjarnö, 1976; Mendelievich, 1979; Rogers and Standing, 1981) and of societies still in transition (for example, Soviet Central Asia). The introduction of the compulsory school system is significant in several respects. It represented a growing demand for more educated labour, larger costs for families in bringing up children – due to the disappearance of the child's contribution to the household economy and a prolonged stage of dependence – an increased economic interest in children by society, and a change in the character of children's activities, now transformed into school work.

Currently, there is a dearth of information about children's organised activities outside school. For example, the extent of child labour and its economic impact is hardly researched. One reason for this may be that sociologists have been persuaded by psychologists to regard 7 to 14 year olds as 'unproblematic'. If we focus on the school system, its meaning for society and children, from the perspective of the social division of labour, schools constitute that part in which the labour force is reproduced, endowed with skills, qualifications, and so on. Schools offer a wide range of subjects, reflecting society's requirements for a specialised labour force, just as previously the content of children's activities were conditioned by the needs of parents. Thus the changes which have occurred in time-tables demonstrate the close connection between children's organised activities and the demands of society. For instance, micro-electronics has become an obligatory subject in many countries, reflecting the economic demand for a new skill.

Schoolchildren are subject to heavy demands on their time by the education system. They are obliged to attend compulsory school, and although they may benefit from education, their efforts are also beneficial to society. Indeed, they are even indispensable. An analysis of the rationale behind education and its necessity for society should prevent us from assuming that 'free' education is simply a 'gift' for children. Children work hard several hours a day; they apply energy, diligence, creativity, intelligence, both in school and when doing homework. To a large extent, children are part of organised, rational, achievement-oriented society, both in and outside of school.

There is a lack of adult recognition of the part played by children in modern society, and a divergence between the typical way of depicting children (as immature, incompetent and affective) and their constructive place in the social division of labour. Children's contribution to the reproduction of labour power is not acknowledged, and as such they do not receive social recognition equivalent to their efforts. As they grow older, children are able to perceive that they, but no one else, participate in organised social activities without remuneration. Like adults, they take this for granted. However, the possibility exists that inter-generational conflict begins with a more or less conscious reaction towards the under-lying inequalities and inequities which exist between children and adults.

The preceding points about the links between the mode of production and the character of child labour can be summarised as follows. In pre-industrial societies the activities of children were conditioned by the demands of the family and local community. Schooling was not required for the reproduction of the labour force since children 'learned' by doing farm work, handicrafts, and so on. Under industrial capitalism, the new working class had an interest in child labour as a supplement to the low incomes of fathers. Employers favoured child labour because of its low cost as a factor of production. The progress of the division of labour and of specialisation eventually resulted in the replacement of child labour by compulsory schooling. Modern society demanded that children's work was done in schools. The demand was not an expression of changed sentiments or emotions towards children, but was dictated by developments which took place with industrialisation. There has been an historical change in the institutions which have had an economic interest in children, starting with the family and local community, passing to the social classes of capitalism (employers, poor workers, farmers, and so on), and eventually to the state (the total community). These changes have been centrally important to children as far as the content and character of their work is concerned. However, in principle, their dependency, continuing subjection to forces outside their control, and lack of social, economic and political rights, have not changed.

While one way of understanding work as it developed during the phase of industrialisation is in terms of specialisation and occupational differen-tiation, a supplementary interpretation can be made in terms of the prole-tarianisation of labour. This process has quite distinct implications, in that it is closely connected with issues of power and authority. In the earlier parts of the chapter, dramatic metamorphoses in the character of children's activities were discussed. Specialisation, as a paramount phenomenon of societal development, came to encompass children. Arguably, a kind of proletarianisation has taken place for children as well as for adults. Children as a separate section of society have become increasingly powerless[2].

This argument should not be taken too far. A relative stability in the qualitative aspects of children's dependency relationships with adults and teachers can be observed. Children are now, as before, subjected to authority, dependent, dispossessed and without rights. Ariès has noted the close connection between the notions of childhood and dependency, arguing that childhood ends when dependency does. Available evidence on the surveillance, subjection and disciplining of children (Stone, 1979; Foucault, 1977) shows that the main agent of authority has simply changed in line with changes in the mode of production.

In modern society, a crucial question is the relationship between position in the social division of labour and subordination. In other words, what are the mechanisms by which people gain human and social rights but which prevent children from obtaining such entitlements? While the literature on 'children's rights' assumes that children enjoy legal protection and certain welfare rights, in terms of the law children are deprived of the right enjoyed by adults which allows them to determine their own lives.

Our legal systems draw dividing lines between children and adults. Adults have the right to vote, work gainfully and to lead autonomous lives, but children do not. On the other hand, it cannot be claimed that children have no duties (an argument which might be forwarded to justify the discrimination), even though some of the *duties* we have imposed on children are labelled *rights* (the right to schooling, for example). Moreover, whatever the power relations might be in individual families, the law equips parents with the freedom to exert authority over their children according to their discretion. In cases where children earn money, parents have the right to dispose of it.

The purpose here is not to make a contribution towards social policy, but to pinpoint some neglected issues concerning children which are of theoretical interest. The point is that children are deprived of their rights and are dispossessed in terms of economic and political power, despite their constructive position in the social division of labour. In his excellent book *Exit, Voice and Loyalty*, Hirschman (1970) analyses three choices which most people face in many situations during their lives. As producers, consumers, marriage partners or whatever they can choose to leave, object or remain loyal. Hirschman presents his theory as one with wide applicability, but children are a group that the theory excludes. They do not normally have all three options. They may 'voice' their opinions, but without the possibility of exerting power, because the choice of 'exit' is not available. They cannot leave their families, schools or other institutions in which they have been placed by their parents and the state. In practically all respects, they are left with only the 'loyalty' option. If the position of children is compared with the position of women (a group whose subordination is widely discussed) there is a great difference in the range of

choices available. Women are able to voice their objections against subordination. Moreover, they have the possibility of combining their protest
with the choice of 'exit'.

Although children's status as dependents has remained stable over time,
there have been changes in the agencies which have exerted power over
them and in the kind of power exerted. Developments in the occupational
structure have compelled us to organise a system of active protection
where one did not exist previously. Shifts in the forms of taking care or
taking charge of children are only logical consequences of the societal
transformations which have occurred over the last two centuries. Foucault
(1977, p. 128) argues they were part of a general trend towards 'time
tables, compulsory movement, regular activities, solitary meditation, work
in common, silence, application, respect, good habits'. Specialisation in
the division of labour necessitated new forms of discipline, regulation and
normalisation.

The institutionalisation of childhood was an important component of
this whole development, which was a question not only of security and
protection but also of education, socialisation and discipline in relation to
new demands set at a macro-level as compared with the previous ones at
a local or family level. There are no signs that children are in the process
of being credited with the part they actually play in society, despite the
highly organised nature of their lives, and their participation in the social
division of labour in traditional settings which resemble those of the adult
world[3]. This reflects the persistent tendency for society to label them as
immature, irresponsible and incompetent.

It is imperative for sociology to investigate children's status on the basis
of what they do, and to examine the consequences of the discrepancy
between their activities and their dependency relationships. We must learn
to recognise that society is dependent on children as much as children are
dependent on society. The prevailing assessment of children not only
furthers indifference towards them (Edgar and Ochiltree, 1983, p. 14), it
supports the kind of colonial paternalism which Doris Lessing pertinently
describes in her characterisation of Karen Blixen's[4] attitudes to indigenous
Africans: 'For while the idea that a man has rights was not one she could
hold, she could not stand that he should be hurt or insulted' (Lessing 1971,
p. 87).

However, children are neither colonial subjects nor slaves, even though
we might be forgiven for thinking that the following definition of a 'slave'
would seem to apply to children:

A man whom law and custom regard as the property of another. In extreme cases he is wholly without rights, a pure chattel; in other cases he may be protected in certain respects, but so may an ox or an ass . . . if he has by his position certain countervailing rights, e.g. to inherited property, from which he cannot (except for some default) be dislodged, he becomes . . . no longer a slave but a serf. (Bottomore, 1981, p. 185)

Bottomore comments that 'slavery thus represents an extreme form of inequality, in which certain groups of individuals are entirely or almost entirely without rights' (ibid).

The way people perceive themselves largely depends on how they are perceived by others. While their contribution to society may be indispensable, if it is not acknowledged as such they may feel alienated and disillusioned. This is best exemplified by the working class and women. Over a long historical span, their powerlessness influenced their self-conception to the extent that they took for granted the 'natural' order which prevented them from enjoying their appropriate share of goods and rights. Lack of self-confidence, lack of resources, subscription to dominant ideology, and social and political apathy accompanied their social perception.

The history of the labour movement and the women's movement reveals considerable resistance to their aims from potential support groups. It is still a problem that large sections of allegedly subjugated groups cannot be won over for the movements. In the women's movement, there is a conviction that 'the anger and revolt had necessarily to emerge from the discriminated and subjected themselves' (Backe, 1984) because it is clear that those in power are not willing to accept nor even acknowledge the complaints and demands from the subjugated. The same arguments could apply to children.

Two important preconditions for the transformation of a section of a society into a social and political force are *both* its objective, material position in the social structure *and* its subjective realisation of this position. Sociologists often take employment to be a basis for distinguishing between people according to their status or class, but recently a discussion of class and surplus value has emerged in connection with women's non-waged labour in the home. It has been argued that women's domestic labour should be included in a broadened concept of surplus labour, since it contributes towards maintaining and reproducing the labour force. The Domestic Labour Debate could be extended to include some of children's activities.

I maintain that children's *objective* position in the social division of labour would justify, on theoretical grounds, the childgroup being assigned a distinct status or class. Children take part in socially necessary activities, contribute towards the accumulation of knowledge and labour power to be used in society, are permanently a part of social renewal, and from an early age are an integral part of social organisation.

Subjectively, children are so firmly encapsulated within the paternalism which pervades society that it is not surprising to discover that they do not constitute a social force. Children have a clear consciousness of themselves as 'children', but not as a group with distinct social attributes. Their lack of social consciousness stems from the views and arguments about childhood which adults have imposed on them. In this way, they remain ignorant about society's dependence on them. A real factor inhibiting the consititution of the child-group 'for itself' is its continuous automatic dissolution. Most workers remain workers throughout their lives, women remain women, but children stop being children when they obtain rights and potential power. Although childhood is a permanent phenomenon, the demographic metabolism which causes complete mobility during one age-span stultifies any socio-political possibilities.

The economic and political strength of childhood has never been realised and it may not be calculable. However, some indicators may be stipulated to guide future study. In economic terms, children have importance, but a distinction has to be made between who will be the main beneficiary and who will bear the main economic burden of children. It is evident that in the past the family invested in and benefited from children, but not while the family and the public economy share the investment, only the latter benefits.

Zelizer argues that from the parents' point of view, 'Children's lives become economically worthless but emotionally priceless' (1981, p. 1050). Other writers (Ariès, 1973; Shorter, 1977) have similarly observed that children have become emotionally more valuable. This fact is not without significance, since it suggests that parents are willing to make more sacrifices for children than formerly. Whether this has been cynically exploited by 'the economy' and the state or not, it can be demonstrated that children nowadays are not only economically worthless for parents, they are very expensive. In Denmark, in 1976, for instance, net income per member in families with children was less than two-thirds of the corresponding income in families without children (Börnekommissionens betaenkning (Report from the Government's Committee on Children), 1981, p. 40). The composition of consumption is systematically influenced by the number of children and the average income. In Denmark, as the number of children in families increases, the share of income per family member apportioned to savings, housing and household equipment falls, but the share spent on food, clothing, electricity and heating rises (ibid, p. 41).

It may be concluded that a larger portion of children belong to the lower income groups than do other age-groups in the population. This was not always the case, and in subsistence economies there is still a positive relation between number of children and affluence. The contribution by children to the family economy in modern societies has not been established empirically. Factors which require analysis are their participation in domestic labour and in paid employment outside the home — which in many cases provides income to cover leisure activities which otherwise would be paid for by parents or not enjoyed. A recent Danish report on 9 to 12 year old children shows that 'daily tasks and duties' made up 4.08 hours per day. This includes not only domestic duties but also paid jobs outside the home. A little more than a quarter of children in this age-group had such a job (Forchhammer and Petersen, 1980, pp. 57, 64).

The importance of children in relation to the national economy is considerable. It may appear that they only represent costs, if the investment in day-care institutions, schools, leisure time activities and family policy measures are considered. However, investments should be regarded as *investments*: that is, they will pay off later. It is to the credit of human-capital theorists that they have turned our attention to this problematique. This theory:

> rests on the proposition that there are certain expenditures (sacrifices) that are made deliberately to create productive stocks, embodied in human beings, that provide services over future periods. These services consist of producer services revealed in future earnings and of consumer services that accrue to the individual as satisfactions over his lifetime. (Schultz, 1973, p. S5)

The societal importance of children can be seen in other respects. Children as consumers represent a very big market. In Denmark, children up to the age of 18 get approximately fifteen billion Dkr. in pocket money, and the yearly turnover of consumer goods for children is more than seven billion Dkr. — an amount which is almost equivalent to all the sales from Danish textile and clothing industries. This huge demand has, of course, been exploited by business. In a way, one could argue that no single section of society has 'discovered' children more effectively than business, so that a major part of the economy is now directed towards the children's market.

Finally, children's economic importance is indirectly demonstrated in the development of new occupational sectors. Calculating the number of professional child-carers depends on how they are defined, but if we restrict ourselves to the most relevant groups (such as teachers in schools and those in pre-school arrangements) we discover a group with a size of around 10 per cent of the gainfully employed people in Western countries. Apart from the immediate economic importance for those so occupied, the very existence of this sector and of the investment in it indirectly signals the economic importance of children. But, while professional carers are paid wages and have economic status, the children they care for are excluded from such rewards. This brings us back to one of the main issues surrounding the study of children; namely that they are treated as nothing but a raw material and investment object (an assumption also made by human-capital theorists) as though there is no input into the economic circuit from them.

The low status children enjoy economically has repercussions in the realm of politics. Children are excluded from politics in the sense that they do not have political rights. This raises the question of which, if any, political parties or pressure groups lobby on behalf of children. Children are badly represented, as studies from the United States indicate (Steiner, 1976). The situation is becoming more critical, because children are, relatively speaking, a diminishing group – the proportion of households with children is decreasing. In West Germany in 1981, for example, less than 50 per cent of households had any children in them. The falling birth-rate may not make it any easier in the future to promote a child-oriented political policy.

In view of the cost of rearing children, it is not surprising that the birth rate is falling. But, their emotional pricelessness will probably help ensure the birth of children and the willingness of parents to make the necessary economic sacrifices to bring them up. It is perhaps curious that traditional family ideology can survive, given that the economic benefits provided by children are now enjoyed not so much by parents as by the state. Most parents are still inclined to invest heavily in something which has no economic pay-off for them, simply to symbolise *their* 'possession' of their children. This may be understandable on an emotional level, but from the point of view of 'family economy' it is an anachronistic paradox. To the extent that there is ideological support for children being parents' property, there is legitimation for the situation in which the state leaves the final responsibility for children with the parents, while retaining for itself the material benefits. The skills and knowledge embodied in children are represented as a 'gift' to families rather than as a state investment. This makes it an easy matter for the state to cut child-support benefits, since parents cannot justifiably make claims on resources to enhance the value of their *own* property. Under the pretext that children belong to the parents, it is politically convenient to place the bulk of the costs, burden and responsibilities onto the family. To the extent that public expenses on children are considered in budgetary terms as expenses (and therefore as costs) we are prevented from recognising that children's activities are of value to society. If this recognition was forthcoming it would make it politically difficult to circumvent its material acknowledgement.

In conclusion, I have tried to spotlight some neglected aspects of childhood and children — aspects which sociologists so far have failed to develop. The sources of some of the problems faced by children can be traced to recent radical social change, and our inability to understand that children have played an integral part in this process. It has been forgotten — or never discovered — that historically children have been constituent and constructive agents in social development and have never been credited with this importance. I believe it is *sociologically* necessary to acknowledge the role which children have had in history and still play in society. Currently, society's combined indifference and paternalism towards children is not conducive to the effective motivation which children need to perform those activities which are expected of them.

NOTES

1. In the following analysis I refer to children mainly of school age.
2. I would like to stress that I am not discussing intra-familial matters, but only macro-sociological issues: the child-group at the societal level.
3. For Foucault, schools came to resemble factories, barracks, hospitals and prisons. The difference in the character of intervention in people's lives is one of degree (see Pratt, 1983, p. 340).
4. Karen Blixen was a Danish writer and baroness who owned a coffee farm in Kenya at the beginning of this century.

7 Paid Work and Unpaid Caring: A Problem for Women or the State?

CLARE UNGERSON

Over recent years central government, of whatever political persuasion, has become increasingly concerned about problems arising out of the coincidence of two distinct social trends. The first trend is the steadily rising proportion of old and very old people in the British population; by 2001 the number of people over 75 years old is expected to increase by one million to 4.2 million, of whom 1.1 million will be over 85 (*Social Trends*, Issue 14, 1984, p. 18). This trend has coincided with a rapid and continuing growth in women's economic participation rates, such that women now make up about 40 per cent of the labour force, compared with 32 per cent in 1961 (ibid, p. 58). Moreover, much of this change in economic activity has been due to the expansion of the service sector, and within that, the social service sector. While these trends do not in any obvious way depend upon each other, their coincidence gives rise to profound problems for the policy-makers of the 'welfare state'.

Given the state's ultimate responsibility for the welfare of the nation's old people, embodied in legislation laid down over the past eighty years, someone has to care for them. There are two possible answers to the problem. First, the state could develop, whether on its own or in conjunction with profit-making private agencies, some form of collective care of old people, paid for directly by the consumers of the care, or indirectly by tax-payers. But — however such care is financed and organised — the people who actually do the caring are paid, at rates subject to market forces. Alternatively, the second possible answer to the problem is to encourage the provision of care, not by paying people to do the caring, but by promoting a consensus of norms and obligations around the issue of dependency and a belief about the lack of alternative forms

146

of caring, such that 'carers' come forward who do not expect to be paid for the work.

The conundrum is that in either case, whether they are paid or not, the carers are likely to be women. There are two main reasons for this. First, since one of the defining characteristics of 'caring' is that, unlike 'curing' or counselling, the tasks involved are unskilled and entail very little training, *paid* carers are likely to be able to command only relatively low wages. Low wages, linked to a lack of credentialism, will mean that employers will seek out women who are untrained but experienced in domestic labour – which in many respects is rather like 'caring' in job content (see below). Once there, the predominance of women will ensure that the work is confirmed as women's work, and in this way, as a reflection of prevailing conditions of the labour market overall, lead to the perpetuation of low wages. Second, *unpaid* carers will be women rather than men largely because it is women who are regarded as the infinitely elastic pool of domestic labour, dressed up ideologically as the 'angels in the house' (see below). Women, as I shall argue fully, are peculiarly sensitive to the demands made on them to extend their domestic labour into caring for dependents for whom they have a sense of obligation and, in many cases, care about.

Thus the state itself seems to contribute to its own problems of generating enough carers, both paid and unpaid. For if it is the case that women are the chief carers, both informally as part of their normal domestic 'responsibilities' and formally through their employment as cheap labour in the caring services, then it would seem that, given limits on the numbers of women available at any one time, informal caring is in competition with formal caring for labour power, and vice versa. In other words, if women are working in the labour market (and some of them will be working in the caring services) then ostensibly they will be unable to contribute their free domestic labour to the task of caring for the nation's elderly at home.

There is one further element in the problem, which is a reflection of specific policies pursued by the state in recent years. Over the past twenty years considerable efforts have been made to reduce the rate of increase of places available in residential institutions for the care of old people, and to replace them by care in and by the 'community'. These policies began at a time when there was increasing criticism of the circumstances of people who live in residential institutions (Jones, 1972). Both policy-makers and pressure groups concerned with the welfare of old people came to believe it would be more humane for the dependent elderly to be cared for, if possible in their own homes, and certainly in circumstances more like the domestic setting that most of us occupy. But these policies, which do not necessarily entail savings in expenditure, have recently coincided with further policies that are less to do with the organisation of the social services in particular, than with the direction of economic policy as a whole. As a result of efforts to reduce the public sector borrowing requirement, planned expenditure on social services has been reduced; services designed to replace, in the 'community', the loss of places in residential institutions have not been forthcoming; and numbers of staff working in the social services have been cut back. Increasingly, then, the 'community', which ideally contains a wide range of humane and caring funded services, has become a chimera, to be replaced by the rather more permanent, though not necessarily more humane, 'family'.

It would be foolish to assume that the reduction in jobs in the social services has (by releasing women to work at home and provide caring services for their relatives, friends and neighbours free, gratis and for nothing) solved the problem of competition for caring labour power outlined above. While a few women have been so released (or more accurately 'made redundant') the state, although it employs large numbers of women, is by no means their only employer. The service sector, which includes jobs in retailing, continues to expand and to employ large numbers of women; similarly the decline of traditionally male-dominated heavy manufacturing and the relative expansion of micro-chip technology in manufacturing processes is likely to increase future demand for female rather than male labour. Thus apparent competition for women's time as informal carers in the home or as cheap labour in manufacturing and service sectors is likely to continue; the only foreseeable change in the situation is that, in future, the role of the state as a competing employer is likely to be somewhat reduced, but replaced in many cases by the development of privately funded services, staffed by women, that take up the demand for caring left unsatisfied by declining social services.

Ostensibly, then, the problem for policy-makers remains the same. If women continue to use their time to earn money for themselves and their families, how are they going to be persuaded to give up time to care for the increasing numbers of old people, who, as a matter of policy, are increasingly being left to their own devices? It is, however, arguable that posing the question this way conceals the true nature of women's lives. For it implies that there are finite limits to the concept of time, and that there are no ways in which 'time' can literally be stretched. It is part of the purpose of this chapter to show that, in the case of women's domestic labour, time is a social construct, determined by the operation of a common ideology about women's role in the domestic divison of labour and mediated by feelings of guilt on the part of individual women. Moreover, the operation of a discriminatory labour market means that, under certain circumstances, there is a greater incentive for women than for men to give up time in paid work in order to spend it in unpaid caring.

While it is the case that the rapid increase in women's economic activity rates over the past twenty years constitutes a major material change in women's lives, there are important ways in which this change has taken place, namely that the effects on those who receive women's domestic services have been carefully minimised. For a start, and most important, a very high proportion of women in Britain work part-time. In 1981, 64 per cent of women aged 16 to 59 were economically active: 33 per cent of women worked full-time, 25 per cent worked part-time. A further 6 per cent were unemployed. The numbers working part-time were much higher for women with children. While 54 per cent of women with dependent children worked, 34 per cent of such women worked part-time, compared with only 15 per cent who worked full-time. The younger their children the less likely were women to work at all, but if they did they were at least three times as likely to work part-time as full-time (*General Household Survey*, 1983, p. 94). Thus, certainly as far as mothering is concerned, women do not appear to have given up this vital job in favour of paid work; rather they seem to have sought out work that they could most easily weave around their perceived primary domestic duties. Employers too have eagerly responded to women's demands for work with shorter hours, for they have been able thereby to pay lower wages and provide less job security (Webb, 1982). One further striking feature of data of this kind, though, is the persistence with which wives continue to work part-time even when they have no children but, according to the data, appear only to have a husband. According to the 1981 General Household Survey, of couples with no dependent children with the wife aged between 30 and 59, 34 per cent of the wives worked full-time but an almost exact equivalent (33 per cent) worked part-time; 31 per cent were economically inactive (*General Household Survey*, 1983, p. 99).

It is not of course possible, with aggregated data of this kind, collected on a national basis, to disentangle all the factors that contribute to the importance of part-time work in women's lives — irrespective of whether they have children. There is bound to be one group of determinants clustered around employers' demand and the nature of particular labour markets, for example, whether work available for women in particular labour markets is of a kind traditionally organised on a part-time basis (retailing, cleaning, ancillary work in hospitals, etc.). But there is also bound to be another group of factors that are to do with women's perception of themselves as primarily housewives and mothers rather than as paid workers. In a survey of attitudes to shift-work, carried out in 1977, working-class wives were asked to comment on a number of classic statements about the position of men and women within the family and their relationship to paid work. Of the wives who were working, 57 per cent agreed with the statement that 'a job is all right but for a woman real fulfilment lies in a home and children'; a further 10 per cent (68 per cent altogether) of the wives who were not working agreed with the statement. But thinking that 'fulfilment' came from caring for their families was not incompatible with having a job: 85 per cent of working wives agreed with the statement that 'a woman and her family will all benefit if she does a job', as did 66 per cent of the non-working wives (Marsh, 1979, table 4.8). These statements are not self-contradictory; evidence from economic studies of women's participation in the labour market indicates that there is good aggregated data to show that, when wages for women went up relative to those of men in the early 1970s, women were increasingly drawn into the labour market, but once there they did not increase the hours they worked even when hourly pay-rates increased (Layard, *et al.*, 1980). In other words, very many women apparently want jobs, but only ones with short hours. In this way they can provide for their household economies by contributing financially to the household resources, and by continuing to contribute their own free labour for the maintenance and well-being of individual members of their families, which, where there are no children, means their husbands alone. In economists' terms, there seems to be considerable quantitative and qualitative evidence that women's participation in the labour market is as much determined by supply factors (the wishes of women themselves) as by demand factors (the wishes of employers). Metaphorically, husbands and children constitute the warp threads in the fabric of family life, while women and their time constitute the weft threads, weaving in and out of the warp threads in diverse patterns, but never (or only very rarely) threatening to disrupt the basic shape.

In effect, the policy-makers' concern that the increase in women's participation in paid work will mean that they will no longer be available to perform their ascribed domestic duties, is founded on a masculinist view of the concept of time. For, when it comes to women's time, women are prepared to push and pull it until they can force time – or rather themselves – to conform to the servicing and financial needs of their families.

But it might be objected that 'mothering' and 'wifing' are rather different from 'caring'. By definition, biological mothers and wives have to be female; 'caring' is apparently sex neutral. Similarly, traditionally, domestic services have been donated free to husbands by their wives and to children by their mothers. In contrast it could be argued that the care of the elderly has, certainly since the 1834 Poor Law, been traditionally, although as a matter of last resort, carried out by paid carers. Thus the naturalism that applies to the domestic sexual division of labour as it applies to mothering and wifing seems relatively muted when it comes to caring. But this is to ignore four aspects of caring, and its relationship to the sex roles of men and women. First, if women still regard themselves primarily as workers in the home, then if there is someone at home in need of care and attention, a woman will see herself as the most appropriate person to provide that care. If at first she resists that definition of herself, she will find herself racked with guilt feelings (often exacerbated by the assumptions that are made about her 'proper' role by social policies and social services personnel) as she attempts to fend off the pressures of the prevailing ideology of woman's 'proper' place. Second, the actual tasks of caring for the elderly are construed by women to bear a strong resemblance to the tasks of mothering. Moreover, there are aspects of caring which seem to be the touchstone of the sexual division of domestic labour. In other words, they raise issues of taboo and pollution that can only be contained by the maintenance of a strict division of labour. And finally, the relatively low wages of women and the relative ease with which they can enter the labour market in a part-time capacity means that, when it comes to calls on their time that entail reducing their hours of work or giving up work altogether, the opportunity costs of becoming a full-time carer are not as great as they would be for a full-time reasonably paid man.

These issues of guilt, mothering, taboo, and opportunity costs will be discussed with reference to caring.

The dictionary definition of 'guilt' is 'failure of duty, delinquency; offence, crime, sin'. Thus, in order to *feel* guilty, one has to have internalised general rules of duty; the sanctions for failure to fulfil one's duty are thence self-imposed. The source of these rules of duty can be manifold, ranging from the criminal law, through ideology about what constitutes appropriate behaviour as put forward by powerful social institutions such as the Church or the State, to familial norms surrounding the concept of love and how love should properly be expressed through action.

When it comes to 'caring', the main source of these rules, which carers then internalise, are social institutions and the norms of 'family life'. As far as Church and State are concerned, Judith Oliver reports that wives caring for husbands feel constrained to do so by the special nature of the marriage relationship and, in particular, the marriage ceremony. Indeed, she suggests that for many wives the power of vows made at the ceremony is so strong that it overwhelms all other feelings, even the ending of love:

> Most wives quoted 'in sickness and in health' and, whilst admitting
> that they had probably felt when they took the vow that it was going
> to cover the odd bout of 'flu, could not see themselves breaking it
> when reality turned out to be far worse. Indeed, there is evidence that
> ill-health and disability are more likely to keep a failing marriage going
> than the reverse. Several wives mentioned that their marriages had been
> on the point of breaking up when the accident had occurred or illness
> been diagnosed, and that they had felt that they could not *in all con-
> science* abandon a sick person. (Oliver, 1983, my emphasis)

The State, too, takes a direct view of the nature of the marriage relationship, although in this case it lays down rules, not only about the continuity
of marriage, but also about the division of labour within it (Land, 1978).
In particular, by denying the Invalid Care Allowance (ICA) to married
women who are caring for a dependent, the State makes it clear that, on
marriage, a woman takes on primary responsibility for the care of who-
ever happens to be living in her household, even when that person is a
non-relative (Groves and Finch, 1983). There is some evidence that, in
this instance, the operation of the rules for the ICA has not in fact very
effectively promoted a sense of guilt among married women, since the
rules seem to be generally regarded by such women as unfair (Equal
Opportunities Commission, 1981). Nevertheless, such rules for cash benefits
legitimate the view, commonly taken by other arms of the State which
allocate services in kind, that married women are not normally in need
of the help of such services, since this burden is no different from the
normal housewifely duties that a woman is assumed to have taken on in
marriage (Oliver, 1983). Indirectly, the refusal of services in kind is likely
to add to the burden of guilt since it is made so obvious by the allocators
of the social services that the woman is the carer in the first — and last —
resort.

But the Church and the State are not the only purveyors of social
rules: classically the family forms the most important locus of the reproduction of ideology, and, not surprisingly, carers report a sense of familial
obligation and the traditional domestic division of labour as their most
pressing constraints. Fay Wright implies that this can cut two ways, in that
women, whether they are carers or cared-for, feel compelled by guilt to
fulfil traditionally allocated caring tasks. In cases where mothers were
being cared for by their unmarried sons, Wright found that the mothers

were 'both more active domestically and had fewer personal care disabilities than those living with daughters'. Some of these mothers went to extraordinary lengths to maintain their caring and parental role, as in the case of Mrs Green, who took an hour to move from her sitting-room to her kitchen in order to get to the stove to cook her son's evening meal. Wright suggests, the 'point of dependency' is itself dictated by a sense of guilt internalised by women, who would prefer to care for their sons rather than be cared for by them. On the other hand, mothers have different expectations of their caring relationship with daughters, and hence become 'dependent' at an earlier stage in the process of physical deterioration (Wright, 1983). Moreover, the cared-for themselves often operate the social rules of familial obligation by making explicit demands of their potential carers. But Wright has evidence that men and women carers respond differentially. Many women find the demands of their dependent relative irresistible: 'my mother just kept ringing me up at work and asking me to go home to be with her. I felt I had to give it up then'; men, on the other hand, found it far easier to put their work first: 'if she ever gets so that I need to give up my job, she will have to go into a home. I am never giving up my job and that's it' (Wright, 1983, pp. 100, 102)

Before leaving the topic of guilt, it is worth making the point that the social rules that determine guilt are not unchanging and permanent. It is interesting to note that Beatrice Webb, writing nearly seventy years ago, discussed family obligations in terms of 'an invalid wife (or husband), a superannuated father or widowed mother, an orphan brother or sister, aged grandparents, uncles and aunts, often more distant relations and, indeed, in some cases, friends who are crippled or in distress' (Webb, 1919, p. 68). Clearly, the prevailing view about which relationships dictate a caring response have considerably altered since 1919 (and could change back again). It is also clear from the debates surrounding the rules for allocating the ICA that the test issue appears to be the obligations or otherwise of those caring for those who are neither relatives through marriage nor kin. This issue has been raised, not on behalf of the large numbers of caring married women, but rather for the three hundred or so men who are caring for women with whom they are cohabiting (Groves and Finch, 1983). Although one might object to the sexist parameters of the debate, it nevertheless indicates that the basis for rules and obligations can be discussed, and eventually changed. One final point about guilt and the care of the elderly: where there is more than one adult child available to do the caring, how is the chief carer selected? In the case of sons versus daughters, it is clear that daughters are far more likely to feel impelled to take on the task. But what of the case where there is more than one daughter? Then, perhaps, other emotions come into play, especially the emotions of love and affection. It may be the case that those who are fondest also feel the most guilty when it comes to the observation of an elderly parent in trouble. In other words, there comes a point when love and guilt coalesce, and it is no longer possible to point to the purely social construction of the caring relationship and the obligations that surround it. If need be, some daughters rather than others would prefer to look after their aged parents. It is precisely this element of voluntariness that so muddies the debates about which individuals, which relatives and which institutions should care for the nation's elderly.

There is little doubt, as I have argued elsewhere (Ungerson, 1983a), that the tasks of caring for any dependant, including the elderly, bear strong resemblance to the care of normal children. In their study, *Family Care of the Handicapped Elderly: Who Pays?*, Nissel and Bonnerjea (1982) list the following tasks that they identified as necessary when it comes to caring for elderly people:

Bathing and washing cared-for
Dressing cared-for, including undressing or dressing for bed
Getting into or out of bed
Lifting, turning, assisting with stairs or getting about house
Putting on, helping with or taking to commode/toilet
Giving, overseeing or helping with medication in home (includes exercises)
Feeding, including a snack, when it means actually physically feeding or assistance, not merely placing tray in front of cared-for
Shopping, specifically for cared-for
Listening out for
Accompanying cared-for in travel
Obtaining medical care in home for cared-for
Obtaining medical care outside the home
Toilette: hair care, nails, shaving, make-up, and so on
Attending to correspondence, bills, paperwork, and so on, of or for cared-for
Meal or snack preparation specifically for cared-for
Cleaning specifically for cared-for
Care of clothing of cared-for
Leisure activity performed with or on behalf of cared-for

But while all these tasks bear some resemblance to the tasks necessary for the care of a child (sometimes, as in the case of 'lifting', a very young child), they do not necessarily invoke mothering as the model. Indeed, in the case of 'attending to correspondence', lifting, 'accompanying cared-for in travel', and leisure activities, they bear more resemblance to the conventionally defined tasks of fathering. Despite this, Nissel and Bonnerjea found a quite remarkable disparity in the amount of time that husbands and wives spent in caring for their elderly relative. On average, wives spent a total of 191 minutes of their day engaged in one or other of the caring tasks; husbands spent 13 minutes.

The reasons for this enormous difference in responsibility for caring are, as this chapter is intended to demonstrate, multi-faceted and complex. But one of the important reasons is that women themselves define many caring tasks as specifically female in orientation and do not expect their husbands to help:

> none of the husbands in the sample contributed substantial direct care. On the other hand, many supported the wife's caring role in other ways and this was much appreciated. Wives particularly liked their caring roles to be acknowledged and praised. When more direct help was needed, female relatives or nurses and doctors were seen as the appropriate sources to turn to. Since much of this care involved 'tending' in the sense of personal care involving touch, there was a perceived barrier between adult males and the relatives. This was true regardless of whether the relative was male or female or the wife's or husband's parent. (Nissel and Bonnerjea, 1982, pp. 40–1)

Similar results are reported in studies of the care of other dependants, such as mentally handicapped children (Wilkin, 1979; Glendinning, 1983). The sharpest division of labour seems to occur with the tasks described above as 'personal care involving touch'; in particular, the tasks concerned with keeping the cared-for clean. It is not simply a case of men refusing to do this kind of work. Both Nissel and Bonnerjea, and Wilkin, found that women carers went to some lengths to exclude their male relatives from the more intimate caring tasks; for example:

> Children, on the whole, were less directly affected. Most women felt that boys should not be directly involved; for example, 'Boys can't be expected to do things – it's not right for a boy to be taking an old lady to the toilet.' Husbands too were excused from the same 'personal' care. (Nissel and Bonnerjea, 1982, p. 36)

What is the explanation for this strict enforcement, by women, of the sexual division of labour when it comes to the more intimate tasks of caring? There are, I think, two possible and related explanations. The first is that these particular tasks bear most resemblance to the tasks of parenting, and thence to mothering. In late twentieth-century Britain, intimate parenting has become a very exclusive activity, usually involving the biological parents only. Similar processes seem to apply to caring, especially its most intimate aspects; there seem to be particular difficulties about accepting the help of those who are not, in reality, parents or who, as in the case of the children of the confused elderly, can be accepted as legitimate parent surrogates. Glendinning found, when it came to asking neighbours and friends to look after a handicapped child, that parents were reluctant to do so on the grounds that only the parents properly understood their child's needs (Glendinning, 1983). Similarly, unless some form of additional incentive is offered — usually in the form of payment for the work — there is no reason why others should feel that they should get involved with what are commonly regarded as the least pleasant tasks of intimate caring (or quasi-parenting):

> The isolation of women with severely handicapped relatives was particularly marked. One woman, who had been talking about the problems she had in getting out to go to the dentist, said, 'You see neighbours shy away because of this incontinence: they're frightened. No one will sit an incontinent grandma. Never.' (Nissel and Bonnerjea, 1982, p. 24)

But the use of the word 'parenting' implies that it is sex-neutral activity. This, of course, is not the case. Innumerable studies indicate that, in practice, 'parents' are mothers (see, for example, Oakley, 1974). Moreover, despite the women's movement, prevailing ideologies do nothing to undermine the practice; Hilary Graham has shown how quickly the rhetoric of sex-neutral parenting can disappear, even from statements with a clear 'liberal' intent:

> Parenthood and mothering of pre-school children should be recognised as the extremely important, skilled and demanding job it is . . . a home responsibility allowance . . . should be paid to her as a matter of right and not charity. (Pringle and Naidoo, 1975, cited in Graham, 1979)

Not surprisingly, mothers find it difficult to resist this maternal model of parenting (Oakley, 1974). Parenting, as it relates to the most intimate tasks, involves two levels of exclusion'. First, it excludes relative strangers and non-parents, unless — generally through payment for their services —

they can be legitimately accepted as surrogate parents. Second, parenting continues to be identified by the prevailing ideology and ideologues as mothering; hence, a further level of exclusion operates, often mediated by women themselves, to exclude men, even fathers, from the parenting process. In terms of caring, given that so many aspects of the tasks involved are similar to parenting and mothering, they become identified as necessarily, and generally exclusively, 'women's province'.

A second, and related, explanation for the exclusion, by women, of men from the caring process seems to be something to do with what can be most accurately described as a 'taboo' system concerning the regulation of incontinence. If such a taboo exists, and it certainly seems to as far as children are concerned (Oakley, 1974), then it appears to be based on a consideration of an appropriate, and firmly bounded, sexual division of labour. Should the taboo be broken, the effect would be extremely upsetting, not just for the male carer breaking the taboo, but also for the incontinent elderly person being cared for. Thus one can hypothesise that the taboo is reinforced, when it comes to the care of the elderly, by old people's own feelings, of what tasks it is appropriate for carers of different sexes to undertake. Women carers, no doubt sensitive to the feelings of their elderly relative, will avoid the crossing of this important boundary, so that order and the self-esteem of all concerned are maintained.

I have so far suggested that there are numerous factors which, at an ideological level, combine to present women with an image of themselves as 'natural' carers. But it would be mistaken to underestimate the effect of material factors, in particular the position of women in the labour market, that also dictate a sexual division of labour when it comes to informal caring at home. The point is a simple, and apparently intractable, one. Women's earnings in work are considerably less than men's: in 1980, female gross hourly earnings from part-time work were 51 per cent of men's gross full-time hourly earnings, and their full-time earnings were only marginally better, at 61 per cent of men's full-time earnings (Webb, 1982). Where there is any doubt about the expenditure of time when it comes to caring for an elderly relative, married couples will almost certainly find it cheaper if the wife reduces her working hours or stops work altogether and the husband continues to 'bring home the bacon' through his full-time work (Ungerson, 1983b). Indeed, one might speculate that husbands, in order to compensate the household's finances which have been depleted through the loss of the wife's earnings, will take on more paid work in the form of overtime or second jobs, thus reducing their availability for caring even further.

It is not beyond the bounds of possibility that the fact that it is cheaper for women than for men to give up paid work in favour of unpaid caring has come to the notice of the policy-makers who devised the rules for the allocation of the Invalid Care Allowance (ICA). As indicated earlier in this chapter, the ICA, which is intended to compensate carers for loss of earnings, is payable to single and married men, and single women. Married women are specifically excluded. The official reason given for this exclusion is that married women 'have, in any event, reason for staying at home which are not connected with the need to care for a severely disabled relative' (a Minister of the DHSS, quoted in Groves and Finch, 1983). But it may also be the case that DHSS Ministers are fully conversant with the effects of a discriminatory labour market. They understand that there are already financial incentives, in the form of reduced opportunity costs supplemented by husbands' earnings of a 'family wage', such that married women do not need an additional incentive to persuade them, where necessary, to give up paid work and take up unpaid caring. The managers of State benefits and the rules for their allocation can rest assured that material effects derived from the relative positions of men and women in the labour market reinforce and coincide with the ideological effects of the rules themselves.

It is ironic and paradoxical that the current cluster of proposals that the ICA be extended to married women (see, for example, EOC, 1982; Nissel and Bonnerjea, 1982; Oliver, 1983) would actually make the material incentives for married women to stay at home to care for their relatives even stronger than they already are. The arguments in favour of such an extension are posed in terms of two considerations. First, married women have just as much need as anyone else for recognition for the work of caring, and that the work is distinguishable from the more onerous than 'normal' housework. Second, most carers report that the direct costs of caring are considerable and not fully compensated for by the range of State benefits, such as Supplementary Benefit and the Constant Attendance Allowance, payable to the elderly dependent relative (Nissel and Bonnerjea, 1982). Thus, it is suggested, the payment of the ICA to married women would be a recognition of their labour of love and raise their sense of self-esteem. At the same time, it would be a welcome and needed supplement to household income. One cannot quarrel with either of these arguments. But it is important to bear in mind that, while the extension of the ICA would reduce the promotion, by the State, of the ideology that a married woman's place is primarily in the home, it would also materially increase the incentive for married women to stay in the home and care for a dependant. It is the operation of the labour market that places women on the horns of this cruel dilemma: however State benefits are arranged in future, the relative difference in men's and women's earning power will continue to ensure that married women, if they perceive that there is someone at home who needs their constant care and attention, are subject to a powerful incentive to stay there.

There are, however, two groups of potential carers of the elderly who are not likely to be subject to these constraints imposed by the labour market. These are, first, the carers who are the spouses of the elderly infirm and who, in many cases, are elderly themselves and retired from paid work, and second, the group of potential male carers who are of working age, but are unable to find paid work. In neither case will the material effects of male and female wage differentials come into play. Very little is known about either group. One can speculate, however, that in both cases the ideology of women's proper place will be amplified rather than reduced, and that the absence of powerful material factors is likely to make very little difference to the allocation of primary caring tasks to women.

In the case of elderly carers, one can hypothesise that in many cases the man will be defined as the 'dependant' and the woman defined as the 'carer'. This partially derives from reality, since women live longer than men and are generally slightly younger than their husbands; hence it is likely that they will become chronically ill at a later date than their husbands. But these classifications are also likely to be constructed, often by the elderly married couple themselves, since the idea that the husband is 'dependent' on the wife for her supportive services merely replicates the relationship they will have experienced throughout their married lives. The older people are, the less likely are they to want, or be able, to relinquish and change well-trodden paths: in these cases, a woman who may be regarded to outsiders as a 'carer' may prefer to see herself as the 'ordinary housewife' that she has always been. In order to maintain the order of their longstanding relationships, such women will maintain rigid sex roles, even at great personal cost to themselves (see above). Of course, where chronic illness strikes the wife rather than the husband, it is probable that special difficulties will arise since the servicing relationship will have to be turned on its head: in such cases there is plenty of evidence that the State, in the form of the social services, is likely to offer material help at a relatively early date in the dependency process (Hunt, 1970).

In couples of working age, where the man is unemployed, one might expect that this would give the couple the opportunity to experiment with role exchange, and, where there is an elderly dependant, for the man to take on the role of primary carer. However, the ideology of 'women's work' seems likely to become even more powerful in these circumstances.

Couples might well maintain traditional sex roles so as not to undermine the role of the man as chief breadwinner even further, for, should they do so, his sense of his masculine self might disappear altogether. Thus one can speculate that it is even less likely that, during the present high levels of male unemployment, men will adopt and adapt to domestic caring tasks. There are only sketchy pieces of evidence to confirm this view, but research in this important area is in progress. Should the hypothesis be confirmed, it will demonstrate that, in certain circumstances, particularly male unemployment, the ideology of domestic labour carries relatively more weight than material factors in the labour market.

I have argued in this chapter that, given the nature of the ideologies of the sexual division of labour, it is unlikely that men can be persuaded to take on the task of caring for the nation's elderly on an informal basis at home. Moreover, material factors in the labour market combine with these ideological factors to make doubly certain that women will continue to carry out these tasks. In a sense, then, the State has nothing much to worry about. The coincidence of the two social trends of increasing numbers of old people and, at the same time, the growth of women's participation in the labour market, will simply mean that women will, whether contemporaneously or consecutively, increasingly find themselves taking on a 'triple shift': the care of their husbands and children, the care of an elderly dependent relative, plus paid work (generally in a part-time capacity). When the task of caring for the elderly relative becomes too time-consuming and exhausting many women will decide that the relatively small wages they can command on the labour market are not worth the general stress that they experience, and reduce their hours in paid work or give it up altogether, thus depleting their own and the household's financial resources. Even where their men are unemployed women are unlikely to find the situation much altered.

The one group who will suffer are the women carers. We will find ourselves engaged in harder and harder work, in isolated circumstances, and faced with the prospect of caring for someone who will increasingly be unable to respond to our ministrations. Exhaustion and depression are almost bound to follow. What is to be done? Neither the State nor men have much interest in ameliorating the situation. It is, I am afraid, once more up to women to fight on a collective basis for the maintenance and expansion of the social services that are designed to help informal carers: home helps, community nursing, 'respite' care, aids for the disabled, home improvements for the disabled. On both an individual and collective basis we will have to resist definitions of ourselves as archetypal 'copers' and refuse to be fobbed off with the idea that the needs of men carers, of whom there will always be a few, should automatically come first. As Elizabeth Wilson has put it: 'We need more . . . campaigns' (Wilson, 1982). Women, as actual carers, and more particularly as potential carers (since they at least, have some time and energy left), must combine to obtain and ensure the maintenance of the social services we need.

NOTE

I am grateful to Sally Baldwin, Caroline Glendinning and Martin Knapp for their comments on an earlier version of this chapter. None of them is responsible for what remains.

8 Returning to Work

JUDITH CHANEY

There is extensive literature on women and employment which is largely based on census data and official employment statistics. It provides a cross-sectional, aggregated picture of the overall position of women in the labour market detailing the familiar picture of the concentration of women in low-paid, unskilled jobs and their segregation in a comparatively smaller number of industries[1]. The focus is on outcomes rather than processes. A further characteristic of this literature is that aggregated figures, whether regional or national, hide the variations in local markets both in the number and type of jobs available for women and in the relative balance between employment opportunities for men and for women. These differences have been considerable in the past, and remain so today; they are significant because of the immobility of most women workers[2]. It is hard to see how the relationship between paid employment and domestic responsibilities can be investigated without relating the employment of women to the development and organisation of industry in a given labour market, but, in general, this approach has not been followed in the sociological literature on women and work.

Since the mid-1950s a substantial number of studies of married women who work have been carried out. These include Myrdal and Klein (1956); Jephcott, Seear and Smith (1962); Klein (1965); Fogarty, Rapoport and Rapoport (1971); Rapoport and Rapoport (1971); Young and Willmott (1975). Veronica Beechey (1978) has written a critical analysis of the theoretical framework within which these studies have been undertaken. She argues that the *ad hoc* adoption of Parsonian functionalism led to a focus on the supply side of labour and diverted attention away from the type of jobs women took. In these studies industrialisation tends to be seen as a generalised cause of change without there being any analysis of how individual elements bring about particular kinds of change and how this might affect the employment of women. The return to work is not seen in terms of the jobs which women get but in terms of the implications of their employment for role-relationships within the family.

Another criticism which can be made of these studies is the comparative invisibility of working-class women. The Rapoports (1978) are explicitly interested in dual-career, professional families. But in other studies, for example Young and Wilmott (1975), this bias derives from the argument that the employment of wives is associated with the development of a more democratic, egalitarian family structure and that this structure filters down from the middle class to the families of manual workers. Many critics of Young and Wilmott have pointed out how flimsy the evidence is in relation to this thesis. None the less, implicitly, the main interest is upon the middle-class model of the future, the experience of working-class women is less well documented than that of middle-class women and some vague notion of 'cultural lag' fills the gap.

A very different perspective on women and work derives from the women's movement. Recent feminist writing has moved from a narrow concern with domestic labour to an analysis of the relationship between the sexual division of labour in the home and the production process. The value of male labour power is premised upon the existence of a family unit in which women perform domestic labour; thus when women become waged workers they represent a source of cheap labour which is subsidised by the family wage of their husbands. These advantages to employers can only be retained as long as women continue to have prime responsibility for childcare and the home. Humphries (1977) argues that this sexual division of labour became entrenched in the nineteenth century when, as part of the fight for a family wage, wives were pressured to stay at home thereby restricting the labour supply and driving wages up. In this analysis, discrimination against women is seen as being intensified by class struggle. In order to restrict the labour supply, trade-union pressure is for women to stay at home or act only as a reserve labour force in times of expansion. If this is not feasible, then Rubery (1980) argues that there will be trade-union pressure to segregate women occupationally, thereby lessening competition and maintaining skill status in male-dominated industries.

This approach offers a way of overcoming the traditional dichotomy between studies of women at work and studies of women at home and a theory which explains the vertical segregation of women in the labour market. However, comparatively few empirical studies have been undertaken utilising this perspective. In part this is because the theory locates the source of the inequality of women in employment so firmly in the sexual division of labour. It is easy to move from this argument to the assumption that studies of women entering paid employment have secondary importance because the outcomes are predetermined. Used in this way, patriarchy implies a structure which is fixed, or as Sheila Rowbotham has neatly put it, 'a kind of feminist base-superstructure model to contend with the more blinkered forms of marxism' (1979, p. 970).

The brief review presented here raises a number of questions:

(1) Within a general context of subordination, to what extent is it possible for women to manoeuvre for a better position in a local labour market? What resources do they have? What constraints exist?

(2) Do the constraints operate with most force at the point of initial entry to the labour market or when a return to work is made after a period of domesticity?

(3) What role do family and wider social network relationships play in the process of women returning to work?

(4) Using occupation as a partial indicator of class, what is distinctive about the experience of women re-entering semi-skilled and unskilled employment?

The chapter is based on an EOC-financed study, which in looking at the experiences of a group of working-class women in Sunderland, concentrates on the process of returning to work in a local labour market and attempts to discuss these issues (Chaney, 1981). The major part of the research was a survey of women who had returned to work since 1970 after a period at home. The fieldwork was carried out in a working-class area of Sunderland known to have a high female activity rate; 20 per cent of all households were contacted in order to identify women who had made at least one return since 1970 to paid employment, after a period at home; 175 women (83 per cent of those eligible) were interviewed.

Sunderland grew rapidly in the nineteenth century with an industrial structure based on shipbuilding and coal-exporting. In spite of the depression in the late 1920s and early 1930s, the dominance of shipbuilding and marine engineering was maintained until 1951 when 26 per cent of the male working population worked in this industry. From 1951 onwards the shipbuilding industry has declined; in August 1976 only 7.7 per cent of employed persons in Sunderland were working in shipbuilding[3]. These jobs have been replaced, but whereas the declining heavy industries were predominantly employers of male labour, the expanding industries provided a high proportion of jobs for women. Thus, according to census figures, between 1951 and 1971 the number of men employed in Sunderland rose by 5 per cent while the number of women in employment rose by 41 per cent. Department of Employment figures, calculated for a slightly smaller area than the County Borough, show make employment falling by 5 per cent between June 1971 and June 1976 and female employment rising by 8 per cent[4].

Table 8.1 compares the economic activity rates of men and women in Sunderland with national (England and Wales) figures. It shows, first, the persistently high male unemployment rate throughout the period, a rate which has since risen to 17.3 per cent in August 1980.[5] Second, it shows that Sunderland is distinctive in having a female labour market which has expanded faster than the national average, in conjunction with a labour market for men which stagnated and in recent years has actually declined. In 1976 the proportion of women in the labour force was 43 per cent — slightly above the national figure of 40 per cent. However, married women form a lower percentage of women workers (49 per cent) than is the case in Britain as a whole, where the figure is over 60 per cent.

The extent of male unemployment and the low wages of unskilled manual workers in Sunderland are such that, since the 1950s, the economic pressures on women to enter employment have been strong. Women returning to work in the 1970s were trying to enter a labour market which expanded in the two preceding decades but is now in decline. The number of jobs in the comparatively well-paid manufacturing sector has contracted rapidly and the segregation of women in low-paid service industries is

TABLE 8.1   *Economic activity rates, males and females,*
Sunderland County Borough (1971 boundaries) and England and Wales 1951—71

Economic activity as % of population aged 15 and over	1951		1961		1971	
	Males	*Females*	*Males*	*Females*	*Males*	*Females*
In work						
Sunderland	83.0	30.3	79.9	32.4	71.2	38.1
England and Wales	85.8	34.6	83.8	36.5	77.2	40.8
Economically active, out of work						
Sunderland	5.4	0.9	6.7	1.1	8.9	2.7
England and Wales	1.8	0.3	2.4	1.1	4.2	2.0
Overall economic activity rate						
Sunderland	88.4	31.2	86.6	33.5	80.1	40.8
England and Wales	87.6	34.9	86.2	37.6	81.4	42.8

SOURCE   *Census, 1971*

intensifying. These structural constraints of the local labour market were perfectly apparent to the women interviewed and influenced their attitudes towards work and their job-search behaviour.

As a background to the discussion of one particular return to work, respondents were grouped according to their patterns of movement in and out of employment, and the characteristics of women in each cluster were then compared. Five main patterns were identified:

(1) the two-phase pattern: 26 per cent of respondents approximated to the traditional sequence of a long break from work while their children were young followed thereafter by continuous employment;

(2) a long break for children followed by an interrupted work pattern: 20 per cent of the sample fell into this category;

(3) a short initial break followed by a longer period at home and then a discontinuous work pattern: this group (32 per cent of the sample) returned to work after the birth of the first child but then left work because of further pregnancies or childcare difficulties;

(4) continual movement between home and paid employment: 15 per cent of respondents were in this group which was the only cluster in which the skill levels tended to rise slightly;

(5) housewives with only one brief return to work: only 5 per cent of the sample were in this group, none were working or wished to work at the time of the interview.

These groups illustrate the varied work patterns of working-class women and the extent to which movement between home and paid employment is a recurrent feature of their lives. The patterns were not related to the kind of employment finally obtained. A diversity of jobs was found in each group but a decline in the skill level of employment characterised four out of five of the groups. Nor were these participation patterns related to skill levels or point of entry into the labour market. This suggests that factors other than simply the extent of discontinuity in a work history influence the position of women in the labour market.

In a low-income area the need to earn is self-evident, and factors such as the opportunity to meet people or the characteristics of jobs themselves appeared to have a negligible influence on the actual decision to return to work. It has been conventional in studies of women at work to distinguish between economic and social or emotional reasons for returning to work. Not only does this distinction enshrine the assumption that paid work is secondary to housework and that therefore women can be expected to give a special reason for working, but also it is too crude a distinction. It ignores the fact that money is a primary social reason for anyone working in this society. Paid employment gives a person a different status. When giving money as their reason for return to work women went on to talk about the change in their lives associated with this. Since husbands generally equated work with paid work, a return to work sometimes legitimated husbands sharing household labour. Paid employment was also regarded as an adequate reason for asking relatives to look after young children, thereby giving mothers a break. This was a request they did not feel able to make if they were at home and 'not working'. In a similar way, contributing to the household income, even if the amount was small, gave them a greater independence in buying items for the house and in their social life – 'it's a bit of fun and it's my money'. In short, when women take paid employment their effort is made visible in the same way that men's labour always has been. This recognition is a strong motivating factor.

Although paid employment brings improvements in status and living standards which are highly valued, there was an acceptance that men and women are defined by different responsibilities. Work was, at best, an increase in their independence of action, and the expectation that work should be a source of self-realisation was not widely held. Very few women therefore identified their family responsibilities as frustrating them from taking a job which they wanted. Instead they provided the boundaries within which jobs had to fit. For this reason, a quarter of women with husbands had not discussed returning to work with them prior to actually getting a job. The characteristics that respondents looked for in a job were, a job near home, part-time hours, and flexible work hours – all items relating to the fit with domestic responsibilities. Other women were seen as especially reliable sources of job information because they understood the problems. Job-search behaviour was passive, and informal: 50 per cent of the sample got their post-1970 return job directly or indirectly through friends or relatives, most of whom knew about the vacancy because they themselves were doing the same job.

There was a strong belief in the value of being 'spoken for', because the women were aware that they were not offering employers scarce skills but personal qualities, like reliability and conscientiousness – not qualities easily established in an interview where the ritual questions are asked and the requisite answers given:

> At your interview they ask you if you have someone to mind the children if they are bad. You say 'yes' to get the job knowing damn fine you haven't.

For this reason, women prefer to apply direct to former employers where their reputation is known. Where this is not possible the help of friends can be very important, and chains of recommendation develop.

It is clear that family and other social networks influence the process of returning to work in two ways. First, they influence attitudes towards work. The acceptance of the roles of wife and mother as the most important roles for women is accompanied by the expectation that men should be breadwinners. The majority of women interviewed were very anxious to emphasise that their own employment was no reflection on the willingness or ability of their husbands to provide. It appeared that the affirmation of their traditional domestic role was a way of protecting their husbands' status. Social networks reinforce these values, and the effect in terms of influencing ideas about employment was to find jobs which entailed a minimum disruption of family roles.

Second, networks act as a major channel of information about jobs. Information about jobs at all levels, from skilled non-manual to unskilled manual, came through social networks. However, jobs obtained in this way were found to be disproportionately concentrated in food preparation and domestic work, to be local, the hours worked to be short, and the jobs rated poorly by the re-entrants themselves. Women getting jobs in this way were not distinguished by any particular set of social characteristics. Their use of networks was related to the deterioration of the job market; as it deteriorates, competition for jobs increases; networks are efficient channels of information about forthcoming vacancies. Women for whom the formal channels have failed to produce jobs are inclined, when they hear through a friend that a workmate is leaving, to go after that job on the grounds that any employment is better than none. In any case the contraction of the manufacturing sector has meant that a higher percentage of available jobs are in unskilled service work of the kind that traditionally recruits workers through the grapevine.

What needs to be taken into account in any explanation is the acceptance of the primacy of women's domestic role and the need for jobs to fit in with domestic responsibilities. Combinations of circumstances — for example, help from husbands, older children who can look after themselves in school holidays, and help from relatives — reduce the pressure from these responsibilities and enlarge the range of jobs that could be considered. It therefore becomes a practical matter to search for jobs, within the limits of the labour market, on the basis of preferences for different types of work, or reward and setting. Women getting jobs through formal agencies and direct application are more likely to rate them interesting, well paid and the working conditions good. Where domestic responsibilities are not lightened, social networks produce, in the manner previously described, more realistic information about jobs.

The information on childcare arrangements illustrates the extent of this kind of restriction. Husbands and mothers account for 50 per cent of all childcare arrangements. Another 17 per cent did not work until at least one child was old enough to look after the others, and 13 per cent only worked during school hours.

The study also provided information about the extent to which the position of the women interviewed had improved or deteriorated in the course of their working lives. Life-history material is always difficult to analyse if respondents are at different points in their life-cycle. One method of analysis used was to take three fixed points in each work history: the job held between leaving school and first stopping work, the first return to work, and the post-1970 return to work. The distribution of occupations in the sample was then compared at these three points. Even this simple procedure presents some difficulties, because for 104 women, 59 per cent of the sample, their first return to work and the post-1970 return are identical.

The second method of analysis was to look at the number of individuals who have experienced various changes between these three points. Jobs were classified using the Registrar General's definitions of social class and socio-economic groups, the Standard Industrial Classification and CODOT classifications. The CODOT groups were subsequently amalgamated to form nine job-descriptive categories (see Table 8.3) which were particularly useful in analysing the jobs covered in this survey.

The average interval between leaving school and first stopping work was six years; 70 per cent stopped between the ages of 18 and 22, usually because of their first pregnancy. Most women had left school with no educational qualifications at all (95 per cent) and only three completed a training course after school. Of the sample, 55 per cent went into semi-skilled work — skilled non-manual and manual being the next largest categories. These jobs were concentrated in manufacturing industries (electrical engineering and clothing) and the distributive trades. All these jobs were full-time, but on their first return to work only 28 per cent worked full-time.

The results of the fixed-point comparison in Tables 8.2 and 8.3 show that a downward shift is associated with the number of returns made but that the greatest decline occurs at the first return. The movement out of semi-skilled manufacturing jobs appears abruptly at the first return to work, whereas the movement out of clerical jobs increases gradually with subsequent returns to work. The increase in the number of cleaners is

TABLE 8.2   *Comparison of jobs held by respondents using Registrar-General's categories of social class*

	Job 1	1st Return	Post-1970 Return
Intermediate occupations	1.2	0.6	0.6
Skilled non-manual	22.8	18.9	15.4
Skilled manual	6.4	1.7	1.7
Semi-skilled manual	55.0	41.1	38.3
Unskilled manual	14.6	37.6	44.0
	100%	100%	100%
	N = 175	N = 175	N = 71*

* This figure excludes the 104 for whom the post-1970 return was also the first return to work.

dramatic, up from 3.4 per cent to nearly a quarter of the sample at the first return to work and the increase continues with subsequent returns.

The data was used to see whether the decline in work profile was related to changes in the labour market rather than the number of times a woman stopped and started work. Since 1970 the job market for women

TABLE 8.3   *Job descriptions at three points in a work history*

	Job 1	1st Return	Post-1970 Return	Total Sample Post-1970 Return
Intermediate white collar	1.2	1.1	–	1.1
Routine white collar	23.4	21.2	12.7	19.4
Food preparation	3.5	15.4	16.9	18.9
Domestic/cleaner	3.5	24.0	42.3	30.3
Personal service	7.0	3.4	2.8	2.9
Assembly line worker in factory/machinist	47.4	18.9	15.5	13.1
Quality controller/checker	4.1	3.4	1.4	2.9
Unskilled packer	7.6	12.5	7.0	10.9
Miscellaneous	2.3	–	1.4	0.6
	100%	100%	100%	100%
	N = 175	N = 175	N = 71*	N = 175

* This figure excludes the 104 for whom the post-1970 return was also the first return to work.

in Sunderland has deteriorated. Any increase in jobs has been largely in low-paid, unskilled non-manufacturing jobs; the biggest loss of jobs has been in the comparatively well-paid manufacturing sector. The experience of women who made their first return to work *before* 1970 was compared with those who returned *after* 1970. The results show that the labour market changes are reflected in the distribution of jobs held after leaving school but that the pattern of movement from Job 1 to first return is very similar in both groups. The pre-1970 returners were more likely to have had their first job in manufacturing and were less likely to have started off in clerical work. The reverse was true for those returning after 1970. However, in both groups most losses occurred in manufacturing and most gains in cleaning jobs.

Another way of looking at this is to take the post-1970 returns made by all women in the sample and compare the jobs obtained by first returners with those obtained by women making a second or subsequent return. Such a comparison indicates that first-returners do better but that the pattern is not uniform. One-fifth of first returners got skilled non-manual jobs in comparison to 8 per cent of other women; 38 per cent as opposed to 52 per cent got unskilled manual jobs. However, among the multiple returners there are fewer in food preparation and more semi-skilled and skilled factory workers. The information on job changes made by individuals shows that in each of the work-history periods roughly half of the women change their jobs but do not change their skill level. Approximately one-third change to jobs of a lower skill level, leaving a minority who improve their skill level.

These results are in accord with those obtained from a re-analysis of National Training Survey Data undertaken at Warwick University (Elias and Main, 1982). This research indicated that with the exception of the teaching and nursing professions, the possession of qualifications was not significantly related to a woman's subsequent work experience. Women who initially enter low-skill occupations have fundamentally different work histories from other women workers; they experience more breaks in employment which are less evenly distributed throughout their lives.

Three broad points emerge from this discussion. First, the increase in employment opportunities for women in Sunderland between 1951 and 1976 has not changed the balance of economic dependence among this group of working-class women. In the area studied there is a high economic activity rate among women but their segregation in low-paid, unskilled jobs, their short hours and insecurity of employment, have meant that their economic dependence on men has changed little. This position corresponds to the classical idea of a reserve army of labour.

Second, the attitudes towards returning to work are related directly to the reality of the constraints of the local labour market. This knowledge of job opportunities and the evaluation of different jobs come largely from observing the experiences of other married women. Thus attitudes towards work are generated and sustained within a particular community; they are closely linked to ideas about the relationship between husband and wife and the nature of wider family obligations.

Third, the conjunction of these two sets of factors results in women seeing themselves as having a different relationship to work from that which men have. Work is the male sphere, work is essential for men; but for women, work complements their primary domestic role. For any individual woman, paid employment may represent increased independence, greater recognition of her contribution to family life, or even self-expression, but it does not undermine her primary responsibility for the home and the family. This is evidenced in the high priority given to part-time hours, flexible working hours, and other factors which relate to the 'fit' with home. This view of their relationship to work increases the vulnerability of women in the labour market. Differences in the bargaining power of groups of workers are influenced by the extent to which workers have alternative employment opportunities. The need for jobs to fit in with domestic responsibilities is an additional barrier to mobility and the pay and opportunities available to women will inevitably reflect this.

The findings of the study do suggest a number of areas where further research would be useful. There is a basic lack of information on work-history patterns among women. A lot of assumptions are made about interrupted work histories but we have very little knowledge of the nature and extent of the differences which exist among women, or of the extent to which class differences are related to particular patterns of labour market participation. Earlier in the chapter the comparative neglect of the empirical study of family and network relationships by 'feminist' writers was noted. The term 'feminist' has been used very loosely here and there are many different strands within this approach. However, it is fair to say that within this tradition the source of the inequality of women entering paid employment is located firmly in the sexual division of labour in the home. This research suggests that the extent of network support of different kinds — practical help, information, friendship — crucially affects the choices available to an individual. Networks can be seen as providing a social space which women can use to manoeuvre for a better position against the constraining forces of the labour market and the restrictions of conventional sex-role definitions. One way of beginning to study this is to look at the services which are exchanged between women, the patterns of reciprocity which exist, the relationship of these exchanges to the sphere of paid employment and the circumstances under which unpaid services become paid work.

Such an approach emphasises the supply side of labour and would be inadequate without equal emphasis being given to the demand for women workers. Two useful areas for further research would be the recruitment practices of firms in relation to married women, and the extent to which trade unions are prepared to foster the movement of women into jobs hitherto regarded as the preserve of men. The latter question is of great importance in the continuing debate about the explanation of the segregation of women in low-paid occupations. It has been argued (Rubery, 1980) that trade-union actions in protecting the living standards of the organised working class, create the segmentation of the labour market which affects women, young workers, and immigrants to a disproportionate extent. The ambivalence involved in the expectation that trade unions can protect the aspirations of women workers to move out of the ghettos of low-paid women's jobs, is especially acute in the present employment crisis.

NOTES

1. See, for example, Hakin (1979). One exception is a comparative study of policies relating to women re-entering employment in nine countries: see Seear (1971).
2. In 1912, for example, between 40 and 50 per cent of wives in Blackburn were employed, at a time when the national figure was only 10 per cent.
3. In addition to the Census, and Department of Employment Gazette, the main sources for this section are the two major studies of the industrial and economic structure of Sunderland: Robson (1969); Barron and Norris (1976).
4. Figures for Sunderland, Pallion and Southwick-on-Wear.
5. Published figures are for the Wearside Area which includes Seaham.

9 Women, The Family and Unemployment

JENNIE POPAY

For more than two decades following the Second World War the mass unemployment of the 1930s appeared to be a thing of the past, never to return. Hopes ran high as official figures for unemployment between 1948 and 1968 averaged around 1.6 per cent of the labour force, or 360,000 people. These golden days seem as distant now as the black days of the 1930s must have appeared to people during the 1950s and 1960s. In the past decade, unemployment has risen at an alarming rate, from 2.6 per cent of the labour force, or 600,000 people, in 1974, to over three million people, or one in seven of the labour force, in 1984.

As the numbers out of work have risen, so attention has focused, as it did in the 1930s,[1] on the economic, social and psychological consequences of being unemployed in a work-oriented society. But the research endeavours that have been stimulated, and the public debate that has ensued, are limited in two important respects. In the 1980s, unemployment is still largely perceived as an individual experience and one which predominantly affects men.

In the first place, official figures of the numbers of people who are unemployed do not give us an indication of the number of people who are actually experiencing unemployment — and how that experience is distributed. The overwhelming majority of the 3,004,600 people officially unemployed in February 1984 — be they men or women, adults or teenagers — are members of families. Whether they are husbands or wives, fathers or mothers, brothers or sisters, daughters or sons, even aunts, uncles and grandparents, an individual's experience of unemployment and its social and economic consequences can be expected to flow over and affect other family members. Given the division of labour within the domestic unit (which has been discussed in earlier chapters), the unemployment of any family member will place a disproportionate burden on women in the family — a burden which to date has been largely neglected.

The second flaw in the research and public debate focused on unemployment is that it is largely perceived as something which predominantly affects men. It is undoubtedly the case that, according to official figures, the majority of the unemployed *are* men. In February 1984, for instance, Department of Employment figures show that out of a total of 3,004,600 people unemployed, 2,117,200 of them — or just over 70 per cent — were men. But official figures underestimate the total number of women who are affected. However, the belief that unemployment is essentially a male experience does not only arise from the undercounting of unemployed women. It has also been argued that, given the very different relationship which women — particularly married women and those with responsibility for children and other dependents — have to the labour market compared with men, women's perception of their employment status and therefore their actual experience of unemployment will be very different from that of men.

The rest of this chapter explores these two issues in more detail. To begin with, a family perspective on unemployment and its effects is developed, exploring in particular the implications of this for women in families. Later, the extent and effects of female unemployment *per se*, again with particular reference to married women with dependents, are considered.

Using data from the British Government's General Household Survey (GHS) we are able to gain a picture of the family circumstances of unemployed men. It should be noted that the definition of unemployment used in this survey is broader than the official definition, in that it includes people actively seeking work in the week prior to the interview rather than only those receiving social security benefits because of unemployment.

Table 9.1 illustrates the incidence of unemployment for men aged 16 to 64, in different marital status groups, in 1980. It is clear from these data that the risk of being unemployed was less for married men than for men in all other marital status groups. While only 8 per cent of all married men were unemployed in 1981, this compares with 14 per cent of all single men and 14 per cent of all widowed, divorced and separated men. However, if married men only are considered, the rate for those with dependent children was slightly higher than those with no children. For men with four or more children it was more than three times as high as for those with none.

In addition to the incidence of unemployment among men in different marital status groups, it is also important to consider what proportion of all unemployed men are married with dependent children. As Table 9.2

TABLE 9.1　*The incidence of unemployment for men aged 16 to 64*
by marital status and number of dependent children, 1981

Single	14%
Widowed, divorced, separated	14%
Married	8%
Married without children	7%
Married with children	8%
with one child	6%
with two children	7%
with three children	14%
with four or more children	24%
All marital statuses	10%

SOURCE　*General Household Survey 1981* (HMSO, 1983) tables 4.3 and 4.8, pp. 92, 96.

illustrates, in 1981 a third of all unemployed men were married with children, 10 per cent of unemployed men were married with one child; 12 per cent were married with two children; 8 per cent were married with three children; and 5 per cent were married with four or more children.[2]

Both tables present data on what is known as the 'stock' of unemployed – that is, those men who are unemployed at one point in time. We also need to consider the flow into and out of unemployment: the groups of men which are at greatest risk of becoming unemployed and of remaining

TABLE 9.2　*The distribution of unemployed men aged 16 to 64*
by marital status and number of dependent children, 1981

Unmarried	46%	(29%)
Unmarried without children	45%	(28%)
Unmarried with children	1%	(1%)
Married*	54%	(71%)
Married without children	20%	(29%)
Married with children	34%	(42%)
with one child	10%	(16%)
with two children	12%	(19%)
with three children	8%	(6%)
with four children	5%	(2%)
All unemployed	100%	

* Figures refer to men living with wives of working age (that is, aged 16 to 59).
NOTE　Figures in brackets refer to respective proportions of economically active males.
SOURCE　*General Household Survey 1981* (HMSO, 1983) table 4.20, p. 103.

unemployed once they have lost their job. Longitudinal studies of the unemployed (studies which have followed a group of people over time) show that the unmarried experience the greatest risk of becoming unemployed. But they also show that married men with children (especially those with large families) are more likely to remain unemployed for long periods. A Manpower Service Commission Survey in 1980, for example, found that two-thirds of a sample of long-term unemployed men were married, and just over a third of married men and women had dependent children (see MSC, 1980, para. 4.1).

The effects on this picture of rising unemployment are complex. Between 1966 and 1971, when unemployment doubled, there was a marked shift towards families with dependent children. According to DHSS benefit data, the proportion of the unemployed with dependent children declined during the 1970s – a process perhaps partly explained by the quite dramatic increase in youth unemployment. But comparisons of recent years of GHS data show little change in the proportions of men in different marital statuses among the unemployed. GHS data do however suggest that fathers with three dependent children have experienced a sharp increase in the risk of unemployment compared with fathers with smaller families. In 1973 and 1975, for example, there was little difference in the incidence of unemployment for married men with between one and three dependent children. But in 1981, 14 per cent of fathers with three children were unemployed compared with 6 per cent of those with one child and 7 per cent of those with two children. GHS and DHSS benefit data then continue to demonstrate that men with large families are overrepresented among the unemployed, and that there has been an increase in the total number of children experiencing the unemployment of a parent. In December 1980, for example, there were three-quarters-of-a-million dependent children in families where the 'head' was receiving benefit because of unemployment. By May 1983, this figure had increased to 1.2 million.

There is also some evidence that unemployment is actually concentrated in some families. According to the 1981 GHS, while 61 per cent of the wives of working men were in work, only 33 per cent of the wives of unemployed men were. The unemployment rate among wives of unemployed men was also higher: 11 per cent compared with 3 per cent among those with a working husband (see *General Household Survey 1981*, p. 80). These data confirm the findings of earlier research which showed that:

The average family suffering unemployment is not cushioned by the earnings of secondary workers (at least wives) to anything like the extent suggested by the high incidence of secondary workers in the economy as a whole. The cushion is particularly thin for the families of unemployed unskilled workers, especially those with three or more children (Smee and Stern, 1978, p. 14)

There is also some evidence of other dimensions to this family con-centration of unemployment. For example, a recent small-scale survey of participants in the Community Industry Scheme found that 30 per cent of a sample of unemployed young people had one or both parents unemployed (Shanks and Courtenay, 1982). Given these family figures on unemployment, the question arises 'what do we know about the financial and other consequences for the families involved?'

The research suggests that unemployment results in a considerable drop in income (see Moylan and Davis, 1980, pp. 830–2). Among a 1978/9 DHSS cohort sample, for example, nearly 50 per cent were re-ceiving less than half the income they had been getting when they were in work. Only 6 per cent were, in fact, better off on benefit than they had been – a figure which according to the Institute of Fiscal Studies had dropped to around 2 per cent of the unemployed by 1983. Given these sorts of figures, it is not surprising that financial difficulties are a common experience among the unemployed. In a study carried out in 1980 by W. W. Daniels of the Policy Studies Institute, around 80 per cent of the respondents cited shortage of money as one of the worst aspects of being out of work (Daniels, 1981). Clearly, part of the explanation for these financial difficulties is, as mentioned already, the concentration of unemployment within families. Data from the Family Expenditure Survey in 1972 (though now dated) gives some indication of the effects of such concentration. They showed that the average household income of un-employed men with an 'independent' wife was nearly double that of those with dependent children; and where children rather than wives were earning, the household income was higher still (Smee and Stern, 1978).

The concentration of unemployment among previously unskilled and low-paid workers may also be a partial explanation of the financial diffi-culties faced by the unemployed. The 'occupational class' distribution of unemployment is illustrated in Table 9.3, and it reveals that semi-skilled and unskilled manual workers are over-represented among the unemployed. While they formed 26.7 per cent of the population at the time of the 1971 census, they made up over 60 per cent of the unemployed in 1981. This distribution is reflected in the findings from the DHSS cohort study, in that almost half of the sample said they had no

TABLE 9.3   *Proportions of men by occupational class who were
unemployed in 1981*

Professional and managerial	9.5%	(23.0%)
Clerical	6.3%	(11.9%)
Craftsmen	18.8%	(28.5%)
Semi-skilled	27.0%	(18.1%)
General labourers	35.5%	(8.6%)

NOTE   Figures in brackets refer to respective proportions of all men in the population in 1971.
SOURCES   Department of Employment Gazette, January 1982; Census, 1971.

savings at all. Contrary perhaps to popular opinion, redundancy payments did not help many unemployed. In the 1980 survey of the unemployed carried out by the Policy Studies Institute, for instance, 90 per cent of the sample received either no redundancy money or less than £500, and only 4 per cent had left their previous jobs with a total of £2,000 or more from all sources. But perhaps the most important factor explaining the financial difficulties associated with unemployment is the inadequacy of benefit provision, especially that for families with children and for the long-term unemployed.

The provision for children under the National Insurance Scheme and that for children under Supplementary Benefit differ from one another. In the case of the National Insurance related 'Unemployment Benefit', a Child Dependency Addition is paid at the same level for each child (regardless of age) on top of Child Benefit. However, this addition (which stood at fifteen pence per week per child at the end of 1983) is being phased out in 1984 in order to establish a single benefit for all children — Child Benefit — regardless of whether a parent is in or out of work. Child Benefit, however, is not being increased to compensate families experiencing unemployment for the loss of income this means. In order to be eligible for Unemployment Benefit, people who lose their jobs must have built up enough National Insurance contributions, and in any case Unemployment Benefit is only payable for one year. With over a third of the registered unemployed having been out of work for more than a year, and many others who having been in and out of work are unable to build up enough contributions, it is inevitable that an increasing proportion of the unemployed will have to depend on the means-tested Supplementary Benefit System (which provides different additions for children of different ages). At the end of 1983 over 50 per cent of the unemployed were receiving some supplementary benefit and 41 per cent were entirely dependent on it. On current rates of Supplementary Benefit (SB) a married couple with two children under 11 receive £61.80 a week to live on, excluding a housing benefit which nominally covers rent. In 1981, the average two-child family spent £124.75 a week, excluding housing costs, according to the Family Expenditure Survey. Many unemployed people are therefore expected to live on around 50 per cent of average expenditure.

The inadequacies of the child additions under the Supplementary Benefit scheme have been the focus of a great deal of criticism. In 1981, for instance, David Piachaud of the London School of Economics argued that these rates 'are below – for some ages substantially below – the estimated cost of modern minimum requirements for young children' (Piachaud, 1979). At that time, the rate for a child under 11 equalled £1.03 per day. By November 1983, it had been increased to £1.30 per day. The inadequacy of this provision is also recognised by the government-appointed Social Security Advisory Committee. In their first report in 1981, they argued that unemployment claimants with dependent children:

> must include people who are amongst the worse off of all supplementary benefit claimants. Families are bound to encounter all sorts of pressing needs for additional spending after a year on benefit (Social Security Advisory Committee, 1982)

In their second report in 1982, they reiterated their concern for the financial situation of people – especially families experiencing long-term unemployment (Social Security Advisory Committee, 1983). The particular problems of surviving for a long period on benefits are recognised within the social security system through the provision of a long-term rate paid after one year on benefit (worth £11.15 a week to a couple receiving supplementary benefit in 1984). However, with the exception of those people over 60 years old who do not register as unemployed, people experiencing unemployment are never entitled to this long-term rate. In December 1982 there were 600,000 unemployed claimants receiving supplementary benefit for over a year with responsibility for nearly half-a-million children.

We know surprisingly little about the effects of this limited income on the life-style of people experiencing unemployment. However, the DHSS cohort study found that a quarter of unemployed people living on Supplementary Benefit were in arrears with rents, rates or mortgages. More recently, research by Jonathan Bradshaw has demonstrated that people experiencing long-term unemployment spend a greater proportion of their income on food, housing, fuel and tobacco than do low-paid workers, and a smaller proportion on clothing, shoes, alcohol, transport and consumer durables. Only 25.5 per cent of the unemployed had a phone compared with 59.6 per cent of the employed, and only 11 per cent had a car compared with 66.7 per cent of those in employment (Bradshaw *et al.*, 1983). Research has indicated that poor families will try to make ends meet by cutting back on food. While this is unlikely to lead to *absolute* shortages in most cases, the effects on diet can be severe. A study of sixty-five families living on Supplementary Benefit conducted by Louie Burghes in 1980 found that overall consumption was low, meals were monotonous, and nutritional balance was lacking. Fruit and vegetables of any form – fresh, tinned or frozen – were missing from their diet, and in some cases parents missed a meal altogether (Burghes, 1980). As Martyn Harris has suggested:

> The general picture . . . is of a more housebound family, unable to afford trips to the pub, cinema, relations or friends, and unable even to phone them up. They watch a lot of television, smoke too much and have to spend too much money on laundrettes, pay phones, food from the corner shop and electric fires. (Harris, 1984)

Hilary Graham has pointed out that statistics on family income and expenditure deal with households and not with individuals:

> In so doing the assumption is made that income is pooled and shared out in such a way that all members of the household live at the same level of income . . . that all family members share equally in the command over resources and share equally in the benefits that these resources bring. (Graham, 1984)

However, research which sheds light on the nature of income distribution within the home suggests that assumptions such as these are not easily supported. Jah Pahl has elaborated a four-part typology of allocative systems within households, and these are illustrated in Table 9.4. The type of system which a particular couple 'chooses', appears to be determined by a number of factors, such as income level, source of income, and the normative expectations of the culture within which the household is located. In a recent review of research in this field, Rowena Burns suggests that among low-income families a 'whole wage' system managed by the wife is the most common (Burns, 1983/4). Jah Pahl postulates that this may be because 'when money is short, managing and budgeting become chores rather than a source of power within households' (Pahl, 1982a). Conversely, other research concerned with families in poverty suggests

TABLE 9.4   *Allocative systems within households*

A. *The whole wage system*, in which one partner, usually the wife, is responsible for managing all the finances of the household, except for the personal spending-money of the other partner.

B. *The allowance system*, in which, most commonly, the husband gives his wife a set amount of money and she is responsible for paying for specific items of household expenditure. The remainder is controlled by the husband, who pays for other specific items.

C. *The shared management system*, whose essential characteristic is that both partners have access to all household monies and share responsibility for house-hold expenditure.

D. *Independent management*, in which both partners have an income and retain separate responsibility for specific items of household expenditure. Neither has access to all household funds.

SOURCE   Pahl (1982a).

that in many cases it is the father who controls the income, passing a fixed amount to the wife (Land, 1977; Pahl, 1982). Whatever allocative system is chosen, however, it does appear that in low-income families it is the woman who typically assumes responsibility for meeting the family's collective needs – paying for food, fuel, rent and clothing. It is this division of responsibility which may mean that in families experiencing unemployment it is the woman who bears the brunt of the financial strain it can bring.

In a preliminary report from one of the few studies of family relations during times of male unemployment, Lorna McKee and Colin Bell describe how this division of responsibility may work:

> it was often the wives who had to live on their wits, variously hunting down bargains, devising new 'economic meals', locating borrowing sources, placating hungry children, refusing children spending money on treats, patching or mending clothes, going without food or taking less nutritional meals themselves and sometimes dealing with creditors. There is too some evidence of wives protecting their husbands from the financial reality or concealing their own worries about money. (McKee and Bell, 1983, p. 26)

McKee and Bell also suggest that the financial constraints associated with unemployment cause not only anxiety: for some women they may also mean a heavier 'managerial' role as women endeavour to 'make ends meet':

Shopping was reported by many to be a very elaborate routine involving visits to numerous stores and to an array of markets, rummage sales, charity events, buying one item here and one item there, finding the lowest price. (McKee and Bell, 1983, p. 29)

Clearly a time-consuming and exhausting process.

Research into the impact of unemployment consistently suggests that for a sizeable majority of men the experience is one of loss of self-esteem and identity, and of increasing social isolation imposed by financial constraints, shame, and the loss of the social networks of work. As the quote from Martyn Harris suggests, many unemployed men spend much of their time around the house, frequently bored and frustrated. Indeed, in the report of their survey of the unemployed in 1982, the Economist Intelligence Unit argues that:

The overall picture . . . is of half of all unemployed feeling that they have undergone character changes of some severity . . . It is alarming to consider the possible implications for a society which could have one in 16 households with a depressed or despairing member. 36% of those interviewed said that unemployment had made them less easy to live with. (Economist Intelligence Unit, 1982, p. 68)

The authors of the report could just as well have asked one to consider the implications of such a situation for women in the home.

As male unemployment has increased, there has been increasing speculation that men may be taking a greater share of domestic responsibilities. At least in low-income families, however, research exploring the division of responsibility in the home when *women* are unemployed does not support such a view. As women have moved into the labour force, it does not appear that they have in proportion shared their domestic responsibilities with the 'man in the house'. As one study of women factory workers found:

Employment had to be fitted in with household duties and child care arrangements, which they and their families regarded as unquestionably their responsibility . . . Most of the women interviewed received little assistance with housework from their husbands or older children. (Shimmin *et al.*, 1981, pp. 344–9)

It would seem that male unemployment has had little effect on this situation. The previous discussion suggests that wives retain responsibility for managing many domestic financial transactions. The work of McKee and Bell also suggests that they retain prime responsibility for childcare and housework, while having an unemployed male around may actually introduce additional work. Housework, for example, was frequently thwarted by the husband's presence, and child-rearing practice could become a source of conflict. For some women, the husband's intervention in the domestic domain represented an unwelcome and perhaps threatening intrusion into areas where they had previously been able to exercise sole control (McKee and Bell, 1983, p. 28). Women's 'job satisfaction' in their domestic role may, therefore, be reduced during times of male unemployment.

The work of McKee and Bell also indicates that male unemployment may adversely affect the social life of wives above and beyond the effects imposed by financial constraints. In some cases, for example, 'wives' social ties and interaction patterns could be devastated [as] friends stay away . . . as wives were discouraged by husbands from pursuing an independent social life' (McKee and Bell, 1983, p. 28). We do not know what effects these types of situation are having on the health and well-being of the women involved. Research does indicate, however, that the wives of unemployed men are at increased risk of developing symptoms of depression and anxiety. In one American study the wives of unemployed men were found to have developed an increased incidence of peptic ulcers (Cobb and Kasl, 1977, p. 180).

A partner's unemployment *may* not be a wholly negative experience for some women. Domestic tasks may be shared or roles within the home actually reversed. In his case study of twenty-two families experiencing male unemployment, Leonard Fagin suggests that for a few of the wives this was so:

> the reversal of roles with husband staying at home cooking, cleaning and shopping and often looking after the children while they went out to work, was taken as an opportunity for self discovery and used to change assumptions about themselves. (Fagin, 1981, p. 710)

But in these cases, wives' new-found assertiveness and freedom may be difficult for the husband to accept, and there is some suggestion that unemployed men may actively discourage their partners from finding employment, or at least women may choose not to seek work for the sake of their partners' self-respect.

Reference has already been made to the reduced economic activity rate among the wives of unemployed men. There are several possible explanations for this. The earnings rules attached to the receipt of benefit — particularly supplementary benefit — may discourage wives from working, especially when their opportunities are restricted to low-paid jobs. Alternatively, it is known that both unemployment and employment opportunities tend to be concentrated in certain geographical areas, and this may be a more important influence on the lower participation rate (the high rates of unemployment among wives of unemployed men). Data from the cohort studies of the unemployed suggest that husbands' unemployment had little effect in the short term on wives' participation in the labour market. But it cannot be concluded that it had no effect in the longer term, for a high proportion of the men in these samples had had previous spells of registered unemployment and it is possible that wives had responded to a situation prior to the one being studied (Moylan and Davis, 1980, p. 832). The research of McKee and Bell does show that male unemployment can have profound implications for female employment. They identified a complexity of influencing factors:

> The fragmentation of wives orientation to and participation in waged work was bound up not just with the structural opportunities for women's work, or with the period in the life cycle and availability of child care facilities, but also importantly with the operation of the social security system and with social values about 'proper' marital and parental roles. (McKee and Bell, 1983, p. 23)

The evidence that is available, therefore, suggests that far from being an individual male experience, unemployment can have profound ramifications for other family members and in particular for women. In many cases they may be carrying a disproportionate burden of the financial worries, and their position as wife—mother (along with the social networks they have developed) may be threatened. The data that have been presented have focused on the unemployment of a male partner, but it would be logical to expect that the unemployment of teenage children may have similar repercussions. Indeed, unemployment has been aptly described by McKee and Bell as men's loss but women's problem. But what of women's unemployment *per se*? How does their own unemployment affect them and the families of which they are a part? To quote from *The Times*:

> We have entered a period of long term world wide unemployment and the essential question is who is not to work. High amongst such candidates must be married women who have work to do at home but prefer not to do it. (Butt, 1982)

This statement reflects a widespread devaluation of the importance of the paid work done by women — especially married women — to both themselves and their families. Given such a view, it is perhaps not surprising to find that female unemployment is neither as visible nor perceived to be as important as male unemployment. But what we do know about the extent of women's unemployment; how do women themselves perceive unemployment; and how does a woman's unemployment affect her and her family?

According to Department of Employment figures, women represented just under 30 per cent of all those unemployed in February 1984, and the majority of these were single women. However, official figures are widely acknowledged to be an underestimate of the number of people actually looking for work, and this underestimate appears to be particularly large for women, especially for married women.

Official unemployment statistics are now derived from DHSS benefit data, the monthly count being the number of people in receipt of benefit through unemployment. This change was introduced in October 1982, and comparisons indicate that it depressed the figure for male unemployment by 4 per cent and for female unemployment by 12 per cent. More recently, changes in the position of men over 60 (who are now allowed to claim the long-term rate of supplementary benefit provided they do not register for work) appear to have increased the difference between the old and new counts for men to over 9 per cent.[3] Data based on receipt of benefit will inevitably disqualify many married women from the figures, because their benefit entitlement is often adversely affected by their particular pattern of employment. Over 80 per cent of all part-time workers are women, whose pay may be insufficient for them to have to pay National Insurance contributions and so for them to have unemployment benefit entitlement. The possibility that part-time female workers will earn below the threshold is quite high, because women are disproportionately concentrated in low-paid jobs. Women are also more likely to leave the labour market for child rearing — though the length of time they are out of the labour market has been falling significantly in recent years. An intermittent employment history will also affect benefit entitlement. Even when in work and earning over the threshold for National Insurance contributions, about 60 per cent of married women in 1978 were nevertheless paying the reduced 'married women's stamp', which does not entitle them to benefit in their own right. To compound the difficulty, in most cases women in two-parent families have no independent right to supplementary benefit if their national insurance contributions are too low or their entitlement to Unemployment Benefit runs out.

Women's right to register as unemployed and to claim Unemployment Benefit has also been adversely affected by changes in the regulations concerning 'availability for work' tests, as well as reluctance by some Department of Employment officials to accept a desire for part-time work (or restrictions on time and mobility) as 'availability'. In a recent study of two groups of women clothing workers made redundant by a large textile company, Angela Coyle documents how such discrimination against women operates:

> The majority of working women have pressures on their time arising out of domestic responsibilities and so, many limit the hours they are prepared to travel for reasons of time and cost. Several women in the sample reported that they had been disqualified from benefit because they had refused to take jobs offered:
>
> > 'I did register. I started getting Unemployment Benefit in February. I got about £27. I don't get that now though, I got suspended for refusing two jobs . . . They offered me a job at Allerton, well that meant getting two buses which wasn't worth my while.'
>
> Men are also selective about the work they are prepared to do. All of the male cutters were still out of work twelve months after redundancy. Yet they still continued to restrict their availability to work requiring those (increasingly obsolete) skills without incurring the same penalty as women. (Coyle, 1983/4, p. 76)

In the event of the removal of these restrictions, married women would still be less likely to register as unemployed because 'unemployment' is a concept which many of them do not apply to themselves, even though they may be 'looking for work'. The most common reason for not using such a definition would seem to be that women regard working within the home to be 'work' in its own right. Angela Coyle suggests that this is combined in some cases with a nervousness about job centres and employment offices. In fact, some of the women in her sample did not know how to register, or thought they had registered when they had claimed a tax rebate. Given this situation it is likely that a significant number of women who are eligible for benefit and 'available for work' may not be claiming. It is difficult to get a precise figure for this, but a campaign to encourage women to register as unemployed for the purpose of claiming benefit in the London Borough of Greenwich (in 1983) discovered that 20 per cent of women had wrongly thought themselves ineligible for benefit.

These barriers to married women registering as unemployed effectively create a self-fulfilling prophecy. Women are actively discouraged from registering since unemployment is deemed to be less important for them than it is for men. Yet when they do not register it is seen as a reflection of *their own* view of its unimportance. But there is strong evidence to suggest that official figures seriously underestimate the number of married women who are actively looking for work outside the home. According to 1981 General Household Survey data, for example, 41 per cent of *married* women who had been actively seeking work in the week before being interviewed were not officially registered as unemployed, compared with 6 per cent of men and 16 per cent of unmarried women. In addition, an unknown number of women would take employment if it were available, even though they would not define themselves as actively seeking work.

One of the principal factors behind assumptions that married women's employment is not really important is the widely held belief that most of them are working for 'pin money' — for the extra luxuries or frills that can easily be forgone. But how accurate is this assumption? There has been, over recent decades, an increase in the number of two-parent families where both parents work. The proportion rose from 54 per cent of all couples of working age in 1973 to a peak of 58 per cent in 1979. The figure then fell to 53 per cent in 1982, reflecting the impact of higher unemployment. Nevertheless, in the same year it was still the case that 50 per cent of families with one or two children, 37 per cent with three children, and 28 per cent with four or more children, had two earners.

Obviously, the fact that these families have both parents in work does not by itself dispel the 'pin money' myth, but figures for trends in family income over recent decades do. As married women have moved out in the labour market, their earnings have compensated to some extent for the combined effect of the failure of Child Benefit to consistently keep up with an increasing cost of living and of changes in the tax system which have disproportionately affected families with children. For those on average earnings, for example, the amount of income tax paid between 1960 and 1983 increased by 74 per cent for a single person, by 110 per cent for a married couple, by 308 per cent for a married couple with two children and by 696 per cent for a couple with four children (Study Commission on the Family, 1983). Married women's unemployment may therefore have a significant effect on family income in two-parent families. In the late 1970s the earnings of one-third of wives made up between 30 per cent and 50 per cent of family income, and one recent small-scale study of families caring for handicapped people estimated that the cost of losing a wife's earnings in this situation could amount to some £4,500 per annum (Nissel and Bonnerjea, 1982, p. 56).

With the increasing rate of divorce, there are also more and more women who are sole breadwinners in families. One child in seven is now living in a one-parent family, and over 87 per cent of these parents are women (Popay, 1983). If a lone-parent is able to find employment, the risk of that family living in 'poverty' (in the sense of having an income less than 120 per cent of supplementary benefit entitlement) is much reduced. In a study conducted by Richard Layard and David Piachaud, only 37 per cent of working lone-parents were in 'poverty', compared with 87 per cent of 'non-working' one-parent families (Layard *et al.*, 1978).

Interview-based research with unemployed women supports the conclusion that female unemployment can have severe financial consequences. In a survey in Lewisham, for example, female unemployment had affected family income immediately and severely. Over 58 per cent of the women in the sample said that their wages made up half of family income (Macrae *et al.*, 1981). In Angela Coyle's research on women textile workers, the women all received redundancy pay, which meant that the financial impact was not so sudden. But as unemployment continued, the effects gained strength. Both of these surveys involved small samples of women, and so do not give the same kind of results as the three large-scale cohort studies of male unemployment, but they do indicate that female unemployment can have severe financial consequences for the women involved and their families.

There are further consequences when women lose their jobs. It has already been noted that research into the psychological consequences of unemployment has concentrated almost exclusively on men. The results of these studies indicate that unemployed men are at much greater risk of mental illness and depression than men in work. What little research has been done on the psychological consequences of female unemployment suggests that the effects are generally less severe. However, it also shows that the impact on single women is significantly different from that on married women, with the experience of single women more closely paralleling that of men. It is to be expected that women with a stronger attachment to the labour market would feel the loss of a job more than those for whom employment is less important. But there are grounds to question the all-too-common response that 'married women don't *need* to work in the same way that men do'. Angela Coyle argues that:

a woman's wage purchases for her a crucial independence within the family and the loss of that independence is commensurate with the difficulties unemployed men experience over the loss of their bread-winner status. (Coyle, 1983/4, p. 80)

Her survey of women textile workers revealed that, initially at least, un-employment gave many of the women an opportunity to 'catch up' on domestic tasks, so providing relief from the stress of combining two jobs. But in this sample of women the sense of relief, and the protection afforded by being able to fall back on the domestic role, lasted only a limited time: 'After a while, the unemployed women faced a surplus of unstructured time.'

These women do appear to have had a strong attachment to the labour market, often working much of their adult lives in the same factory. But there is further research which supports the view that employment is important to the psychological well-being of many married women. In a study by George Brown and Tirril Harris of depression among working-class women, it is cautiously suggested that having employment outside the home may protect women against depression when other factors in their circumstances predispose them to it (Brown and Harris, 1978). The research of Raymond Cochrane and Mary Stopes-Roe confirms this finding. In relation to the much higher incidence of psychological dis-turbance among women compared with men which has been reported in a number of studies, these authors suggest that:

many fewer women than men are in employment and it is towards unemployment rather than marital status, that we should be looking as a major determinant of sex differences in psychopathology. (Coch-rane and Stopes-Roe, 1981, pp. 373–81)

One final consequence of female unemployment should be noted, and again one which is most commonly discussed in relation to male unemployment alone. This is the phenomenon of 'deskilling'. Research into the effects of periods out of the labour market related to child-bearing suggests that women frequently re-enter the labour market at levels of skill below those of when they left. It would appear that un-employment reinforces the process whereby women are restricted to low-paid unskilled and insecure jobs, with few if any employment rights or career prospects.

Both the Lewisham study and the study of women textile workers discovered this process. The latter showed that:

After one year, only 19 of the 30 women were back in work, eight in full time work and two as homemakers. The majority found work as domestics in hotels, hospitals and old people's homes and without exception they had accepted lower pay and less favourable conditions. (Coyle, 1983/4, p. 82)

In this chapter I have argued that unemployment is not, as it is usually depicted, an 'individual' experience affecting only men (and *perhaps* single women). As far as female unemployment is concerned, it is important for research not to conflate the experience of women in one marital status with that of women in another. It is essential that research is sensitive to the anomalous position of women who are married or who have dependents in relation to the labour market. As Angela Coyle has pointed out, it is anomalous 'not because women do not know their own minds, but because their dual role contains its own ambiguities'. However, although the research base is not as extensive as it is in the case of male unemployment, it is possible to identify more similarities than differences in the economic, social and psychological consequences of male and female unemployment. In addition to their own unemployment, there is also much evidence that women carry a further burden. Within families experiencing unemployment – whether women are themselves employed or not – it would appear that very often they take the main responsibility for managing a severely reduced family income, for performing the domestic and child rearing tasks, and for providing emotional support to other unemployed family members be they partners or children. These perspectives on unemployment need to be taken much more seriously both within public policy and within research.

NOTES

1. For a flavour of the research conducted during the 1930s, see Bakke (1937); The Pilgrim Trust (1938); Jahoda (1972).
2. The following discussion draws heavily on work undertaken with Lesley Rimmer of the Family Policy Studies Centre. For further data relating to Tables 9.1 and 9.2 see Rimmer and Popay (1982).
3. The Unemployment Unit, London, compares unemployment figures produced by the Department of Employment with those based on the old method of counting.

10 Do We Really Know What 'The Family' Is?

JON BERNARDES

The theme of this book not only implies a relationship between family life and economic life but also presupposes a clear understanding of the two concepts of 'family' and 'economy'. This chapter focuses upon the former concept and will present evidence and argument to support the contention that we are, as scholars and as everyday participants, remarkably ignorant about family life. Following this, it will be made clear that a critical reappraisal of the nature of family life is a fundamental prerequisite for the development of an adequate understanding of the relationship between family life and economic life. Further, it is concluded that the issues of ideology and the social construction of reality are both central to any examination of this relationship.

One of the most interesting facets of studying family life is the surprisingly protean nature of the central concept of 'the Family'. Quite simply the concept can and does refer to a wide range of disparate phenomena, from organised crime (the Mafia is sometimes known as 'the Family') to humanity itself ('the Family of Man'); from mere consanguinity (people related by blood) to much more limited procreative units ('starting a family'); and from sacred institution (the major religions) to vilified tyranny (some radical feminists: see Greer, 1970, pp. 219–38; Firestone, 1971, pp. 183–224; Oakley, 1976, pp. 222–41). Recently, family life has re-emerged not only as an area of growing academic interest (Rapoport *et al.*, 1982) but also as both a fit symbol for political slogans (Craven *et al.*, 1982, p. 11) and the subject of popular public interest (Mount, 1982; Berger and Berger, 1983).

Among the range of topics addressed by sociology, family life is perhaps the single most taken for granted. The bulk of the population grow up in situations referred to as 'families', and most members of our population are eager to discuss their own first-hand experience and knowledge of family life. Much academic literature on 'the Family' seems to take this popular familiarity for granted as a common 'knowledge base' from which to commence discussion and analysis. However, far from making family life easy to explore sociologically, this popular familiarity makes the subject one of the most difficult areas of human social life to study. This is perhaps why a social scientific discipline, which has a long tradition of critical analysis of 'social institutions', has itself been criticised for failing to develop a critical theory of family life (Morgan, 1975, p. 3). More recently there have emerged criticisms of 'the Family'[1], criticisms of previous debates about 'the Family'[2], an attempt to 'capture the middle ground' between those attacking and those defending 'the Family' (Berger and Berger, 1983) and some criticisms of extant family theory (Bernardes, 1981). Unlike any of these strategies this chapter is intended to open the way for the development of a critical theoretical approach to understanding behaviour within everyday families and the relationship between everyday family life and the wider society.

While one hesitates to characterise an entire field of sociological study there does seem to be a fairly clear recent view that 'traditional family sociology'[3] has adopted a central 'ideal type' model of a presumed dominant 'nuclear family' or 'typical' family. The major assumptions underpinning this model are perhaps best described by the Skolnicks (1974b, pp. 7—8) who also present a neat summary of the image of this 'normal' family:

> During the 1950s and 1960s, family scholars and the mass media presented an image of the typical, normal or model American family. It included a father, a mother, and two or three children. Middle class, they lived in a single-family home in an area neither rural not urban. Father was the breadwinner, and mother was a full-time homemaker. (Skolnick and Skolnick, 1974a, p. 435)

While this model was formulated in American terms, most scholars in the United Kingdom felt that such an image was also true of the British scene and adopted very similar models[4].

Since the beginning of the 1960s, however, there have emerged several different bases for a critical analysis of the adoption of a simple model of the family. First, the emergence of what Morgan calls the 'radical psychoanalytical' approach to the family (Morgan, 1975, ch. 5) epitomised in the work of R. D. Laing and David Cooper (Laing, 1971; Cooper, 1972).

Second, and perhaps more important, was the emergence of radical feminism. Morgan argues that:

> Undoubtedly, one of the main challenges to mainstream sociology of the family has come from the body of writing associated with the Women's Liberation or radical feminist movement. (Morgan, 1975, p. 134)

Beyond these two particular sources, it is important to recognise the 1960s as being characterised, at least in part, by criticisms and rejections of the 'status quo'[5]. It is vital to grasp that criticisms, from radical feminism and radical psychoanalysis as well as less specific sources, did not criticise the adequacy of the ideal-type model as an accurate description of reality. Until very recently it was not unusual to find authors like Talcott Parsons (Parsons, 1971a, pp. 53–66) and Ann Oakley (Oakley, 1976, pp. 222–41) in apparent agreement as to what the family *is*, despite obvious conflicts over the virtue of the family.

A third base for critical analysis emerged in the early 1970s under the auspices of Marvin B. Sussman. His contribution is remarkable in that he actually posed the question of how common is the single wage-earner nuclear family. The attempt to answer this question involved the use of US census date to reveal that such families represented around 30 per cent of American family situations (Cogswell and Sussman, 1973, p. 139). This approach was subsequently adopted by the Rapoports who published the same table relating to American data in their discussion of 'Diversity of Parental Situations' (Rapoport *et al.*, 1977, p. 93). The Rapoports attempted to move beyond simple census-based counts of particular family structures to include an assessment of more qualitative variant or diverse family forms, such as stepfamily arrangements and families with handicapped children. I have estimated, using 1971 UK census data, that the proportion of 'normal families' was around 18 per cent of all family situations in the early 1970s. The estimate was, however, deliberately conservative in terms of the limited number of dimensions recognised as constituting variant family forms (Bernardes, 1981, p. 91). This approach was also adopted and developed by the Study Commission on the Family (Rimmer, 1981, pp. 61–2), which has performed the valuable task of popularising the idea that there is no single form of 'typical' family but rather complex and subtle variation and diversity. I have estimated that there are at least two hundred items relating to variations within, and alternatives to, 'typical' family life (Bernardes, 1981, pp. 423–5).

It is not enough, however, to simply observe variation and diversity.

Much past sociological theory about family life has been based upon the notion of a 'typical' pattern or 'ideal type' of family. Clearly we need to locate when and how a central 'ideal type' notion of the family became suspect in order both to ascertain which elements of previous theory remain valid and, of course, to understand the historical relationship of family and economy.

Strangely, few commentators have actually addressed the issue of how and when the 'typical' or 'ideal type' pattern of the family became redundant. The Rapoports, in acknowledging a 'lag between behaviour and the appropriate conceptual models' (Rapoport *et al.*, 1977, p. 129), seemed to imply that behaviour had changed fairly recently. Rimmer, drawing upon another comment by the Rapoports, supports the view that the model of the typical family is 'increasingly unrealistic' (Rimmer, 1981, p. 61). Perhaps clearest, though, is Peter Laslett's assertion that 'there is now no single British family' (Rapoport *et al.*, 1982, p. xii). Laslett also argues that 'This [nuclear model] had prevailed almost universally in our country until the 1950s' (ibid, p. xi).

On the other hand, Jessie Bernard has explicitly recognised the error of speaking of 'the "American family" as an institution' (Bernard, 1942, p. 245). Harris has recognised that 'the British family' was only the 'name of a constructed model, and not of a social fact' (Harris, 1974, p. 36). Harris has also argued 'It is not likely, then that there will be found one distinctive type of urban family' (Harris, 1970, p. 35). Moreover, Sussman has argued:

> Undoubtedly, in this society from its very beginning, there has been an assortment of family structures . . . [in] which the nuclear family unit . . . is but one. (Sussman, 1973, p. 3)

To summarise this review of 'the Family' in sociological literature. During the 1960s and 1970s various radical bodies of thought criticised 'the Family' itself. During the latter decade evidence of diversity and variation in family forms emerged. These recognitions have begun to gain widespread acceptance but are, it must be admitted, by no means universally accepted even today. Among those who accept variation and diversity there have emerged two views as to how and why single central concepts of the 'typical' or 'ideal type' family are now redundant. One view holds that recent social trends (divorce, rise of single parenthood, and so on) have generated diversity and variation. A second view holds that family life has always been diverse and varied and that we have only recently come to recognise the inadequacy of our theoretical tools. Clearly there is something of a dilemma here. There exists not only the competing analyses of the existence and demise of 'the Family' but also a further dilemma not yet made explicit in the literature, namely how to proceed with the theoretical analysis of family life if we do abandon the central notion of a 'typical' family pattern.

While it is tempting, and sometimes fashionable, to assert that both parties in a controversy are in a sense 'right' and vary only in terms of differing 'theory', I believe that this controversy about the demise of 'the Family' can be resolved. Research reported elsewhere has convinced me that family life has been a diverse and varied phenomenon, at least throughout the twentieth century in the United Kingdom and United States (Bernardes, 1981, ch. 3). The issue is not whether 'the Family' once existed, but how sociologists have ever believed that there existed a single central dominant 'type' of family, be it labelled 'nuclear', 'conjugal' or whatever. It has already been noted that popular familiarity with 'the Family' makes the issue of family life an extremely difficult topic to explore sociologically. In 1945, Komarofsky and Waller observed about those who study family life:

The worker in the field is shackled by taboos and ancestral superstition, which he has the more trouble combatting because they are in his mind as well as his environment. We are able to observe only what the mores permit us to see. (Komarofsky and Waller, 1945, p. 443)

Similarly, Moore has argued that:

In reading these and similar statements by American sociologists . . . I have the uncomfortable feeling that the authors despite all their elaborate theories and technical research devices, are doing little more than projecting certain middle-class hopes and ideals onto a refractory reality. (Moore, 1965, p. 161)

At the simplest level, then, it is important to recognise that the term 'the Family' is far from being a simple neutral descriptive label. One strategy is to recognise that the term itself can and does have a variety of levels of meaning. This approach involves two serious risks. In the first place, it is simply very difficult to continually distinguish different uses of the term. Second, such an approach does not enable one to deal with the very wide range of variation and diversity in family forms which is becoming apparent. At some point one particular meaning of the term 'the Family' must still mask a host of different kinds of family situations. An alternative strategy to understanding the emphases placed upon 'the Family' is to explore the way in which both popular and sociological attempts to understand family life have tended to compel commentators to adopt a single central concept.

First and foremost one must recognise the nature of what has become known as family ideology. In the United States in 1973, Skolnick discussed 'the nuclear family ideology' which 'includes assumptions about the naturalness, emotional intensity, self-sufficiency and balance of the nuclear family unit' (Skolnick, 1973, p. 13). More recently in the United Kingdom, Segal has neatly summarised the core of contemporary family ideology:

Our traditional family model of the married heterosexual couple with children – based on a sexual division of labour where the husband as breadwinner provides economic support for his dependent wife and children, while the wife cares for both husband and children – remains central to all *family ideology*. (Segal, 1983, p. 13)

Clearly, everyday actors draw upon this extant ideology in forming their own opinions and moral evaluations of family life. From dominant sections of society such as the media, emerges what Skolnick refers to as a distinct 'usage' of the term 'nuclear family' (Skolnick, 1973, p. 13). These distinct non-sociological usages present a two-fold problem in that they may be incorporated into working theoretical constructions by family sociologists and may also be used as an interpretive device by non-specialists reading the work of family scholars. Thus, of course, there arises a full circle of complexity and confusion. Being at least partially submerged in his or her cultural setting, the family sociologist inevitably abstracts parts of family ideology in his or her use of language and, language being as ambiguous as it is, it is very difficult to sustain a 'purely theoretical construct' use of a word throughout an argument. Further, non-specialists (and even some specialists) are likely to employ (albeit unwittingly) some parts of family ideology as interpretive devices in reading and seeking to understand theoretical arguments. In this way, then, family sociology has been unable to avoid actually incorporating, or appearing to incorporate, at least part of the notion of 'the Family' as enshrined in family ideology.

While the nature of family ideology clearly does have something to do with the power of a central concept of 'the Family', this can only be a part-explanation. The sociologist often confronts concepts deeply enshrined in everyday ideology in several fields: why should the concept of 'the Family' be particularly potent? I believe that we need to seek further explanations of the immense symbolic power of the notion of 'the Family'.

The working assumption of this chapter is that traditional family sociology made a central theoretical mistake in assuming the existence of 'the
Family', and a further mistake in constructing ideal-type models of 'the
Family'. The nature of, and reasons for, these mistakes will be explored,
not only because it is obviously important to 'correct' previous errors, but
also because the reasons for such mistakes are likely to illuminate the
process of theory formulation. Moreover, given the role of 'the Family' in
contemporary ideology and morality, an exploration of the reasons behind
such mistakes is likely to illuminate the nature of ideology in contemporary
society.

   The explanatory analysis here will proceed by examining four areas of
the sociological attempt to understand family life. The aim is to identify
ways in which these areas of sociology have both incorporated elements of
popular family ideology and also tended to be formulated in such a way
as to make a single central conception of 'the Family' indispensable.

   The first area to examine is that of macro-theoretical approaches to
family life. To consider family life, one is inevitably also involved in considering central and fundamental issues about the nature of society, not
least of which issues are reproduction and childrearing, the 'purpose' or
'function' of the family unit, and changes in family life associated with
major socio-historical events. Quite simply it would not have been possible
to consider these issues *without* a single central ideal-type notion of 'the
Family'. Three issues will be examined here: universality; functionality;
family and industrialisation.

   The major sources for the debates about the universality of the nuclear
family is the work of George Murdock. As a result of examining data on
250 societies throughout the world, Murdock asserted that:

> The nuclear family is a universal social grouping. Either as the sole
> prevailing form of the family or as the basic unit from which more com-
> plex familial forms are compounded, it exists as a distinct and strongly
> functional group in every known society. (Murdock, 1967, pp. 2–3)

There have been very many discussions about the universality of the
family, and a great many qualifications have been added, but relatively
few scholars have rejected Murdock's thesis. Of the doubters, Hendrix is
the most elegant. After identifying conceptual and empirical weaknesses
in Murdock's work, Hendrix notes that Murdock's thesis had a deep in-
tuitive appeal because it enabled sociologists to 'cope with the variation in
family systems of which they were aware' (Hendrix, 1975, p. 166). Given
an awareness of the distinction between biological and social roles in

parenthood and an awareness of the variation of child-rearing practices over time as well as cross-culturally, it would seem that Murdock actually observed little more than the universality of sexual reproduction. That this is the case is clear when one reconsiders Murdock's point that the 'nuclear family' may be 'the basic unit for which more complex familial forms are compounded' (Murdock, 1967). One merely has to ask whether there would be any cases for which the 'nuclear family' was not the basic unit; Murdock himself seems to believe that single parenthood and polygamy are somehow basically examples of the 'nuclear family'.

Ultimately developed into a comprehensive theoretical approach to the family by Talcott Parsons (Parsons and Bales, 1956, pp. 3–33, 35–131), structural-functionalism became one of the major theoretical means of discussing family life in human society. Morgan has said of Parsons:

> It would not be too much of an exaggeration to state that Parsons represents *the* modern theorist on the family. (Morgan, 1975, p. 25)

It has been argued that the Parsonian functional analysis must be seen as being 'political' (Skolnick and Skolnick, 1971, p. 389). As such, functional analysis may have drawn upon a concept enshrined in family ideology rather than having drawn upon empirical observation. Even so, like Murdock, once possessed of the notion of a central functioning unit called 'the (nuclear) family' it is extraordinarily difficult *not* to adjust observations to fit the concept. Perhaps more telling though is the observation that without a central unit of 'the (nuclear) family' a large portion of structural-functionalism would not have been theoretically viable, nor would it have had the same simple and logical appeal to scholars (Bernardes, 1981, p. 13).

Related to the structural-functional debate, and even partly related to the universality debate, a third major area of theoretical controversy in traditional family sociology involves the issue of industrialisation and family forms. In very crude terms, most analyses suggest that the development of industrialisation is accompanied by a shift from rural extended families to isolated urban nuclear families. Recently this debate has been reformulated (Laslett and Wall, 1972), but most textbooks still rehearse a variant of the original format presented by William Goode. He conducted a wide-ranging cross-cultural study and argued that the 'conjugal family' as an acknowledged abstraction or ideal type somehow 'fitted' the modern industrial system (Goode, 1963, pp. 7–10). The essential argument suggests that the character of urban industrial life leads almost inexorably to the development of a family unit comprising of and revolving around the conjugal pair and their children. Goode's work was criticised by Lenero-Otero as having contributed to an 'ideological perspective' validating and idealising the nuclear family (Lenero-Otero, 1977, p. 3).

These three macro-theoretical approaches to family life all took for granted the existence of 'the Family'. Each debate would not have been possible, or perhaps would have been far less elegant, if the originators had had to acknowledge and accommodate diverse family situations. Each of these debates not only draws upon but also serves to reinforce family ideology in explaining, justifying or legitimating a particular central family form.

The second area of the sociological attempt to understand family life to be examined here concerns the problem of communication in terms of the use of language between sociologists (and between sociologists and the public) and the way in which language, theory and everyday commonsense interact. Looking at the issue of simply 'thinking about' family life it is clear that the researcher in this field faces a set of linguistic and intellectual problems by virtue of being simultaneously a member of society, enmeshed in its values and ideology, and also attempting to be a dispassionate analyst, setting aside the values and ideology of society. Many of the previously mentioned theorists have been explicit in stating that the notion of 'the Family' which they individually employ is an ideal type, in the sense of being, as Goode writes, 'a theoretical construction, derived from intuition and observation' (Goode, 1963, pp. 7–10). To use such a construct is, of course, a regular and accepted means of pursuing the intellectual endeavour in a wide variety of fields right across the natural and social sciences. The social sciences, however, suffer from one problem which, among others, confuses our language a good deal. In short, it takes a tremendous effort to maintain and distinguish, on the one hand, 'the family *may be seen as*, in a theoretical construct sense', and, on the other hand, 'the family *is*'. This is to say that there exist a series of linguistic and intellectual problems which, in a discussion of family life, make it extremely difficult to clearly distinguish between theoretical constructs and empirical reality. This problem has been recognised by Morgan:

> I do not intend to offer a definition of the 'family' . . . It will, I hope, become clear that it is difficult to talk about 'the' family at all. (Morgan, 1975, p. 7)

In a subsequent paper, Morgan is more explicit, identifying the problem as that of reification:

> Since we cannot constantly use roundabout phrases referring to cur-

rently overlapping notions of family and household, to 'what the analyst normally understands to be the normally current use of the term', the dangers of reification are ever with us. (Morgan, 1979, p. 15)

The Rapoports have experienced the problem, and have felt it necessary to insert a disclaimer:

> Although . . . we may appear to revert at times to the assumption of a model family type in our treatment of these issues, this is not our intention. (Rapoport *et al.*, 1977, p. 129)

Family sociologists face a tremendous problem in keeping their discussions as to how family life may be theoretically conceived distinct from what may appear to be simple statements of what family life *is like*. One of the best examples of this problem is in that of Talcott Parsons discussing 'The Normal American Family':

> It is of course a commonplace that the American family is predominantly and, in a sense, increasingly an urban middle-class family . . . there has emerged a remarkably uniform, basic type of family. It is uniform in its kinship and household composition in the sense of confinement of its composition to members of the nuclear family. (Parsons, 1971a, p. 83).

The Skolnicks very clearly recognise a fundamental intellectual problem arising from the use of an ideal-type model, which they claim 'impedes us from considering alternative explanations' (Skolnick and Skolnick, 1974b, p. 8). I suggest that the Skolnicks perhaps understate the problem. For a practising sociologist it is extraordinarily difficult *not to use* the term 'the Family', since so many elements of sociological theory involve assertions about the role and nature of 'the Family'. Worse still, as illustrated by Chester, is the ease with which structural variation can be regarded as deviant or pathological (Chester, 1977). Perhaps most serious though is the way in which structural arrangements are assumed to dictate qualitative aspects of family life as is demonstrated by Talcott Parsons in his discussion of 'The Normal American Family'.

Traditional family sociology has quite simply made a fundamental mistake. In treating everyday commonsense as adequate, past theorists have adopted and refined a notion of '*the* Family' without ever asking, in the first place, whether or not such an institution existed. Because the sociological ideal type was based upon everyday commonsense, it was necessarily highly abstract and lacking empirical referents, as do most major concepts enshrined in everyday commonsense. Lacking detailed empirical referents, such ideal-type models of the family appeared to be so self-evidently 'true' that they did not require carefully collected empirical evidence to support them. In this way, traditional family sociology presents a startling case study of the interaction of theorising, language and everyday commonsense.

The third area of sociological attempts to understand family life to be examined concerns the relationship between language, sociology and everyday experience. Implicit in much of the foregoing is the theme that theorists, students and everyday actors actually uphold family ideology, while most of them actually experience a distinct family 'reality'. This is to suggest that actors can and do simultaneously hold two conflicting pieces of 'knowledge' or beliefs: specifically that there exists a single dominant 'type' of family and that their own experience does not (quite) match this 'type'. Clearly any attempt to suggest that traditional family sociology made a mistake must satisfactorily explain this apparent contradiction. The position taken here is to suggest that everyday actors, as a matter of course, hold at least two distinct concepts of 'the Family'. These will be called the 'specific', that is personal or individual, and the 'general', that is a concept used in relation to society at large. One of the many interesting points about language is its extreme imprecision and highly symbolic nature. That is to say that, especially when dealing with very common terms, we rarely actually check that we have properly understood the speaker or writer. Thus, when we hear someone refer to 'the Family' or 'my family' we rarely need to ask what *exactly* the speaker means. Further, marriage, parenthood, and family life are intensely private affairs in our culture. Not only do we not need to ask what a speaker means by 'my family' but we are also inhibited from enquiring by way of cultural mores. Mayer, in discussing 'the invisibility of married life' (Mayer, 1967a), indicates just how little we are likely to know of the married lives of other people, precisely because the greater part of marital interaction is unseen or private, that is 'backstage' in Goffman's terms (Goffman, 1976). Mayer also points out that this 'invisibility' results largely from the 'assumptive world' within which we operate (Mayer, 1967b). That is to say that we do not need to 'see' the marriages of other people in action because we have available a clear image or set of assumptions as to what married life is like. Exactly similar comments may be applied of course to 'the Family' and 'family life'.

The work of Birdwhistell adds an important dimension to this debate. In exploring the behaviour of two related ethnic groups, Birdwhistell found that despite sharing a common language the two groups diverged in the meanings attached to this language, yet one group may never be aware of the other group's different meanings *despite* interaction (even inter-marriage):

> An Upper and Lower Kutenai – they spoke the same language – could go to school together, could engage in business relationships, and could even marry without ever discovering that they held different views of kinship and family relationships. (Birdwhistell, 1966, p. 206)

As Birdwhistell makes clear, this situation is possible because of the natural tendency of any individual to believe that the odd behaviour of another individual is a matter of individual idiosyncrasy, rather than a systematic difference in behaviour. Birdwhistell goes further to suggest that everyday actors can use the same rationale, in that 'The "American Family" needs no examples in real life . . . for those who seek a standard of behaviour' (Birdwhistell, 1966, p. 211).

In the course of my research, I have found evidence to support the possibility that everyday actors can and do hold apparently contradictory 'specific' and 'general' concepts of 'the Family' (Bernardes, 1981, ch. 7). That is, individuals feel no discomfort about describing their own family life as 'unusual', and yet believing that they are seen by other people as having a 'usual' family life, and finally asserting that most families 'conform to a pattern or type'.

It would seem possible, in principle, that there does exist a major sense in which family ideology and family 'reality' diverge. Moreover, everyday language and knowledge are such that this divergence rarely emerges in a 'general' way but rather usually occurs in a 'specific', and therefore non-problematic, way. Moreover, it is interesting to find, as the notion of variation and diversity of family forms is popularised, that everyday actors (and indeed politicians) can happily accommodate diversity as well as offer arguments to support or encourage the 'independence' of 'the Family'. It should now be clear why I believe that attempts to categorise different meanings of the term 'the Family' are not of much practical use to sociology. As the foregoing demonstrates, it is not only extremely difficult to maintain distinctions between different 'meanings' but also such an attempt is not at all helpful in trying to expose the diversity of family life.

The fourth area of sociological attempts to understand family life to be examined originates from the phenomenological study of marriage. The notion of the role played by marriage in the social construction of reality was introduced by Berger and Kellner, who took up the Durkheimian theme that marriage 'serves as a protection against anomie for the individual' (Berger and Kellner, 1971, p. 23). They propose that language is the central medium through which 'the social' is erected. Language is the means by which meaning is constructed and shared by individuals, thus constituting an at least partly shared 'sense of reality'. In the context of such social construction of reality, Berger and Kellner argue that marriage 'occupies a privileged status among the significant validating relationships for adults in our society' (ibid, p. 24). Summarising this process, they argue that:

> the process is . . . one in which reality is crystallised, narrowed and stabilized. Ambivalencies are converted into certainties. Typifications of self and of others become settled. Most generally, possibilities become facticities. What is more, this process of transformation remains, most of the time, unapprehended by those who are both its authors and its objects. (ibid, p. 28)

It would not seem too great a violence to expand Berger and Kellner's work to the wider category of family life in terms of parent—child relationships, and extend the notion of the construction of reality to the process of socialisation, as long as socialisation is conceived of as a two-way process of interaction[6]. As later made clear by Berger, family life is the first place of interaction and the arena in which a child adopts or internalises much of what will become his or her everyday commonsense (Berger and Berger, 1976, ch. 5). In the context of a predominant family ideology it is clear that 'family life' is a prime 'taken-for-granted'. In a very clear sense, the process of reality construction between parent(s), and between parent(s) and child(ren), serves as a bedrock for the individual sense of reality both for adults and for a child as he or she grows to maturity. Beyond these reformulations of fairly conventional ideas, it is crucially important to grasp that this process of reality construction as a child grows is in itself one of the fundamental, almost unquestionable, taken-for-granteds of social life. We *have* to believe that we share most of our family experience in common in some way; this is a prerequisite of accessing a common reality or world of experience. From believing that we share similar experiences it is no great leap to believing that these experiences must have occurred within similar situations, and to believing that 'my family' and 'your family' are fundamentally similar and both examples of 'the Family'[7]. Thus, the work of Berger and Kellner suggests a means whereby the notion of 'the Family' enshrined within family ideology gains credibility and is assimilated by actors within individual family situations.

To close this exploration of the problem of 'the Family', several points need to be made clear. The central thrust of the foregoing section has been to demonstrate that there are a large number of factors which have tended to support a single ideal-type model of the family, and which simultaneously inhibit the recognition of variation and diversity in family forms. Clearly, a prevalent family ideology has tended to portray the notion of a single (literally, ideal) model of what family life *should* be like. It is interesting that the very nature of sociological debates relating to family life has tended to demand an extremely abstract ideal-type model which has, in part, drawn upon and reinforced family ideology. Further, there is a very real problem in attempting to construct sociological theory by using concepts and language in current everyday use. Moreover, everyday language and knowledge are such that individual actors can happily accommodate several different meanings of the term 'family'. Finally, the development of a phenomenological or microsociological approach to family life itself rounded out the exploration, not only by locating the genesis of an individual's sense of social reality in early family life, but also by suggesting ways in which individuals come to accept a single central concept of 'the Family' as real.

It is now apposite to return to the central theme of 'Family and Economy' in the context of the title question of this chapter -- 'Do we really know what 'The Family' is?' The response proposed here is that we do *not* know what 'the Family' is, in any useful sense. Certainly there is in the United Kingdom and United States a prevalent image of 'the Family' which is an important object for sociological analysis in itself. In terms though of attempting to understand family life as experienced by everyday actors the concept is of little use. The notion of 'the Family' is part of a longstanding and sociologically validated body of family ideology that bears little if any relation to family 'reality', or family life as actually experienced by everyday actors. The awesome power of this family ideology, supported by central institutions including government and major religions, rests upon curious conceptual ambiguities. Individuals are able to, indeed must, simultaneously accommodate both 'general' and 'specific' concepts of 'the Family'. Individuals are able to, first, assume that there is a single uniform type of 'the Family'; second, believe that their own family life is divergent from this model; and third, remain unaware that all families may diverge from a single dominant type. This is possible not simply because individuals *can* simultaneously hold 'general' and 'specific' concepts of 'the Family', but because they *must* hold these two concepts in order both to reconcile personal family 'reality' and public family ideology, and to minimise dissonance or ambiguities in everyday social life. The notion of common human experience, and the assumption that this is the result of living in common human structures (Berger and Berger, 1976, chs 3–5), is central to the (assumed) existence of a sense of 'communality' or a sense of the 'social'.

One of the great puzzles for any scholar of family life is 'how is it possible for so many varied, even opposing, parties to have actually agreed as to what "the Family"*is*?' How is it possible that the extreme right and left of contemporary political debate, established religion, a wide range of 'anti-establishment' social movements, structural-functional sociological theorists, and radical Marxist feminists all agree about what 'the Family' *is*, despite wide disagreement over 'it's virtues and widely different programmes of action? Until recently it was possible to believe that 'the Family' was one of the external and ultimate components of human society – indeed a section of the literature is orientated to affirming this universality. However, when considered carefully, recent recognitions and suggestions render this quintessential approach untenable. Hence the need for an attempt to locate and expand upon the genesis of such a fundamental theoretical or conceptual mistake.

To go a little further, it is relevant to consider past attempts at institutional social action and social change *vis-à-vis* 'the Family'. It must be asked: 'why has it required such enormous efforts of government and other lesser institutional agencies to come to grips with, and act in response to, single parenthood, divorce and issues relating to child care, family poverty, and so on, which have existed for centuries?' (Mount, 1982). One (and only one) of the reasons is that dominant groups and institutions have fiercely resisted any public move away from the notion of 'the Family', not only because of the strength of family ideology, but also because of enormously wide-ranging (and astonishingly complex) policy reformulations that would be required if social policy attempted to deal with family 'reality' rather than attempt to corral all families into behaviour and lifestyles conforming to the image enshrined in family ideology. Further, one very important reason for the difficulties in implementing, or the poor 'results' of, family-orientated social policy – for example, in childcare and income maintenance – may be the conceptualisation of 'the Family' as the object of these policies. This may be substantially harder to remedy than first glance might suggest. In the 'Conclusion' and 'Policy Agenda' of the Final Report of the Study Commission on the Family (Study Commission on the Family, 1983, pp. 50–51) the discussion still includes reference to 'the Family' and 'a family policy' as well as references to 'families' and 'family life'. This might be seen as pedantic criticism but does, I suggest, well illustrate the peculiar difficulties even of writing clearly in this area, let alone ensuring that meaning is clearly and precisely understood. The Study Commission on the Family, despite its title, is clearly aware of variation and diversity in family forms (ibid, 1983, p. 43) and the difficulty of even speaking of 'the Family' (Rimmer, 1981, p. 61). However, a casual reader of the Final Report could easily interpret the Policy Agenda as relating to a single dominant form of 'the family'. Similarly, Segal clearly recognises that current family ideology may 'obscure the nature of how we live' (Segal, 1983, p. 11) and yet this author adopted the title 'What is to be Done About the Family?', as if there does exist one single dominant form[8].

How is it that such otherwise sophisticated authors can perpetuate such confusions? The key to answering this question lies I believe in a very much closer examination of the nature of the relationship between Family and Economy. We have so far failed to adequately grasp the complexity of this relationship. The recognition of family ideology has been a vital step on the path to a critical understanding of family life, but has diverted attention away from a much wider range of issues. What is required is a much broader understanding of the relationship between family life and economic life and a more sophisticated appreciation of the role of ideologies. There are a vast number of ideologies — which shape our attitudes, beliefs and opinions — ranging from contemporary family ideology and traditional sex-role ideology to much broader notions of dominant ideology. It has been a mistake to isolate a set of family-related values, or family ideology, rather than recognise the centrality of the notion of 'the Family' to a much wider class of types and levels of ideologies. While different theoretical positions would involve varying emphases, we must clearly recognise that there is a link between the structure of economic life, models of behaviour enshrined within various ideologies, and the day-to-day activities of actors within family situations.

I wish to include two speculative discussions in so far as they relate to the concept of 'the Family'. The first area to examine is the role and place of ideology as it relates to family life and economic life. Recently, Nava in examining feminist critiques of the family noted how feminists have focused upon the ideological rather than the economic as the central determinant of women's oppression (Nava, 1983, p. 86). Nava specifically refers to the ideologies 'of femininity, of wifehood and motherhood'. It does not seem unreasonable, however, to relate this idea to a discussion of family life, since the particular ideologies identified clearly relate to family ideology as discussed in this chapter. Nor does it seem unreasonable to extend the analysis in terms of Mannheim's typology of ideology (Mannheim, 1972, ch. 2). His work is attractive, at least at a superficial

level, for its simplicity. Mannheim, in exploring the Sociology of Knowledge, distinguished a 'particular conception of ideology [which] denotes
that we are sceptical of the ideas and representations advanced by our
opponent', from a 'total conception of ideology' which refers to the
'ideology of an age or . . . historico-social group [here] we are concerned
with . . . the total structure of the mind of this epoch or of this group'
(ibid, pp. 49–50). Mannheim's work partly concerns what individuals
'know', and does not seem incompatible with the work of Berger and
Kellner in discussing how individuals come to construct and share a sense
of reality.

Clearly Mannheim's particular conception of ideology equates well with
the ideologies Nava identifies as relating to women's oppression. The same
is true of contemporary debates 'for' and 'against' 'the Family' as explored
by Berger and Berger. However, the concept of 'the Family' itself would
appear to be much closer to Mannheim's 'total' conception of ideology.
The very existence of 'the Family' seems to be part of the 'total structure
of the mind' (Mannheim, 1972, p. 50) of contemporary society in much
the same way as notions of ownership and wage-labour seem to be. Put
another way, the (total conception of) ideology that legitimates our
current economic structure also legitimates the idea of a single dominant
form of 'the Family'.

To take another speculative step in relating Mannheim's work to that of
Berger and Kellner, clearly language and conversation as discussed by Berger and Kellner involve ideology in both of Mannheim's senses. Thus, the
social construction of reality, the prime location of which would appear to
be family situations, must surely involve the social construction or social
reproduction of ideology. Certainly there is room for debate about the
exact relationship between ideology and a sense of reality. None the less,
in constructing or reproducing ideology in mature adults and developing
children, inter-action within family situations must play a part in determining social, political and economic relationships. If not actually 'determining' these relationships, it at least predisposes individuals to behave in
certain ways. In reproducing 'particular' ideologies, family life perhaps
contributes to sustaining, for example, partisan political divisions, class
divisions and gender role divisions. In reproducing 'total' ideology, family
life may contribute directly to the relatively uncritical acceptance of
current economic structure by the majority of the population. Further, in
reproducing 'total' ideology, family situations themselves may be a
crucial component in the process leading to the very widespread adoption
of the term 'the Family' and the belief that it is real. This may partly
explain why otherwise sophisticated writers do not seem able to avoid re-

introducing the term 'the Family', no matter how clear their rejection of the concept may be.

In the broader terms of the theme of this book, this discussion suggests the need to add the issues of ideology and the social construction of reality to any exploration of the relationship between economic and family life. Clearly needed is an empirical examination of how individuals come to adopt certain elements of family ideology and, say, gender role ideology. Also needed is a macro-thoretical or conceptually orientated analysis of the way in which family life, economic life and various types or levels of ideology are related.

A second speculative discussion also relates to the power of the central image of 'the Family' enshrined in family ideology. There seems to be little room to doubt the point that everyday actors do accept 'as real' the existence of 'the Family'. It would appear, then, to be important to present some account of why this image is so popular. Quite simply, I would suggest that this image plays a vital role in maintaining contemporary economic structures, despite (or even *because* of) the relative rarity of families that actually match the image. Family units, whether diverse in type or of a single form, are literally an ideal arrangement both for producing wage-labourers and for the purchase and consumption of material and non-material goods. Beyond this, though, the individual struggle to achieve a family life which comes even remotely close to the image portrayed in family ideology is surely one of the most powerful of stimuli to ensure 'conformity' to standards of social and economic behaviour in contemporary society. In this context it seems likely that one of the major reasons for the dominance of the idea of 'the Family' is a near-universal unwillingness to recognise that such a central life-goal is illusory, or non-existent. The dominance of the concept also obstructs the attempt to discover what life is actually like within those things we call families. We do not know, perhaps, what family life is actually like because we fear the consequences of any exposé. The very idea of 'the Family' is one of the cornerstones of our mutual sense of reality. This would appear to be a further important reason why even those who can intellectually grasp the difficulties of speaking of 'the Family' lack the conviction to so radically challenge everyday commonsense and hence re-adopt the term.

The response to the title question of this chapter, then, is twofold. First, there exists in contemporary society a very powerful central image of what 'the Family' *is* enshrined within family ideology and ideology more broadly conceived. Second, family situations in contemporary society society are so varied and diverse that it simply makes no sociological sense to speak of a single ideal-type model of 'the Family' at all. Consequently, since scholars within traditional family sociology have adopted flawed theoretical tools, we know very little indeed about family life in contemporary society. Indeed, the sociological use of a central model of 'the Family' has actually sustained family ideology and ensured our continued ignorance.

In attempting to understand why and how traditional family sociology has relied upon a central concept of 'the Family' several features of sociological debates become apparent. Not only was the existence of 'the Family' taken for granted in several macro-theoretical debates, but moreover such a single central concept was essential to the themes of those debates. The very notion of 'the Family' — embedded as it is in ideology, language, morality, and everyday commonsense — has proved to be extremely difficult to critically analyse. The microsociological study of family situations suggests a means whereby individuals come to accept the notion of 'the Family' as being real.

In addressing the issue of Family and Economy, attention was turned to the question of why sophisticated authors, aware of the inadequacy of the notion of 'the Family', are none the less found to re-introduce this term. The role of ideology was identified as central here. Recognising family ideology has been valuable, but has obscured wider issues relating economic life, ideology, and family life. In a speculative discussion I have sought to demonstrate the crucial importance of ideology and the social construction of reality in studying the relationship between economic life and family life. In a second discussion I have sought to demonstrate that the idea of 'the Family' is one of the cornerstones of our mutual sense of reality. This contention supports the view that a more sophisticated exploration of ideology and family life may add an important element to the explanation of the persistence of contemporary economic structures.

This chapter has emphasised the location of the image of 'the Family' not only at the heart of family ideology but more widely conceived. While we do know a great deal about this image of 'the Family' it is increasingly clear that we, as scholars and as participants, are remarkably ignorant of the nature of family life in modern societies. My own sociological conviction is that we must abandon the sociological use of the term 'the Family', and eschew this term in all future literature. This term can and must only have one possible use in future: specifically we must relegate the term 'the Family' to denoting only the usage of everyday actors. It is only by this means, I believe, that we shall be able to locate and critically examine the complexities of the relationship between family life, the social construction of reality, ideologies and economic structures.

NOTES

1. See later comments regarding the challenges presented by radical psychoanalysis and radical feminism. A useful recent summary of feminist critiques may be found in Segal (1983, ch. 3). For a recent example see Barrett and McIntosh (1982).
2. See Mount (1982) and the attempt to construct 'An Alternative history of Love and Marriage'.
3. The term 'traditional family sociology' is intended to denote that body of mainstream family studies addressed by Morgan (1975); the Rapoports (1977 and 1982); Bernardes (1981, pp. 2–30); and the Study Commission on the Family (1983).
4. See Rapoport *et al.*, (1977, p. 88); Study Commission on the Family (1980, p. 16). Rapoport and Rapoport (1982, pp. 475–99) discuss the transition from such a model and accept that it did and does exist.
5. For a readable short account of this period see Segal (1983, ch. 2).
6. See Bell and Harper (1977, pp. 212–14). The notion of socialisation as a two-way process is implicit in some modern textbook approaches (see Berger and Berger, 1976).
7. It may be that we do not share a common reality at all, but rather spend a good deal of our lives negotiating not 'common understandings' but compromise situations, in which the conflict between dissonant senses of reality are rendered unapparent. Indeed, Birdwhistell's work would seem to imply exactly this.
8. The same is also true of Barrett and McIntosh (1982, p. 81).

Bibliography

P. Abrams, 'Rites de Passage. The Conflict of Generations in Industrial Society', *Journal of Contemporary History*, 5 (1970) 175–90.

P. Abrams and A. McCulloch, *Communes, Sociology and Society* (Cambridge: Cambridge University Press, 1976).

B. N. Adams, 'The Social Significance of Kinship', in M. Anderson (ed.), *The Sociology of the Family* (Harmondsworth: Penguin, 1971).

C. Adams and K. Winston, *Mothers at Work: Public Policies in the United States, Sweden and Canada* (New York: Longman, 1980).

D. Adler, 'Matriduxy in the Australian Family', in A. F. Davies and S. Encel (eds), *Australian Society: A Sociological Introduction*, vol. 1 (Melbourne: Cheshire, 1965).

L. Althusser, 'Ideology and Ideological State Apparatuses', in B. R. Cosin (ed.), *Education: Structure and Society* (Harmondsworth: Penguin, 1972).

A. Amsden, *The Economics of Women and Work* (Harmondsworth: Penguin, 1980).

F. Anthias, 'Women and the Reserve Army of Labour: A Critique of Veronica Beechey', *Capital and Class*, 10 (1980) 50–63.

P. Ariès, *Centuries of Childhood* (Harmondsworth: Penguin, 1973).

A. B. Atkinson and A. Harrison, *The Distribution of Personal Wealth in Britain* (Cambridge: Cambridge University Press, 1978).

L. Backe, *Politiken*, 5 Feb. 1984.

E. W. Bakke, *The Unemployed Man* (London: Nisbet, 1937).

D. L. Barker, 'The Regulation of Marriage: Repressive Benevolence', in G. Littlejohn *et al.*, *Power and the State* (London: Croom Helm, 1978).

M. Barrett, *Women's Oppression Today: Problems in Marxist Feminist Analysis* (London: Verso, 1980).

M. Barrett and M. McIntosh, *The Anti-Social Family* (London: Verso, 1982).

R. Barron and G. Norris, *Studies of Poverty Among the Unemployed*, SSRC Research Report (1976).

M. Bayley, *Mental Handicap and Community Care* (London: Routledge & Kegan Paul, 1973).

V. Beechey, 'Women and Production', in A. Kuhn and A. Wolpe (eds), *Feminism and Materialism* (London: Routledge & Kegan Paul, 1978).

R. Q. Bell and L. V. Harper, *Child Effects on Adults* (New Jersey: Erlbaum, 1977).

B. Berger and P. L. Berger, *Sociology: A Biographical Approach* (Harmondsworth: Penguin, 1976).

B. Berger and P. L. Berger, *The War Over the Family* (London: Hutchinson, 1983).

P. L. Berger and H. Kellner, 'Marriage and the Construction of Reality: An Exercise in the Micro-Sociology of Knowledge', in B. R. Cosin, *School and Society* (London: Routledge & Kegan Paul, 1971).

R. A. Berk and S. Fenstermaker Berk, *Labor and Leisure At Home: Content and Organisation of the Household Day* (Beverly Hills: Sage, 1979).

S. Fenstermaker Berk (ed.), *Women and Household Labor* (Beverley Hills and London: Sage, 1980).

L. Berkner, 'Recent Research in the History of the Family in Western Europe', *Journal of Marriage and the Family*, 35 (1973).

L. Berkner, 'The Use and Misuse of Census Data for the Historical Analysis of Family Structure', *Journal of Interdisciplinary History*, 14 (1975).

J. Bernard, *American Family Behaviour* (New York: Harper, 1942).

J. Bernard, *The Future of Marriage* (Harmondsworth: Penguin, 1976).

J. Bernardes, 'Diversity Within and Alternatives to "The Family"': The Development of an Alternative Theoretical Approach' (University of Hull, unpublished PhD Thesis, 1981).

D. Bertaux, *Destins Personnels et Structure de Classe* (Paris: Presses Universitaries de France, 1977).

R. L. Birdwhistell, 'The American Family: Some Perspectives', *Psychiatry*, 29 (1966) 203–13.

F. Blackaby (ed.), *De-Industrialisation* (London: Heinemann, 1978).

R. O. Blood and D. M. Wolfe, *Husbands and Wives* (London: Collier Macmillan, 1960).

M. Bondfield, 'Women as Domestic Workers', in E. Malos (ed.), *The Politics of Housework* (London: Allison & Busby, 1980).

Börnekommissionens betaenkning (Report from the Government's Committee on Children) No. 18 (Copenhagen, 1981).

C. Bose, 'Technology and Changes in the Division of Labor in the American Home', *Women's Studies International Quarterly*, 2 (1979) 295–304.

C. Bose and P. Bereano, 'Household Technologies: Burden or Blessing?', in J. Zimmerman (ed.), *The Technological Woman: Interfacing with Tomorrow* (New York: Praeger, 1983).

E. Bott, *Family and Social Network: Roles, Norms and External Relationships in Ordinary Urban Families* (London: Tavistock, 1957).

T. B. Bottomore, *Sociology* (London: George Allen & Unwin, 1981).

T. B. Bottomore and M. Rubel, *Karl Marx: Selected Writings in Sociology and Social Philosophy* (Harmondsworth: Penguin, 1963).

J. Bowlby, *Maternal Care and Mental Health* (Geneva: World Health Organisation, 1951).

J. Bradshaw, K. Cooke and C. Godfrey, 'The Impact of Unemployment on the Living Standards of Families', *Journal of Social Policy*, 12 (1983) 433–52.

I. Brennan, 'Marxism and the Family', *Marxism Today*, 17 (1973).

C. Brown, 'Mothers, Fathers and Children: From Private to Public Patriarchy', in L. Sargent (ed.), *Women and Revolution* (London: Pluto Press, 1981).

G. Brown and T. Harris, *Social Origins of Depression: A Study of Psychiatric Disorder in Women* (London: Tavistock, 1978).

I. Bruegel, 'Women as a Reserve Army of Labour: A Note on Recent British Experience', *Feminist Review*, 3 (1979) 12–23.

L. Bryson *et al.*, 'Working Mothers and Family Life', unpublished report (1965).

L. Bryson and F. Thompson, *An Australian Newtown: Life and Leadership in a Class Suburb* (Ringwood: Penguin, 1972).

M. Buckley, 'Women in the Soviet Union', *Feminist Review*, 8 (1981) 79–106.

L. Burghes, *Living From Hand to Mouth* (London: Family Service Unit/Child Poverty Action Group, 1980).

S. Burman (ed.), *Fit Work for Women* (London: Croom Helm, 1979).

R. Burns, 'Financial Management and the Allocation of Resources Within Households: A Research Review', *Work and the Family*, EOC Research Bulletin no. 8, Winter (1983–4).

R. Butt, 'The Woman Whose Workplace is in the Home', *The Times*, Dec. 1982.

M. Carpenter, 'Left Orthodoxy and the Politics of Health', *Capital and Class*, 11 (1980) 73–98.

G. Causer, 'Some Aspects of Property Distribution and Class Structure', in P. Hollowell (ed.), *Property and Social Relations* (London: Heinemann, 1982).

J. Chaney, *Social Networks and Job Information: The Situation of Women who Return to Work* (Equal Opportunities Commission, 1981).

A. Cherlin, 'Postponing Marriage: The Influence of Young Women's Work Expectations', *Journal of Marriage and the Family*, 42 (1980) 355–65.

R. Chester, 'The One Parent Family: Deviant or Variant', in R. Chester and J. Peel (eds), *Equalities and Inequalities in Family Life* (London: Academic Press, 1977).

A. Clark, *The Working Life of Women in the Seventeenth Century* (London: Frank Cass, 1968).

K. A. Clarke and A. I. Ogus, 'What is a Wife Worth?', *British Journal of Law and Society*, 5 (1978) 1–25.

P. Close, 'The Social Situations of Unmarried Mothers', unpublished PhD thesis, University of Kent, Canterbury, 1976.

P. Close, 'Review of Roberta Hamilton's "The Liberation of Women"', *S.S.R.C. Survey Archive Bulletin*, no. 13, May (1979).

P. Close and R. Collins, 'Domestic Labour and Patriarchy: The Implications of a Study in the North-East of England', *International Journal of Sociology and Social Policy*, 3 (1983) 48–64.

S. Cobb and S. Kasl, *Termination: The Consequences of Job Loss*, NIOSH Research Report (US Department of Health, Education and Welfare 1977).

R. Cochrane and M. Stopes-Roe, 'Women, Marriage, Employment and Mental Health', *British Journal of Psychiatry*, 139 (1981) 373–81.

B. E. Cogswell and M. B. Sussman, 'Changing Family and Marriage Forms: Complications for Human Service Systems', in M. B. Sussman, *Non-Traditional Family Forms in the 1970s* (Minneapolis: National Council on Family Relations, 1973).

P. Cohen, *Modern Social Theory* (London: Heinemann, 1968).

Conference of Socialist Economists, Sex and Class Group, 'Sex and Class', *Capital and Class*, 16 (1982) 28–94.

D. Cooper, *The Death of the Family* (Harmondsworth: Penguin, 1972).

P. Corrigan, *The Smash Street Kids* (London: Macmillan, 1979).

R. Schwartz Cowan, 'A Case Study of Technological and Social Change: The Washing Machine and the Working Wife', in M. Hartmann and L. W. Banner (eds), *Clio's Consciousness Raised. New Perspectives in the History of Women* (New York: Harper, 1974).

R. Schwartz Cowan, 'From Virginia Dare to Virginia Slims: Women and Technology in American Life', in M. Moore Trescott (ed.), *Dynamos and Virgins Revisited: Women in the History of Technology* (New Jersey and London: Scarecrow Press, 1979a).

R. Schwartz Cowan, 'The "Industrial Revolution" in the Home: Household Technology and Social Change in the 20th Century', in M. Moore Trescott *op. cit.* (1979b).

A. Coyle, 'An Investigation into the Long Term Impact of Redundancy and Unemployment Amongst Women', *Work and the Family*, EOC Research Bulletin No. 8, Winter (1983–4).

E. Craven *et al.*, *Family Issues and Public Policy* (London: Study Commission on the Family, 1982).

R. Crompton and J. Gubbay, *Economy and Class Structure* (London: Macmillan, 1977).

A. Curthoys, 'Men and Childcare in the Feminist Utopia', *Refractory Girl*, 10 (1976) 3–5.

R. Dahrendorf, *Class and Class Conflict in Industrial Society* (Stanford: Stanford University Press, 1959).

W. W. Daniels, *The Unemployed Flow*, Stage 1, Interim Report, PSI (1981).

L. Davidoff, 'The Rationalisation of Housework', in D. L. Barker (ed.), *Dependence and Exploitation in Work and Marriage* (London: Longman, 1976).

C. Davidson, *A Woman's Work is Never Done: A History of Housework in the British Isles 1650–1950* (London: Chatto & Windus, 1982).

R. Davies, *Women and Work* (London: Arrow Books, 1975).

K. Davis, 'The Child and the Social Structure', *The Journal of Educational Sociology*, 14 (1940) 217.

C. Delphy, *The Main Enemy: A Materialist Analysis of Women's Oppression* (London: WRRC Publications, 1977).

C. Delphy, 'Sharing the Same Table: Consumption and the Family', in C. C. Harris (ed.), *The Sociology of the Family* (Keele: Sociological Review Monograph, 28, 1979).

R. Dobash and R. Dobash, *Violence Against Wives* (London: Open Books, 1980).

J. Dominican, 'Families in Divorce', in R. Rapoport *et al.* (eds), *Families in Britain* (London: Routledge & Kegan Paul, 1982).

J. Donzelot, *The Policing of Families: Welfare Versus the State* (London: Hutchinson, 1979).

K. Dunnell, *Family Formation 1976* (London: HMSO, 1979).

B. Easton, 'The Decline of Patriarchy and the Rise of Feminism', *Catalyst*, 10–11 (1977) 104–24.

The Economist Intelligence Unit, *Survey of the Unemployed*, 1982.

D. Edgar and G. Ochiltree, 'Family Change and Early Childhood Development', Institute of Family Studies, Melbourne, Discussion paper no. 6 (1983).

S. Edgell, *Middle Class Couples* (London: George Allen & Unwin, 1980).

S. Ehrenreich and D. English, '*"For Her Own Good": 150 Years of the Expert's Advice to Women*' (London: Pluto, 1979).

Z. Eisenstein (ed.), *Capitalist Patriarchy and the Case for Socialist Feminism* (London: Monthly Review Press, 1979).

P. Elias and B. Main, *Women's Working Lives* (Institute for Employment Research, University of Warwick, 1982).

S. Encel, 'The Family', in A. F. Davies and S. Encel (eds), *Australian Society: A Sociological Introduction*, 2nd edn (Melbourne: Cheshire, 1970).

F. Engels, *The Origins of the Family, Private Property and the State* (New York: Pathfinder, 1972).

Equal Opportunities Commission, *Behind Closed Doors* (Manchester: EOC, 1981).

Equal Opportunities Commission, *Who Cares for the Carers?* (Manchester: EOC, 1982).

M. Evans and C. Ungerson (eds), *Sexual Divisions: Patterns and Processes* (London: Tavistock, 1983).

L. Fagin, *Unemployment and Health in Families: Case Studies Based on Family Interviews – A Pilot Study* (London: DHSS, 1981).

H. Fallding, 'Inside the Australian Family', in A. P. Elkin (ed.), *Marriage and the Family in Australia* (Sydney: Angus & Robertson, 1957).

M. M. Ferree, 'Satisfaction With Housework: The Social Context', in Berk (1980).

J. Finch and D. Groves (eds), *A Labour of Love: Women, Work and Caring* (London: Routledge & Kegan Paul, 1983).

M. Finer, 'One Parent Families', Report of the Committee on (London: HMSO, 1974).

S. Firestone, *The Dialectic of Sex* (New York: Bantam, 1971).

E. Fischer, *Marx in His Own Words* (Harmondsworth: Penguin, 1973).

M. Fogarty, R. Rapoport and R. Rapoport, *Sex, Career and the Family* (London: George Allen & Unwin, 1971).

J. Forchhammer and J. Helmer Petersen, *Kulturens Börn* (Children of Culture) (Copenhagen: Kulturminsteriets Arbjdsgruppe on Börn og Kultur, 1980).

M. Foucault, *Discipline and Punish* (London: Allen Lane, 1977).

B. Fox, 'Women's Double Work Day: Twentieth-Century Changes in the Reproduction of Daily Life', in B. Fox (ed.), *Hidden in the Household* (Ontario: The Women's Press, 1980).

R. Fox, *Kinship and Marriage* (Harmondsworth: Penguin, 1967).

F. Fröbel, J. Heinrichs and D. Rowolt, *The New International Division of Labour* (London: Cambridge University Press, 1980).

P. H. Furfey, 'The Group Life of the Adolescent', *The Journal of Educational Sociology*, 14 (1940).

A. Game and R. Pringle, 'Women, the Labour Process and Technological Change in the Banking Industry in Australia', *Intervention*, 14 (1981) 25–53.

J. Gardiner, 'Political Economy of Domestic Labour in Capitalist Society', in D. L. Barker and S. Allen (eds), *Dependence and Exploitation in Work and Marriage* (London: Longman, 1976).

H. Gavron, *The Captive Wife* (London: Routledge & Kegan Paul, 1966).

M. Geerken and W. Gove, *At Home and at Work: The Family Allocation of Labour* (Beverly Hills: Sage, 1983).

General Household Survey 1981 (London: HMSO, 1983).

J. Gershuny, *After Industrial Society: The Emerging Self-Service Economy* (London: Macmillan, 1978).

J. Gershuny, 'Household Work Strategies: Sexual Segregation and Inequality', paper presented at the International Sociological Association Conference, Mexico City, 1982.

J. Gershuny, *Social Innovation and the Division of Labour* (Oxford: Oxford University Press, 1983).

J. Gershuny and I. Miles, *The New Service Economy. The Transformation of Employment in Industrial Societies* (London: Frances Pinter, 1983).

J. Gershuny and G. Thomas, *Changing Patterns of Time Use: Data Preparation and Preliminary Results. UK 1961–1974/5* (Falmer: Science Policy Research Unit Occasional Paper No. 13, 1980).

H. Gerth and C. W. Mills (eds), *From Max Weber* (London: Routledge & Kegan Paul, 1964).

A. Giddens, *Central Problems in Social Theory* (London: Macmillan, 1979).

A. Giddens, *The Class Structure of the Advanced Societies* (London: Hutchinson, 1981).

A. Giddens, *A Contemporary Critique of Historical Materialism* (London: Macmillan, 1981a).

A. Giddens, *Sociology: A Brief But Critical Introduction* (London: Macmillan, 1982).

J. R. Gillis, *Youth and History, Tradition and Change in European Age Relations, 1770 – Present* (New York: Academic Press, 1981).

C. Perkins Gilman, 'The Home: Its Work and Influence', in E. Malos (ed.), *The Politics of Housework* (London: Allison & Busby, 1980).

C. Glendinning, *Unshared Care: Parents and their Disabled Children* (London: Routledge & Kegan Paul, 1983).

E. Goffman, *The Presentation of Self in Everyday Life* (Harmondsworth: Penguin, 1976).

J. Goldthorpe *et al.*, *The Affluent Worker in the Class Structure* (Cambridge: Cambridge University Press, 1969).

P. Goodall, 'Design and Gender', *Block*, 9 (1983) 50–61.

W. Goode, *World Revolution and Family Patterns* (New York: Collier Macmillan, 1963).

H. Graham, '"Prevention and Health: Every Mother's Business": A Comment on Child Health Policies in the 1970s', in Harris (1979).

H. Graham, *Women, Health and the Family* (London: Wheatsheaf, 1984).

P. G. Gray, *The British Household* (Mass-Observation Survey No. 2497, 1947).

G. Greer, *The Female Eunuch* (London: MacGibbon & Kee, 1970).

D. Groves and J. Finch, 'Natural Selection Perspectives on Entitlement to the Invalid Care Allowance', in J. Finch and D. Groves (eds), *A Labour of Love: Women, Work, and Caring* (London: Routledge & Kegan Paul, 1983).

C. Guillaumin, 'The Practice and Power of Belief in Nature', *Feminist Issues*, 1 (1980) 3–28 and 3 (1981) 87–109.

C. Hakin, *Occupational Segregation*, Department of Employment Research Paper no. 9, 1979.

C. Hall, 'The History of the Housewife', in E. Malos (ed.), *op. cit.* (1980).

S. Hall and T. Jefferson, *Resistance Through Rituals: Youth Subcultures in Post-War Britain* (London: Hutchinson, 1976).

R. Hamilton, *The Liberation of Women* (London: George Allen and Unwin, 1978).

M. Haralambos, *Sociology, Themes and Perspectives* (Slough: University Tutorial Press, 1980).

J. Harper *Fathers at Home* (Harmondsworth: Penguin, 1980).

J. Harper and L. Richards, *Mothers and Working Mothers* (Ringwood: Penguin, 1979).

C. C. Harris, *Readings in Kinship in Urban Society* (Oxford: Pergamon, 1970).

C. C. Harris in DHSS, *Preparation for Parenthood* (London: HMSO, 1974).

C. C. Harris, 'Changing Conceptions of the Relations Between the Family and Societal Form in Western Society', in R. Scase (ed.), *Industrial Society: Class Cleavage and Control* (London: George Allen and Unwin, 1977).

C. C. Harris (ed.), *Sociology of the Family: New Directions For Britain* (University of Keele: Sociological Review Monograph, 1979).

C. C. Harris, *The Family and Industrial Society* (London: George Allen and Unwin, 1983).

M. Harris, 'How Unemployment Affects People', *New Society*, 19 Jan. 1984.

J. Harrison, 'The Political Economy of Housework', *Bulletin of the Conference of Socialist Economists*, 3 (1974) 35–52.

H. Hartmann, 'The Unhappy Marriage of Marxism and Feminism', *Capital and Class*, 8 (1979) 1–33.

H. Hartmann, 'The Family as the Locus of Gender, Class and Political Struggle: The Example of Housework', *Signs*, 6 (1981) 366–94.

D. Hayden, *The Grand Domestic Revolution: A History of Feminist Designs for American Homes, Neighbourhoods and Cities* (Cambridge, Mass: MIT Press, 1981).

L. Hendrix, 'Nuclear Family Universals: Fact and Faith in the Acceptance of an Ideal', *Journal of Comparative Family Studies*, 6 (1975) 125–38.

A. O. Hirschman, *Exit, Voice and Loyalty* (Cambridge, Mass: Harvard University Press, 1970).

P. Hirst, *On Law and Ideology* (London: Macmillan, 1979).

J. Hjarnö, *Migration – West Samoa–New Zealand*, vol. 1 (Copenhagen: Copenhagen School of Economics, 1976).

J. Humphries, 'Class Struggle and the Persistence of the Working Class Family', *Cambridge Journal of Economics*, 1 (1977).

A. Hunt, *The Home Help Service in England and Wales* (London: HMSO, 1970).

P. Hunt, *Gender and Class Consciousness* (London: Macmillan, 1980).

U. Huws, *Your Job in the Eighties. A Woman's Guide to New Technology* (London: Pluto Press, 1982).

Institute of British Launderers, *Laundry Usage* (Mass-Observation Survey No. 2315, 1945).

B. Jackson, 'Single-Parent Families', in R. Rapoport *et al.* (eds), *Families in Britain* (London: Routledge & Kegan Paul, 1982).

M. Jahoda, 'The Impact of Unemployment in the 1930s and the 1970s, *Bulletin of the British Psychological Society*, 32 (1979) 309–14.

M. Jahoda *et al.*, *Marienthal: The Sociology of an Unemployed Community* (London: Tavistock, 1972).

P. Jephcott, B. N. Seear and J. H. Smith, *Married Women Working* (London: George Allen & Unwin, 1962).

J. Johnson, 'New Research on Family Violence', *Journal of Family Issues* (1981).

K. Jones, *A History of the Mental Health Services* (London: Routledge & Kegan Paul, 1972).

E. Kaluzynska, 'Wiping the Floor with Theory: A Survey of Writings on Housework', *Feminist Review*, 6 (1980) 27–54.

W. F. F. Kemsley and D. Ginsburg, *Expenditure on Laundries' Dyeing and Cleaning, Mending and Alterations and Shoe Repairing Services* (London: Central Office of Information, 1949).

C. Kerr *et al.*, *Industrialisation and Industrial Man* (Harmondsworth: Penguin, 1973).

V. Klein, *Britain's Married Women Workers* (London: Routledge & Kegan Paul, 1965).

A. Kollontai, 'Communism and the Family', in A. Holt (ed.), *Alexandra Kollontai. Selected Writings* (London: Allison & Busby, 1977).

M. Komarofsky and W. Waller, 'Studies of the Family', *American Journal of Sociology*, 50 (1945) 443–51.

J. Kuczynski, *Geschite der Kinderarbeit in Deutschland 1750–1939*, vol. 1 (Berlin: Verlag Neues, 1958).

A. Kuhn and A. Wolpe (eds), *Feminism and Materialism: Women and Modes of Production* (London: Routledge & Kegan Paul, 1978).

Le Roy Ladurie, *Montaillou* (Stockholm: Manpocket, 1980).

R. D. Laing, *The Politics of the Family and Other Essays* (London: Tavistock, 1971).

H. Land, 'The Myth of the Male Breadwinner', *New Society*, 9 Oct. 1975, 71–3.

H. Land, 'Women: Supporters or Supported?', in D. L. Barker and S. Allen (eds), *Sexual Divisions and Society: Process and Change* (London: Tavistock Publications, 1976).

H. Land, 'Inequalities in Large Families: More of the Same or Different?', in R. Chester and J. Peel (eds), *Equalities and Inequalities in Family Life* (London: Academic Press, 1977).

H. Land, 'Who Cares for the Family?', *Journal of Social Policy*, 7 (1978) 257–84.

H. Land, 'The Family Wage', *Feminist Review* 6 (1980) 55–77.

J. Landes, 'Women, Labour and Family Life', in R. Quinney (ed.), *Capitalist Society: Readings for a Critical Sociology* (Homewood, Illinois: Davey Press, 1979).

G. Lapidus, *Women, Work and the Family in the Soviet Union* (New York: M. E. Sharpe, 1982).

P. Laslett, *The World We Have Lost*, 2nd edn (Cambridge: Cambridge University Press, 1971).

P. Laslett, *Family Life and Illicit Love in Earlier Generations* (Cambridge: Cambridge University Press, 1977).

P. Laslett, 'Foreword', in R. Rapoport *et al.*, (eds), *Families in Britain* (London: Routledge & Kegan Paul, 1982).

P. Laslett and R. Wall, *Household and Family in Past Time* (Cambridge: Cambridge University Press, 1972).

R. Layard, M. Frederking and A. Zabala, 'Married Women's Participation and Hours', *Economica*, 47 (1980) 427–544.

R. Layard, D. Piachaud *et al.*, 'The Causes of Poverty', Background paper no. 5 in *Royal Commission on the Distribution of Income and Wealth* (London: HMSO, 1978).

E. Leach, *A Runaway World?* (London: BBC Publications, 1967).

L. Lenero-Otero, *Beyond the Nuclear Family Model: Cross Cultural Perspectives* (London: Sage, 1977).

D. Lessing in *New Statesman*, Jan. 1971.

S. Lewenhak, *Women and Work* (Glasgow: Fontana, 1980).

F. D. Lewis, 'Fertility and Savings in the United States: 1830–1900', *Journal of Political Economy*, 91 (1983).

D. Lockwood, *The Blackcoated Worker* (London: George Allen & Unwin, 1958).

D. Lockwood, 'Sources of Variation in Working-Class Images of Society', *Sociological Review*, 14 (1966) 249–67.

E Lupri and G. Symons, 'The Emerging Symmetrical Family: Fact or Fiction?', *International Journal of Comparative Sociology*, XXIII (1982).

D. B. Lynn, *The Father: His Role in Child Development* (Monterey: Brooks/Cole, 1974).

A. McCulloch, 'Alternative Households', in R. Rapoport *et al.* (eds), *Families in Britain* (London: Routledge & Kegan Paul, 1982).

L. McKee and C. Bell, 'Marital Relations in Times of Male Unemployment', paper given to the SSRC Research Workshop on Employment and Unemployment, 1983.

L. McKee and M. O'Brien (eds), *The Father Figure* (London: Tavistock, 1982).

A. Macfarlane, *The Origins of English Individualism* (Oxford: Blackwell, 1978).

R. MacKay, 'Conceptions of Children and Models of Socialisation', in H. P. Dreitzel (ed.), *Childhood and Socialisation*, Recent Sociology No. 5 (London: Collier Macmillan, 1973).

W. J. M. Mackenzie, *Power and Responsibility in Health Care: The National Health Service as a Political Institution* (Oxford: Oxford University Press, 1979).

M. Mackintosh, 'Gender and Economics: The Sexual Division of Labour and the Subordination of Women', in K. Young *et al.* (eds), *Of Marriage and the Market: Women's Subordination in International Perspective* (London: CSE Books, 1981).

E. Macklin, 'Nontraditional Family Forms: A Decade of Research', *Journal of Marriage and the Family*, 42 (1980) 905–22.

H. Macrae, S. Emerson and M. Dickens, *Lewisham's Wageless Women: The Invisible Unemployed* (Lewisham Women and Employment Project, 1981).

E. Malos, *The Politics of Housework* (London: Allison & Busby, 1980).

K. Mannheim, *Essays on the Sociology of Knowledge* (New York: Oxford University Press, 1952).

K. Mannheim, *Ideology and Utopia* (London: Routledge & Kegan Paul, 1972).

Manpower Services Commission, *A Study of the Long Term Unemployed* (MSC, 1980).

K. Margolis, 'The Long and Winding Roads', *Feminist Review*, 5 (1980) 89–102.

A. Marsh, *Women and Shiftwork* (London: HMSO for Office of Population, Censuses and Surveys, 1979).

P. Marsh *et al.*, *The Rules of Disorder* (London: Routledge & Kegan Paul, 1978).

K. Marx, *The Economic and Philosophic Manuscripts of 1844* (New York: International Publisher, 1964).

K. Marx, *Capital* (London: Lawrence & Wishart, 1974; London: Dent Dutton, 1974a).

K. Marx and F. Engels, *Manifesto of the Communist Party* (Peking: Foreign Language Press, 1968).

Mass-Observation, *Clothes Washing Motives and Methods – Interim Report* (Mass-Observation, 1939).

J. E. Mayer, 'The Invisibility of Married Life', *New Society* (1967a) 272–3.

J. E. Mayer, 'People's Imagery of Other Families', *Family Process*, 6 (1967b) 27–36.

M. Meissner *et al.*, 'No Exit for Wives: Sexual Division of Labour and the Cumulation of Household Demands', *Canadian Review of Sociology and Social Anthropology*, 12 (1975) 424–39.

E. Mendelievich (ed.), *Children at Work* (Geneva: ILO, 1979).

C. Middleton, 'Sexual Inequality and Stratification Theory', in F. Parkin (ed.), *The Social Analysis of Class Structure* (London: Tavistock, 1974).

C. Middleton, 'Patriarchal Exploitation and the Rise of English Capitalism', paper presented to the Annual Conference of the British Sociological Association, Manchester, April 1982.

R. Miliband, *The State in Capitalist Society* (London: Weidenfeld & Nicolson, 1969).

J. Mitchell, *Women's Estate* (Harmondsworth: Penguin, 1971).

M. Molyneux, 'Beyond the Domestic Labour Debate', *New Left Review*, no. 116 (1979) 3–28.

M. Molyneux, 'Socialist Societies Old and New: Progress Towards Women's Emancipation', *Feminist Review*, 8 (1981) 1–34.

B. Moore, 'Thoughts on the Future of the Family', in B. Moore, *Political Power and Social Theory: Seven Studies* (New York: Harper & Row, 1965).

D. H. J. Morgan, *Social Theory and the Family* (London: Routledge & Kegan Paul, 1975).

D. H. J. Morgan, 'New Directions in Family Research and Theory', in Harris (1979).

F. Mount, *The Subversive Family* (London: Jonathan Cape, 1982).

S. Moylan and B. Davis, 'The Disadvantages of the Unemployed', *Employment Gazette*, 88 (1980) 830–32.

G. P. Murdock, 'World Ethnographic Sample', *American Anthropologist*, 59 (1957) 664–84.

G. P. Murdock, *Social Structure* (New York: Free Press, 1967).

L. Murgatroyd, 'Domestic Labour in a Class Society: Stratification Inside and Outside the Home', mimeo (1981).

L. Murgatroyd, 'Gender and Occupational Stratification', *Sociological Review* (1982a).

L. Murgatroyd, 'Gender and Class Stratification', thesis submitted for the degree of DPhil, University of Oxford (1982b).

L. Murgatroyd, 'The Production of People: Domestic Labour Revisited', *Socialist Economic Review* (1983).

A. Myrdal and V. Klein, *Women's Two Roles: Home and Work* (London: Routledge & Kegan Paul, 1956).

M. Nava, 'From Utopia to Scientific Feminism? Early Feminist Critiques of the Family', in L. Segal (ed.), *What is to be Done About the Family?* (Harmondsworth: Penguin, 1983).

M. Nissel and L. Bonnerjea, *Family Care of the Handicapped Elderly: Who Pays?* (London: Policy Studies Institute, 1982).

A. Oakley, *The Sociology of Housework* (Oxford: Martin Robertson, 1974).

A. Oakley, *Housewife* (Harmondsworth: Penguin, 1976).

A. Oakley, 'Wisewoman and Medicine Man: Changes in the Management of Childbirth', in J. Mitchell and A. Oakley (eds), *The Rights and Wrongs of Women* (Harmondsworth: Penguin, 1976a).

A. Oakley, *Subject Women* (Glasgow, Fontana, 1982).

O. Oeser and S. Hammond (eds), *Social Structure and Personality in a City* (London: Routledge & Kegan Paul, 1954).

W. F. Ogburn and M. F. Nimkoff, *Technology and the Changing Family* (Cambridge, Mass: Houghton Mifflin, 1955).

J. Oliver, 'The Caring Wife', in J. Finch and D. Groves (eds), *A Labour of Love: Women, Work and Caring* (London: Routledge & Kegan Paul, 1983).

L. Olsson, *Da Barn Var Lönsamma* (When Children Were Profitable) (Stockholm: Tiden, 1980).

J. Pahl, 'Patterns of Money Management Within the Family', paper presented at the British Sociological Association Conference, Manchester, 1982.

J. Pahl, 'The Allocation of Money and the Structuring of Inequality Within Marriage', Health Services Research Unit, University of Kent at Canterbury, 1982a.

J. Pahl and R. Pahl, *Managers and their Wives* (London: Allen Lane, 1971).

R. Pahl and C. Wallace, 'Household Work Strategies in Economic Recession', paper presented at the British Sociological Association Conference, Bradford, 1984.

F. Parkin, 'Strategies of Social Closure in Class Formation', in F. Parkin (ed.), *The*

Social Analysis of Class Structure (London: Tavistock, 1974).

F. Parkin, *Marxism and Class Theory: A Bourgeois Critique* (London: Tavistock, 1979).

T. Parsons, *The Social System* (Glencoe, Illinois: The Free Press, 1952).

T. Parsons, 'The American Family: Its Relations to Personality and to Social Structure', in T. Parsons and R. F. Bales, *Family, Socialisation and Interaction Process* (London: Routledge & Kegan Paul, 1956a).

T. Parsons, 'Family Structure and the Socialisation of Children', in T. Parsons and R. F. Bales, *Family, Socialisation and Interaction Process* (London: Routledge & Kegan Paul, 1956b).

T. Parsons, 'The Social Structure of the Family', in R. N. Anshen (ed.), *The Family: Its Functions and Destiny* (New York: Mayer, 1959).

T. Parsons (ed.), *Essays in Sociological Theory* (New York: The Free Press, 1964a).

T. Parsons, 'Evolutionary Universals in Society', *American Sociological Review* (1964b).

T. Parsons, 'The Incest Taboo in Relation to Social Structure', in R. L. Coser (ed.), *The Family: Its Structure and Functions* (London: Macmillan, 1964c).

T. Parsons, 'The Normal American Family', in B. N. Adams and T. Weirath, *Readings on the Sociology of the Family* (Chicago: Markham, 1971a).

T. Parsons, 'Reply to His Critics' in M. Anderson (ed.), *The Sociology of the Family* (Harmondsworth: Penguin, 1971b).

T. Parsons and R. F. Bales, *Family, Socialisation and Interaction Process* (London: Routledge & Kegan Paul, 1956).

T. Parsons and R. C. Fox, 'Illness Therapy and the Modern American Family', in N. Bell and E. Vogel (eds), *A Modern Introduction to the Family* (New York: Free Press, 1968).

I. Philipson, 'Child Rearing Literature and Capitalist Industrialization', *Berkeley Journal of Sociology*, 26 (1981) 57–73.

D. Piachaud, 'The Cost of a Child', Child Poverty Action Group Pamphlet 43, 1979.

The Pilgrim Trust, *Men Without Work* (London: Cambridge University Press, 1938).

I. Pinchbeck, *Women Workers and the Industrial Revolution 1750–1850* (London: Cass, 1977).

J. Pleck and M. Rustad, 'Husbands' and Wives' Time in Family Work and Paid Work in 1975–76 Study of Time Use', Wellesley College Centre for Research on Women, unpublished paper, 1980.

G. Poiner, 'The Good Old Rule: A Study of Social Relationships in a County District of New South Wales', University of Sydney, PhD thesis (1982).

J. Popay, L. Rimmer and C. Rossiter, *One Parent Families: Parents, Children and Public Policy* (London: Study Commission on the Family 1983).

M. Poster, *Critical Theory of the Family* (London: Pluto Press, 1978).

J. Pratt, 'Reflections on the Approach of 1984: Recent Developments in Social Control in the U.K.', *International Journal of the Sociology of Law*, 11 (1983) 340.

M. K. Pringle and S. Naidoo, 'Early Child Care in Britain', *Concern*, 18 (1975).

P. Quicler Davies, 'Pilots and their Families', paper delivered to Seminar, University of New South Wales School of Sociology, May, 1981.

D. M. Rafky, 'Phenomenology and Socialisation: Some Comments on the Assumptions Underlying Socialization Theory', in H. P. Dreitzel (ed.), *Childhood and Socialization*, Recent Sociology No. 5 (London: Collier Macmillan, 1973).

R. Rapoport and R. Rapoport, *Dual-Career Families* (Harmondsworth: Penguin, 1971).

R. Rapoport and R. Rapoport, *Dual-Career Families Re-Examined* (London: Martin Robertson, 1976).

R. Rapoport *et al.*, *Fathers, Mothers and Others* (London: Routledge & Kegan Paul, 1977).

R. Rapoport *et al.* (eds), *Working Couples* (London: Routledge & Kegan Paul, 1978).

R. Rapoport and R. Rapoport, 'British Families in Transition', in R. Rapoport *et al.* (eds), *Families in Britain* (London: Routledge & Kegan Paul, 1982).

R. Rapoport *et al.* (eds), *Families in Britain* (London: Routledge & Kegan Paul, 1982).

D. Read, *Fact Sheet on Home Laundry Appliances* (London: Burton-Marsteller Ltd, 1982).

L. Richards, *Having Families* (Ringwood, Australia: Penguin, 1978).

L. Rimmer, *Families in Focus: Marriage, Divorce and Family Patterns* (London: Study Commission on the Family, 1981).

L. Rimmer and J. Popay, *Employment Trends and the Family* (London: Study Commission on the Family, 1982).

D. Robbins (ed.), *Rethinking Social Inequality* (Aldershot: Gower, 1982).

J. P. Robinson, 'Housework Technology and Household Work', in Berk (1980).

J. Robinson and P. Converse, 'Social Change Reflected in the Use of Time', in A. Campbell and P. Converse (eds), *The Human Meaning of Social Change* (New York: Sage, 1972).

B. T. Robson, *Urban Analysis* (Cambridge: Cambridge University Press, 1969).

G. Rogers and G. Standing (eds), *Child Work, Poverty and Underdevelopment* (Geneva: ILO, 1981).

S. Rowbotham, 'The Trouble with Patriarchy', *New Statesman* (1979) 970.

S. Rowbotham, L. Segal and H. Wainwright, *Beyond the Fragments: Feminism and the Making of Socialism* (London: Merlin Press, 1979).

J. Rubery, 'Structured Labour Market, Worker Organisation and Low Pay', in A. Amsden (ed.), *Economics of Women and Work* (Harmondsworth: Penguin, 1980).

G. Rubin, 'The Traffic in Women: Notes on the "Political Economy" of Sex', in R. R. Reiter (ed.), *Towards an Anthropology of Women* (New York: Monthly Review Press, 1975).

S. Ruddick, 'Maternal Thinking', in B. Thorne and M. Yalom (eds), *Rethinking the Family: Some Feminist Questions* (New York: Longman, 1982).

S. Ruehl, 'Feminism and Economism', *Socialist Economic Review* (1982).

G. Russell, 'Fathers: Incompetent or Reluctant Parents?', *The Australian and New Zealand Journal of Sociology*, 15 (1979) 57–65.

G. Russell, 'Fathers and Men's Role in Caregiving', in D. Davis, G. Caldwell, M. Bennett and D. Boorer, *Living Together* (Canberra: ANU, 1980).

G. Russell, 'A Multivariate Analysis of Father's Participation in Child Care and Play', Macquari University, School of Behavioural Sciences, unpublished paper (1981).

G. Russell, 'Shared – Caregiving Fathers: An Australian Study', in M. E. Lamb (ed.), *Nontraditional Families: Parenting and Child Development* (New Jersey: Erlbaum, 1982).

G. Russell, *The Changing Role of Fathers?* (St. Lucia, Queensland: University of Queensland Press, 1983).

M. Rutter, *Maternal Deprivation Reassessed* (Harmondsworth: Penguin, 1982).

N. B. Ryder, 'The Cohort as a Concept in the Study of Social Change', *American Sociological Review*, 30 (1965) 843.

C. Safilios-Rothschild, 'Family Sociology or Wives' Family Sociology? A Cross-Cultural Examination of Decision Making', *Journal of Marriage and the Family*, 31 (1969) 290–301.

C. Safilios-Rothschild (ed.), *Towards a Sociology of Women* (Lexington, Mass: Xerox College Publishing, 1972).

C. Sandford, *The Economic Structure* (London: Longman, 1982).

L. Sargent (ed.), *Women and Revolution: The Unhappy Marriage of Marxism and Feminism* (London: Pluto Press, 1981).

T. W. Schultz, 'The Value of Children: An Economic Perspective', *Journal of Political Economy*, 81 (1973) S5.

R. von Schweitzer, 'Kinder und ihre Kosten', in K. Lüscher (ed.), *Sozialpolitik für das Kind* (Stuttgart: Klett-Cotta, 1979).

J. Scott, *Corporations, Classes and Capitalism* (London: Hutchinson, 1979).

J. Scott, *The Upper Classes: Property and Privilege in Britain* (London: Macmillan, 1982).

B. Seear, *Re-Entry of Women to the Labour Market After an Interruption in Employment* (OECD, 1971).

W. Seccombe, 'The Housewife and her Labour Under Capitalism', *New Left Review*, no. 83 (1974) 3–24.

W. Seccombe, 'Domestic Labour – A Reply to Critics', *New Left Review*, no. 94 (1975) 85–96.

L. Segal, *What is to be Done About the Family?* (Harmondsworth: Penguin, 1983).

R. Sennett, *Families Against the City* (Cambridge, Mass: Harvard University Press, 1970).

R. Sennett and J. Cobb, *The Hidden Injuries of Class* (Cambridge: Cambridge University Press, 1977).

K. Shanks and G. Courtenay, *Young People, Work and Community Industry* (London: Community Industry, 1982).

G. Sharp and L. Bryson, 'The Family: Maternal Work and the Internal Division of Labour', paper presented to the Sociological Association of Australia and New Zealand, 1965.

S. Sharpe, *Just Like A Girl* (Harmondsworth: Penguin, 1976).

M. Shaw, *Marxism Versus Sociology* (London: Pluto, 1974).

M. Shimmin, J. McNally and S. Liff, 'Pressures on Women Engaged in Factory Work', *Employment Gazette* (1981) 344–9.

E. Shorter, *The Making of the Modern Family* (London and Glasgow: Fontana, 1977).

A. S. Skolnick, *The Intimate Environment* (Boston: Little Brown, 1973 and 1978).

A. S. Skolnick and J. H. Skolnick, *Family in Transition* (Boston: Little Brown, 1971).

A. S. Skolnick and J. H. Skolnick, 'Introduction', in A. S. Skolnick and J. H. Skolnick, *Initimacy, Family and Society* (Boston: Little Brown, 1974a).

A. S. Skolnick and J. H. Skolnick, 'Domestic Relations and Social Change' in A. S. Skolnick and J. H. Skolnick, *Intimacy, Family and Society* (Boston: Little Brown, 1974b).

A. S. Skolnick and J. H. Skolnick, *Intimacy, Family and Society* (Boston: Little Brown, 1974c).

C. Smee and J. Stern, *The Unemployed in a Period of High Unemployment: Charac-*

teristics and Benefit Status, Government Economic Service Working Paper, No. 11 (HMSO, 1978).

D. Smith, 'Women, The Family and Corporate Capitalism', in M. Stephenson (ed.), *Women in Canada* (Toronto: New Press, 1974).

P. Smith, 'Domestic Labour and Marx's Theory of Value', in Kuhn and Wolpe (1978).

R. Smith, 'Sex and Occupational Role on Fleet Street', in D. L. Barker and S. Allen (eds), *Dependence and Exploitation in Work and Marriage* (London: Longman, 1976).

Social Security Advisory Committee, *First Report* (London: HMSO, 1982).

Social Security Advisory Committee, *Second Report* (London: HMSO, 1983).

Social Trends, Issue 11 (London: HMSO, 1981).

Social Trends, Issue 13 (London: HMSO, 1983).

Social Trends, Issue 14 (London: HMSO, 1984).

D. Spender and E. Sarah (eds), *Learning to Lose: Sexism and Education* (London: The Women's Press, 1980).

M. Spring Rice, *Working Class Wives, Their Health and Conditions* (Harmondsworth: Pelican Books, 1939).

SPRU Women and Technology Studies, *Microelectronics and Women's Employment in Britain*, Science Policy Research Unit Occasional Paper No. 17 (1982).

M. Stacey 'The Division of Labour Revisited or Overcoming the Two Adams', in P. Abrams *et al.* (eds), *Development and Diversity: British Sociology 1950–1980* (London: George Allen & Unwin, 1981).

M. Stacey and M. Price, *Women, Power and Politics* (London: Tavistock Women's Studies, 1981).

F. P. Stafford, 'Women's Use of Time Converging with Men's', *Monthly Labor Review*, Dec. (1980) 57–9.

G. Y. Steiner, *The Children's Cause* (Washington: Brookings Institution, 1976).

J. Stephens, *The Transition from Capitalism to Socialism* (London: Macmillan, 1979).

J. Stolzman and H. Gamberg, 'Marxist Class Analysis Versus Stratification Analysis', *Berkeley Journal of Sociology*, 18 (1974) 105–25.

L. Stone, *The Family, Sex and Marriage in England 1500–1800* (London: Weidenfeld & Nicholson, 1977; and Harmondsworth: Penguin, 1979).

S. Strasser, *Never Done: A History of American Housework* (New York: Pantheon Books, 1980).

Study Commission on the Family, *Happy Families?* (London: Study Commission on the Family, 1980).

Study Commission on the Family, *Families in the Future* (London: Study Commission on the Family, 1983).

M. B. Sussman, *Non-Traditional Family Forms in the 1970s* (Minneapolis: National Council on Family Relations, 1973).

A. Szalai (ed.), *The Use of Time* (The Hague: Mouton, 1972).

R. Taft, 'Some Sub-Cultural Variables in Family Structure in Australia', *Australian Journal of Psychology*, 9 (1957) 69–90.

G. Thomas and C. Zmroczek Shannon, 'Technology and Household Labour: Are the Times A-Changing?', paper presented at the annual British Sociological Association Conference, Manchester April, 1982.

C. A. Thrall, 'The Conservative Use of Modern Household Technology', *Technology and Culture*, 23 (1982) 175–94.

C. Tilly, *As Sociology Meets History* (New York: Academic Press, 1981).

M. Moore Trescott (ed.), *Dynamos and Virgins Revisited: Women and the History of Technology* (New Jersey and London: Scarecrow Press, 1979).

N. Tucker, 'Review of "Dream Babies: Child Care from Locke to Spock"', *Theory, Culture and Society*, 2 (1984) 150–51.

C. Ungerson, 'Why Do Women Care?' in J. Finch and D. Groves (eds), *A Labour of Love: Women, Work and Caring* (London: Routledge & Kegan Paul, 1983a).

C. Ungerson, 'Women and Caring: Skills, Tasks and Taboos', in E. Gamarnikow, D. H. J. Morgan, J. Purvis and D. Taylorson (ed), *The Public and the Private* (London: Heinemann, 1983b).

J. Urry, 'Deindustrialisation, Households and Forms of Conflict and Struggle', Lancaster Regionalism Group Working Paper 3, University of Lancaster, 1981.

J. Vanek, 'Household Technology and Social Status: Rising Living Standards and Status and Residence Differences in Housework', *Technology and Culture*, 19 (1978) 361–75.

J. Vanek, 'Time Spent in Housework', in A. Amsden (ed.), *The Economics of Women and Work* (Harmondsworth: Penguin, 1980).

M. Verdon, 'Kinship, Marriage and the Family: An Operational Approach', *American Journal of Sociology*, 86 (1981) 796–818.

K. Walker, 'Homemaking Still Takes Time', *Journal of Home Economics*, 61 (1969) 621–9.

B. Wearing, 'The Ideology of Motherhood', PhD thesis, University of New South Wales, Sydney, 1981.

B. Webb, *The Wages of Men and Women: Should They Be Equal?* (London: Fabian Society, 1919).

M. Webb, 'The Labour Market', in I. Reid and E. Wormald (eds), *Sex Differences in Britain* (London: Grant McIntyre, 1982).

M. Weber, *The Theory of Social and Economic Organisations*, ed. T. Parsons (New York: The Free Press, 1966).

B. Weitbaum and A. Bridges, 'The Other Side of the Paycheck', in Z. Eisenstein, *Capitalist Patriarchy and the Case for Socialist Feminism* (London: Monthly Review Press, 1979).

J. Westergaard and H. Resler, *Class in a Capitalist Society* (Harmondsworth: Penguin, 1976).

A. Whitehead, '"I'm Hungry, Mum": The Politics of Domestic Budgeting', in K. Young *et al.* (eds), *Of Marriage and the Market* (London, CSE Books, 1981).

J. H. Whitehouse (ed.), *Problems of Boy Life* (London: P. S. King, 1912).

D. Wilkin, *Caring for the Mentally Handicapped Child* (London: Croom Helm, 1979).

C. Williams, *Open Cut: The Working Class in an Australian Mining Town* (Sydney: George Allen & Unwin, 1981).

P. Willis, 'Shop Floor Culture, Masculinity and the Wage Form', in J. Clarke, C. Critcher and R. Johnson (eds), *Working Class Culture* (London: Hutchinson, 1979).

E. Wilson, 'Beyond the Ghetto: Thoughts on "Beyond the Fragments – Feminism and the Making of Socialism"', *Feminist Review*, 4 (1980) 28–44.

E. Wilson, 'Women, the "Community" and the "Family"', in A. Walker (ed.), *Community Care, the State and Social Policy* (Oxford: Basil Blackwell & Martin Robertson, 1982).

E. Wilson, *What Is To Be Done About Violence Against Women?* (Harmondsworth: Penguin, 1983).

Women's Employment Rights Campaign, *Women and Unemployment* (Sydney: Chippendale, 1979).

F. Wright, 'Single Carers: Employment, Housework and Caring', in J. Finch and D. Groves (eds), *A Labour of Love: Women, Work and Caring* (London: Routledge & Kegan Paul, 1983).

K. Young, C. Wolkowitz, R. McCullagh (eds), *Of Marriage and the Market: Women's Subordination in International Perspective* (London: CSE Books, 1981).

M. Young and P. Willmott, *The Symmetrical Family* (Harmondsworth: Penguin, 1975).

E. Zaretsky, *Capitalism, the Family and Personal Life* (London: Pluto Press, 1976).

I. M. Zeitlin, *Marxism: A Re-examination* (Princeton, New Jersey: Van Nostrand, 1967).

V. A. Zelizer, 'The Price and Value of Children: The Case of Children's Insurance', *American Journal of Sociology*, 86 (1981) 1036–56.

Index

Index